INSIGHT CITY GUIDE

LasVegas

Part of the Langenscheidt Publishing Group

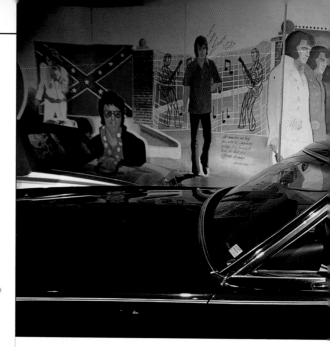

※ INSIGHT GUIDE
Las Vegas

Project Editor
Martha Ellen Zenfell
Art Director
Klaus Geisler
Picture Editor
Hilary Genin
Cartography Editor
Zoë Goodwin
Editorial Director
Brian Bell

Distribution

United States
Langenscheidt Publishers, Inc.
46–35 54th Road, Maspeth, NY 11378
Fax: (1) 718 784-0640

Canada
Thomas Allen & Son Ltd
390 Steelcase Road East
Markham, Ontario L3R 1G2
Fax: (1) 905 475 6747

UK & Ireland
GeoCenter International Ltd
The Viables Centre, Harrow Way
Basingstoke, Hants RG22 4BJ
Fax: (44) 1256-817988

Australia
Universal Publishers
1 Waterloo Road
Macquarie Park, NSW 2113
Fax: (61) 2 9888 9074

New Zealand
Hema Maps New Zealand Ltd (HNZ)
Unit D, 24 Ra ORA Drive
East Tamaki, Auckland
Fax: (64) 9 273 6479

Worldwide
Apa Publications GmbH & Co.
Verlag KG (Singapore branch)
38 Joo Koon Road, Singapore 628990
Tel: (65) 6865-1600. Fax: (65) 6861-6438

Printing

Insight Print Services (Pte) Ltd
38 Joo Koon Road, Singapore 628990
Tel: (65) 6865-1600. Fax: (65) 6861-6438

ABOUT THIS BOOK

This guidebook combines the interests and enthusiasms of two of the world's best-known information providers: Insight Guides, whose titles have set the standard for visual travel guides since 1970, and Discovery Channel, the world's premier source of nonfiction television programming.

The editors of Insight Guides provide both practical advice and a general understanding about a place's history, culture, institutions and people. Discovery Channel and its website, www.discovery.com, help millions of viewers explore their world from the comfort of their own home and also encourage them to explore a destination firsthand.

Insight CityGuide: Las Vegas is carefully structured to help convey an understanding of Las Vegas, the surrounding area and its people, as well as to guide readers through all the fantastic sights and activities Sin City and the nearby desert can offer to visitors:

◆ The **Features** section, indicated by an orange bar at the top of each page, covers the natural and cultural history of the region in a series of informative essays.

◆ The main **Places** section, indicated by a blue bar, is a complete guide to all the sights and areas worth visiting. Places of special interest are coordinated by number with the maps.

◆ The **Travel Tips** listings section, at the back of the book, provides a handy point of reference for details on travel, tours, hotels, car rental, shops, outdoor sports and also has an A–Z of practical information.

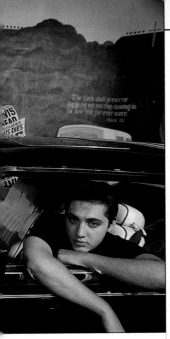

The contributors

The guiding hand behind this book was that of **Martha Ellen Zenfell**, who has been the project editor of most of Insight Guides' North American titles. Zenfell's first task was to recruit **Catherine Karnow**, her favorite photographer and visual collaborator on several books, certain that Karnow's distinctive eye was perfect for capturing the glitz, the glitter and the sheer hard work that goes into organizing and running America's best-known playground for grown-ups.

Zenfell and Karnow ran around the Las Vegas Strip in 110° temperature like a pair of dervishes, and got busted for jay-walking when Karnow spied the perfect shot in front of the Monte Carlo Hotel *(see page 114 for the result)*. Karnow

was also given unique access to take pictures in the gaming rooms of Bellagio, the Venetian, Caesars Palace, Paris Las Vegas and the Aladdin; these images are published here for the first time. When the desert was too hot to handle, **Richard Cummins** and **Glyn Genin** filled in the visual gaps.

Meanwhile, **Gina Cunningham** of the Las Vegas Convention and Visitors Authority smoothed the way for Zenfell to go through what seemed like hundreds of boxes of archive pictures to illustrate the history section, selecting images that for the most part have rarely been published.

At the same time, principal writer **John Wilcock**, who has worked on many Insight projects, including the *Insight Guide to Los Angeles* and the *Insight Compact Guide to Las Vega*s, was pounding away on the keyboard. Little of city life escaped his scrutiny, from showgirls and food to the gaming habits of men versus women. **David Whelan**, too, proved a dab hand at the typewriter, while polishing his techniques at the tables.

Other articles were penned by **Mike** and **Linda Donahue**, writers who currently operate Little Meadows horse farm outside the Valley of Fire State Park. For more than 25 years, the Donahues have written about all aspects of Southern Nevada, including desert wildlife and Las Vegas wild life (nightlife). We are very grateful to all the casino public relations directors who allowed us to document such a fascinating city.

CONTACTING THE EDITORS

We would appreciate it if readers would alert us to errors or outdated information by writing to:

Insight Guides, P.O. Box 7910, London SE1 1WE, England. Fax: (44) 20 7403-0290. insight@apaguide.co.uk

CONTENTS

Maps

Travel Tips

THE BEST OF LAS VEGAS

Lions, pyrotechnics and a roller coaster are among the indoor spectacles. Outside are sea battles, a volcano and a Sphinx. Here are the must-see attractions of the desert

LAS VEGAS SPECTACULAR

Some of the dazzling highlights from this city of fantasy and extremes. Be sure to see:

- **The Fremont Street Experience** Around 2 million lights become a free night-into-day extravaganza *(see page 179)*.
- Cirque du Soleil's astonishing **O show** *(see page 131)* is in a purpose-built theater, with lake, at Bellagio.
- The Arc de Triomphe, Montgolfier balloon and Eiffel Tower at **Paris Las Vegas** *(see page 128)*.
- The **Colosseum** *(see page 136)* at Caesars, built around Celine Dion's show. Elton John fills in on her nights off.
- **Dale Chihuly's** 50-foot (15-meter) high chandelier of stained glass over Bellagio's lobby *(see page 130)*.
- The spectacular nighttime **view of the Strip** from the observation platform on top of the Stratosphere Tower *(see page 162)*.
- **Acrobats** hang from the rafters day and night at Circus Circus *(see page 160)*.
- The **Burger Bar** in Mandalay Bay serves über-burgers with foie gras and truffles *(see page 123)*.
- The bright lights of Broadway and the **Statue of Liberty** at New York-New York *(see page 107)*.
- A glittering galaxy of super-star turns at the Imperial's **Legends in Concert** show *(see page 142)*.
- The **Carnival World Buffet** at the Rio *(see page 174)*, the most sumptuous of Vegas's famous serve-it-yourself feasts.
- Stone-faced and slow-eyed heavyweights square up for big money at the **World Series of Poker**. The Horseshoe *(see page 183)*, every April.
- Blinding glitter at the **Liberace Museum** *(see page 169)*.
- **In-pool blackjack** at the fun Tropicana *(see page 112)*.
- With more magic in Vegas than you can wave a wand at, **Lance Burton's** show *(see page 115)* at the Monte Carlo is still voted the best.

- Tiger Woods is a regular at **Rio Secco** *(see page 172)*, one of the world's premier golf resorts.
- Works by Cézanne, Gauguin, Van Gogh, Matisse, Renoir and others at the **Guggenheim Hermitage** *(see page 155)*.

- The giant pyramid and the enigmatic 100-foot (30-meter) Sphinx of the **Luxor** *(see page 118)*.
- The Doges Palace, the Campanile and the Piazza San Marco, all in one view, with gondolas, at the **Venetian** *(see page 153)*.

BELOW: The bright lights and "performance architecture" of the most exciting city in the United States.

SPAS

- The huge **Canyon Ranch SpaClub** at the Venetian *(see page 153)* is the largest spa in the US. With gorgeous roof-top pools, the spa offers over 30 types of massage, and a variety of treatments.
- **Spa Bellagio**, at Bellagio *(see page 130)* offers hydrotherapy treatments and fine waxing. Massages include aromatherapy and tandem.
- **The Spa** at the Four Seasons *(see page 122)* has 16 treatment rooms, a hydrotone capsule and eucalyptus steam, Balinese and Javanese body rituals, facials and massages.
- Partake of luxurious Egyptian rituals at the **Oasis Spa at Luxor** *(see page 118)*.

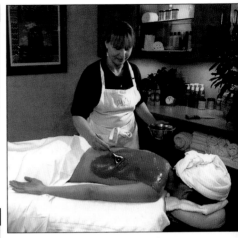

ABOVE: Like a modern Cleopatra, you can sign up for luxurious rituals and mudbaths at the Luxor.

POOLS

- **Bellagio's** pools, set among gardens of vines, offer cabanas with a dressing area, lounge chairs, TV, phone, air mister and a stocked fridge.
- **Caesars'** Garden of the Gods pool area has 4.5 acres of marble statues, shrubs and umbrellas. Three pools and two outdoor whirlpool spas.
- **The Hard Rock** has a two-acre pool area and beach club, complete with beaches, wave pools, underwater music and private cabanas. Beach parties most Wednesdays.

GAMBLING TERMS

Comp: complimentary, or free of charge.

Drop box: a box below a casino game table where dealers deposit paper money through a slot on top of the table.

Eye in the sky: mirrors or concealed video cameras used to monitor table games (dealers and gamblers) to prevent cheating.

Pit boss: the person overseeing table games from behind the dealer.

Shoe: the small box on the gaming table from which poker cards are dealt.

Shooter: the player rolling the dice at a craps game.

Toke: a tip or gratuity.

Whale or **high roller:** a customer with the bankroll to bet large sums of money. Whales may arrive in Vegas by private jet courtesy of the casino, and be given comp food and suites.

ONLY IN VEGAS CAN YOU...

- **Walk** on a Picasso. Claude Picasso, son of the artist, designed the carpets for a fine restaurant in Bellagio *(see page 133)*.
- **Feel** Rain in the Desert at The Palms Casino Hotel nightclub *(see page 173)*.
- **Stand** by a curbside Volcano as it erupts, four times every hour *(see page 148)*.
- **Watch** a perfect dawn and splendid sunset – indoors; every hour at the Forum Shops *(see page 138)*.
- **Hear** an Elvis impersonator perform every hour, on the hour at Elvis-A-Rama *(see page 171)*.
- **See** the world's biggest golden nugget at the Golden Nugget casino, Downtown *(see page 186)*.
- **Ogle** a double-sized David. The statue of David at Caesars *(see page 135)* is twice the size of Michelangelo's original sculpture.

- **Marry** in the place that Britney Spears wed Jason Alexander, in A Little White Chapel *(see page 177)*. Hopefully, though, you'll stay together longer.
- **Plight** your troth on a bungee jump, in a drive-thru chapel, in the back of a limo with hot tub, or over the Grand Canyon *(see page 89)*.

ABOVE: Thrills and cheers at New York-New York.
LEFT: Celebrity chef Wolfgang Puck.

CELEBRITY CHEFS

More than 50 renowned restaurateurs are enhancing their fame in Sin City. Here are a few:

- **Emeril Lagasse** is at Delmonico's in the Venetian, and at his own New Orleans Fish House at the MGM Grand.
- **Wolfgang Puck**, the first of Vegas's brigade of star stirrers, now operates five establishments here.
- **Charlie Palmer** transplanted his super-chic Aureole from New York to the Mandalay Bay.
- **Jean-Marie Josselin** offers a unique blend of Asian and European food at 808 in Caesars Palace.
- **Nobuyuki Matsushia** prepares world-famous sushi at Nobu in the Hard Rock.
- Steve Wynn lured **Julian Serrano** to serve food among the Cubist originals and preside over Picasso at Bellagio.
- **Jean-Georges Vongerichten** cooks beautifully at Prime in Bellagio.
- The celebrity of celebrity chefs is **André Rochat**, whose Andre's French Restaurant, located Downtown, has been consistently voted the best in Las Vegas since 1980.

THRILL RIDES

- The Stratosphere Tower hosts the world's three highest rides by erecting them on the tower's landmark needle:
- **Big Shot** catapults riders at high speed to the top of the tower's mast, 1,000 feet above ground.
- **High Roller** whirls them above the observation platform.
- **X Scream** dangles frightened guests in the air more than 800 feet above ground.
- **Manhattan Express** at New York-New York: as well as the usual flips and loops, this roller coaster twists and spins dizzyingly around the replicated towers of Manhattan.
- **Canyon Blaster** at Circus Circus gives a 60-foot drop, a spiral spin around a mountain and three upside-down spins as it whips riders around and up to 45 miles per hour. All of it is indoors.

SPÉCIALITÉ DE LA MAISON

Here are some of the tastiest highlights from Vegas's wild and varied menus:

Piero Selvaggio at the Venetian's **Valentino** presents parmesan chips called *frico*, and three-colored gnocchi. Also at the Venetian, the **Delmonico Steakhouse** is famous for truffled potato chips dusted with parmesan cheese and rock shrimp salad.
In the Venetian Grand Canal Shoppes, **Postrio**'s signature dish is baked *loup de mer en croûte*.

Creamy scrambled eggs topped with caviar inside a covered ceramic egg delight visitors to Laurent Tourondel's **Palace Court** at Caesars Palace.
Chef David Robins features mahogany roast duck accompanied by pomegranate and crêpes at **Spago** in Caesars' Forum Shops.
Il Fornaio at New York-New York is known for fried calamari with spicy marinara sauce.
Popular at Bellagio's **Picasso** is quail escabèche, a dish chef Julian Serrano

disarmingly claims is "easy to make."
At **Nobu** in the Hard Rock, there's an ample variety of sushi, but don't miss the black cod marinated in white miso.
Off the main menu, but available to those in the know at **Francesco's** is chef Marco Porceddu's tagliolini, served with mullet roe, at T.I. (Treasure Island).
At the MGM Grand, Michael Mina's Gilroy garlic soup filled with spinach and egg ravioli is a favorite at **Nobhill**.
Finish at the MGM Grand with satin-like bread pudding in whisky sauce, a yummy dessert at Emeril Lagasse's **New Orleans Fish House**.

THEMED DINING

- **Buccaneer Bay Club** at T.I. *(see page 151)* offers a continental menu as a battle between Sirens and pirates takes place before your very eyes.
- **ESPN Sports Bar** in New York-New York *(see page 108)* offers diners 150 screens featuring nothing but sport.
- **Harley Davidson Café** on the Strip has around 15 custom-made motorcycles including Elvis Presley's. As the latest Harleys pass by on a conveyor belt, eat tasty American road food.
- **House of Blues**, Mandalay Bay *(see page 123)* is a Southern and blues-themed restaurant offering regional cuisine including Creole and

Cajun staples. A Sunday gospel feature has live music and a country-style buffet brunch.
- **NASCAR Café** at Sahara, *(see page 163)*. This two-level restaurant features NASCAR stock cars, and huge screens showing the best races. Drag-race mechandise is on offer, along with American food.
- **Quark's Bar and Restaurant** is part of *Star Trek: the Experience* at the Las Vegas Hilton *(see page 166)*. The Trekkie-inspired environment features metallic furniture and costumed employees. Snack on gummy worms and other delicacies from Outer Space.

ABOVE: The fountains at Bellagio are choreographed to music and lights. It's lovely, but don't stay in one of the rooms above them as the show gets very repetitive.

VEGAS FOR FREE

- The **fountains** at Bellagio *(see page 130)*. More than 17,000 gallons of water spray from no fewer than 11,000 spouts, all of which are choreographed to music and lights.
- The **sea battle** at T.I. *(see page 149)* is a roadside engagement between scantily clad Sirens and a crew of renegade pirates. The sea battle takes place several times each evening.
- The **Conservatory at Bellagio** *(see page 131)* showcases lilies, orchids, ferns and rare

tropical flowers around water features that seem impossible in the desert.
- At **Ethel M. Chocolates** *(see page 215)*, around a ton and a half of chocolates are enrobed on each employee's shift.
- **Lion Habitat** at MGM Grand *(see page 110)*. The home of the descendants of Metro, MGM studio's signature lion.
- **M & M's World** *(see page 111)*. There are interactive exhibits, a Racing Café and a candy store.
- The **White Tiger Habitat** at the Mirage *(see page 147)* is the home of Siegfried & Roy's tigers.
- The fine **Marjorie Barrick Museum** *(see page 169)* is a natural history museum with live lizards.

VEGAS FOR FAMILIES

- **Circus Circus** *(see page 160)*. Children under 17 stay for free, and cribs are available. The Adventure-Dome and a children's playground are on the premises, too.
- Kids under 12 also stay free at the **MGM Grand** *(see page 109)*, where admission to the Lion's Habitat is free.
- **The Sahara** *(see page 158)*. Children under 12 stay free, and the fun NASCAR Café and Wet 'n' Wild theme park are both within easy reach.

- The **Stratosphere Tower** *(see page 162)* lets children under 11 stay free, and also offers cribs. Three of Vegas' best thrill rides are on the top of the tower.
- In **Excalibur** *(see page 117)*, children under 12 stay free.

A DELIRIOUS DESERT CITY

**Chancers, dreamers, gangsters, and entrepreneurs –
all have been lured across the scorching desert
to try their luck at games of chance**

Desert springs watered Las Vegas, and the hot-house canopy of arid isolation nourished the town's primary business, which was best conducted away from the prying eyes of the outside world. Since 1920, when Mayme Stocker opened the first casino, chancers and gangsters have been lured across the desert to try their luck at games of chance.

The lights, the shows, the fortunes turning on the roll of a die – Las Vegas is a world of neon fantasy and eye-popping architectural illusion. Enticements include an indoor parody of the ancient wonders of Egypt, hourly sea-battles, and surreal reincarnations of Venice and Paris. Lush and lavish pools surrounded by Italian gardens, and museums with treasures from the ancient and modern world provide, among other things, a breeding colony for a rare human sub-species – the Elvi, otherwise known as the people earning a living impersonating the Mississippi rock 'n' roller.

The character of modern Las Vegas has been most obviously shaped by three groups: the casino visionaries, a handful of world-class singers, and the arcane masters of magic and illusion. All of them brought innovations that shaped the way Vegas has evolved by drawing their own crowds of devotees from across the States and beyond.

The gaming entrepreneur who reinvented Vegas hospitality was Jay Sarno. His Caesars Palace was the first of the casinos designed as an integrated, themed fantasy. From the world of entertainment, Frank Sinatra set the tempo, singing songs for swinging lovers in Las Vegas lounges. And then there's magic. Magic is such an integral part of Vegas that no fewer than four museums here are dedicated to the art. The city is itself a vast showcase of sleight-of-hand, and it's no coincidence that the magicians' most basic, intimate illusions often involve the manipulation of playing cards, only the throw of a die away from the gaming tables.

For although 65 percent of visitors claim to be attracted to Sin City by something other than gambling, somehow 87 percent of people find time to play the tables or slots during their stay, contributing an average of $480 each to the casinos' coffers.   ❏

PRECEDING PAGES: at home in the Liberace Museum just off the Strip; showgirls limbering up; everybody dreams of leaving Las Vegas richer than when they arrived.
LEFT: neon fantasy in the desert.

THE EARLY YEARS

For centuries, Native Americans lived peacefully in
the desert, but the discovery of water, precious metals,
and the construction of the railroad changed this forever

L as Vegas – Spanish for "the meadows,"
or fertile plains – grew around an oasis in
the desert, but the valley wasn't always
as harsh and arid as it is today. In 1993, construction workers in Nevada uncovered the
remains of a Colombian woolly mammoth. As
well as halting construction, this beast anywhere from 8,000 to 15,000 years old indicated that in prehistoric times the terrain was
sympathetic enough to nourish life in relative
abundance. Hidden for centuries from all but
Native Americans, the Las Vegas Valley oasis
was protected from discovery by the surrounding harsh and unforgiving desert.

The indigenous Paiute had adapted over the
centuries to survive in what seemed to be a
barren, inhospitable terrain by careful hus-
bandry in a semi-nomadic existence. They
planted corn and squash in the well-watered
areas and timed their return to when the crops
were ready. Judging by remains discovered at
Tule Springs, an archeological site in the
northwest of the valley, they hunted caribou,
mammoth, and bison.

Prehistoric hunters

There are traces of the so-called Archaic Indians, a foraging culture of hunters who har-
vested mesquite and cholla fruit. As early as
300 BC the Anasazi who had settled about 60
miles (96 km) north of the present-day city,

along the Muddy and Virgin rivers, were
known for their basket-making skills. The
prehistoric Native Americans were hunter-
gatherers who collected seeds and pods from
cacti, yucca, and agave, and hunted rabbits,
coyotes, and rodents in the desert, heading
into the mountains after deer and Bighorn
sheep. Annual expeditions led to still higher
elevations to collect pinon nuts.

The first non-native person known to have
discovered the springs was a young Mexican
scout, Rafael Rivera, who came with a party led
along the Spanish Trail to Los Angeles by Mexican trader Antonio Armijo. Rivera was an

LEFT: trapping a woolly mammoth; in 1993 a
prehistoric mammoth was discovered in the desert.
RIGHT: mountainman John Moss and Tercherum, a
Paiute chief, at Fort Mojave in the 1860s.

experienced scout, and in search of water. The exact date of the find is unknown, but he is thought to have left the party around Christmas 1829 and made his momentous discovery soon after. Over the following 30 years, hundreds of traders, miners, soldiers, and pioneers traveled along the Old Spanish Trail, previously known as the Paiute Trail, between what is now Abiquiu, New Mexico and San Gabriel, California. About 135 miles (217 km) of the trail crosses the state of Nevada.

Although the abundant spring water discovered at Las Vegas eased some of the rigors for Spanish traders – and hastened the rush west for California gold – it didn't make the journey much less arduous. For the preceding hundreds, and maybe thousands of years, the whole region had been covered in marshes with vegetation nurtured by the water, but the marsh receded and gave way to desert. Rivers disappeared beneath the surface, and what had been teeming wetlands transformed into an unforgiving baked landscape, though underground water surfaced to nourish luxuriant plants and creating welcome oases.

The incursions of the pioneers were, of course, disastrous for the native Paiute. By the 1830s, the traders and travelers who camped without permission at Paiute home sites near springs and streams were becoming a menace.

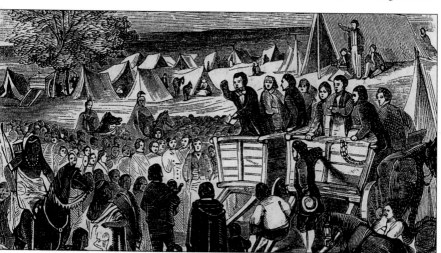

MORMONS IN THE MODERN ERA

By the 21st century, when nearly one quarter of local jobs were in casinos, Mormons – prized for their integrity – filled top posts. John Marz, vice president for corporate marketing at Mandalay Resorts, says: "People just wouldn't be here without these jobs. For me it came down to 'can you function in the job and still be a good Church member?'"

In his book *Saints in Babylon: Mormons and Las Vegas* Kenric F. Ward said that "While Church leaders remain queasy about gambling – regularly denouncing it as a pernicious pastime and fighting its importation into other states – Latter Day Saints in Nevada have played a major role in regulating the business, and in some cases promoting it." In 1959, Senator Jim Gibson helped create the Nevada Gaming Commission. Don Shaw, who ran the Castaways Hotel casino says, "As long as you're ethical and honest in your dealings, that's what counts." His partner Mike Villamor, who converted to Christianity when he was 21 and married in the Las Vegas temple, says, "Yes, I've seen people lose their life savings in casinos. I've also seen a man die from overeating in a restaurant."

Still there are hold-outs, including the globally prominent Marriott Corporation which operates seven local hotels – all free of slot machines or spinning wheels, but with a Book of Mormon sitting in most guest rooms.

Their stock damaged the plant life and they depleted the land's resources by shooting the game, and sometimes the locals too. The Paiutes were prepared to defend their way of life, and mounted raids on mines, settlements, and stagecoaches. When Native Americans attacked the intruders in 1859, troops from Fort Tejon, near what is now Los Angeles, mounted a punitive expedition. From 1866 to 1868 Federal troops engaged in the "Snake Wars," and the Paiutes were ultimately force-marched into a reservation at Fort Tejon.

The US acquired the region after winning the Mexican War in 1848, and just seven years later the Mormons arrived. Leader William Bringhurst was the man in charge of 30 settlers, dispatched by Brigham Young to establish a fort for protection of the mail route between Los Angeles and Salt Lake City. The fruit trees and vegetables that they cultivated failed to thrive in the alkaline soil, and a mining venture at nearby Mount Potosi was also unsuccessful. The lack of water for processing the ore meant that the metal was flaky. Some of the silver-laced lead bullets from the era have turned up in recent years.

Mormon settlement

The adobe brick fort with stone foundations established by the Mormons had thick walls 14 feet (4 meters) high and 150 feet (46 meters) long. Rawhide thongs and wooden pegs secured planks to beams because nails were scarce. Three years later the settlement was abandoned by the Mormons, partly because of raids by native peoples, but more to pre-empt a rising threat from the Federal government to march on Salt Lake City. Buildings which were added to the site and used by successive ranchers have been removed, but the portion of the Mormon Fort that survived, with some added reconstruction, is still maintained as a historic site in downtown Las Vegas *(see "Downtown," page 191)*.

Scientists began an archeological dig on the site in the early 1990s to see what was below. In 2000, a group dressed as Mormons from the 1850s re-enacted the Mormon pioneers' 600-

mile (965-km) route in covered wagons.

Members of the Church of Jesus Christ of Latter-Day Saints (the Mormons) currently make up about 12 percent of the southern Nevada population and in December 1989 a Mormon temple was dedicated in Las Vegas. The temple spires are visible in the foothills of Sunrise Mountain to the east of the city. Although LDS leaders originally were opposed to gaming, they eventually came to accommodate it.

On May 13, 1844, the USA's well-known explorer, John C. Fremont, leading an overland expedition heading west, chose to camp at Las Vegas Springs and subsequently thousands

of copies of the map he drew were freely distributed. His name is remembered today not only in museums and history books but glowingly in neon. The Fremont Hotel-Casino bears his name, as does Fremont Street – the main casino-lined thoroughfare Downtown.

The 19th century was a lawless time. An early historian, Hubert Bancroft, wrote in an 1890 book that between 1864 and 1890 there were 400 murders in Nevada, a very high number when one considers the sparseness of the population. But by the final decade of the 19th century, railroad developers had determined the water-rich Las Vegas Valley would be a prime location for trains to stop. The

LEFT: Mormons preaching in the wilderness, 1853.
RIGHT: explorer John C. Fremont, after whom Las Vegas' Fremont Street is named.

town, along with the ranch and vineyard on the old Mormon site, was eventually acquired by Senator William Clark's railroad. Half a dozen different railroad companies tried to build a track from Salt Lake City to Los Angeles along the old Mormon Trail. Clark's San Pedro Los Angeles Salt Lake Railroad (later the Union Pacific) advertised for workers. The company offered $2 per 10-hour day for white men, $1.75 for Mexicans and Native Americans, with teamsters (union members) promised $40 a month, including board.

Sub-contractors lined up 1,200 workers who were accommodated in groups of 50 to 100 in canvas tents for which they each paid

Helen Stewart, the biggest landowner of the time, owned 1,800 acres (728 hectares) which included the site of the old Mormon Fort on which her ranch stood. Her husband was killed in a dispute with a former ranch hand, but she continued to operate the ranch for another 20 years or so afterwards. Mrs Stewart sold land the railroad needed to Senator William Clark for $55,000. She later deeded around 10 acres (4 hectares) "for the use of Pauite Indians."

From a collection of tented shacks with saloons, stores, and boarding houses, the town grew to a population of 1,500 by early 1905 when the railroad was completed. The railroad

75¢ per day. Each shelter, which could be as small as 7 by 9 feet (2 meters by 3 meters), housed several workers and their cots.

Food and drink

In the railroad workers' kitchens and dining halls, canned fruits and vegetables, syrup, bacon, locally grown potatoes and onions were served. Archeologists have found dome-shaped ovens for bread baking, and blasting powder tins reshaped into cooking pans and sieves. Water was first brought in by wagons. Later the railroad, which merged with E.H. Harriman's Oregon Short Line in the early part of the 20th century, installed a pipeline.

offered free rides to town for the big auction at which 175 lots were sold almost immediately for $450 each. Eventually the land brought in a sum of $265,000, five times as much as Helen Stewart had been paid for her property lining the tracks. On January 20, 1905, trains made their inaugural run from California to points east.

The railroad yards were located at the birthplace of a partially paved, dusty Fremont Street. Today, Jackie Gaughan's Plaza Hotel, located at Main and Fremont streets in downtown Las Vegas, stands on the site of the original Union Pacific Railroad depot. Freight and passenger trains still use the depot site at the hotel as a terminal – the world's only railroad station inside a hotel casino. In 1905, the Las Vegas Land & Water Co. installed redwood pipes to bring water from the main line at Clark and Main streets but there were constant leaks and bursts, which once left the town without water for several days. Artesian wells later solved some of the water problems.

Even after the turn of the 20th century, mining thrived in the region. A mining camp at Searchlight – on what became the main Las Vegas to Los Angeles highway – established by George Colton in 1907, produced $7 million in gold, silver, and other precious metals. It was an era when personal disputes were set-

canvas shirt. A double-crowned hat, or an extra pocket sewn into a trouser leg would hold about 5 lbs (2.25 kg) of ore.

When miners were working high-grade ore, owners would require them to shower and change clothes after coming off shift, but men constantly found new and more ingenious ways to smuggle and steal, like using hollowed-out ax handles.

Mining town

The work of a miner is very different today as most mining uses heavy machinery in open pits. Nevada is still the nation's leading producer of silver, and the state yielded more than

tled with guns, and duels were commonplace. Mugging was also common in Searchlight, and embezzlement was not unknown. In 1906, the front pages of the newspapers followed the case of W.B. Atwell, the town postmaster, who admitted stealing $5,730 in government funds.

Atwell was jailed for four years, but there were lesser crimes, the most common being "high-grading" – smuggling rich ore out of the mine in clothes, hair, or a lunchbox. Ore could be secreted between the layers of a double

8 million ounces (227,000 kg) of gold in 2001. But most of the Searchlight mines were worked out long ago, and the town declined. It serviced travelers on the Arrowhead Highway until 1927, when what is now Interstate 15 bypassed it. Today it is little more than a stop on US 95 for travelers heading from Needles to Las Vegas or visiting Lake Mojave.

Early in the 20th century, Nevada followed the lead of other states and outlawed gambling. As many predicted, the activities simply went underground. For the next two decades everybody knew somebody who knew the right door to knock on and had no trouble joining any one of a hundred games.   ❑

LEFT: railroad depot, waiting room, and ticket office, on a 1905 Las Vegas sidetrack.
ABOVE: Nevada silver-mining camp, 1894.

THE GROWTH OF GAMBLING

The building of the Hoover Dam brought men and money. All that was needed to part them from one another were a few gambling dens

When the city of Las Vegas was incorporated on March 16, 1911, it was hardly a pretty sight. "Anyone who lives here is out of his mind," said newcomer Mayme Stocker from Reading, Pennsylvania. Her husband had come for work as an engine foreman at the railroad yards. In her recollections many years later, Mayme said "There were no streets or sidewalks and there were no flowers, lawns, or trees." In spite of this, Mayme stayed, and in 1920 opened the Northern Club on Fremont Street, for which she was granted Las Vegas's first casino license.

Mr Las Vegas

The first man to be known as "Mr Las Vegas" was Robert Griffith. Griffith helped his father build a home at the southwestern corner of 2nd and Fremont streets, where the Golden Nugget now stands. At the age of 26 he was appointed postmaster and instructed to prepare for an airport. He leveled a site in the desert, near today's Sahara and Paradise roads, where the first flight landed on April 17, 1925, taking letters which were hand-stamped to mark the occasion on the 2½-hour flight back to Los Angeles. The next year, Western Airlines inaugurated passenger flights into Vegas.

The following years saw a lot of artesian wells drilled for water, but after an initial boom the town remained more or less isolated until the early 1930s, when it was revived with the building of the Boulder (later Hoover) Dam.

LEFT AND RIGHT: the Flamingo Hotel was both a desert fantasy and the downfall of mobster Bugsy Siegel.

There were hopes even in those early days that Las Vegas could be turned into a tourist resort, and entrepreneur David Lorenzi dug two lakes in the northwest part of town. His planned "high-class resort" came to nothing, but the lakes are still there in appropriately named Lorenzi Park. Frank Garside, a publisher who had operated newspapers in Tonopah and other boom towns, had seen an opportunity in Las Vegas, buying a struggling weekly, the *Clark County Review*, and hiring Reno-born Al Cahlan to run it. Between 1930 and 1970, Cahlan wrote a column for what became the *Las Vegas Review-Journal*. His busiest time as editor was during the building of Boulder Dam, 34 miles (55 km) away in Black Canyon on the Colorado River.

This enormous project employed 5,300 workers with a monthly payroll of half a million dollars, and by the time it was finished, the population of Las Vegas was up to 5,000. In the decade between 1930 and 1939, the Federal government pumped $70 million into the area, much of it going toward the Boulder Dam. When it was completed, Garside still thought the town would "blow away" like so many of the other boom towns with which he had been associated in the past.

Cahlan married Missouri-born Florence Lee Jones in 1940. She covered the story of a

In August 1931 the workers went on strike complaining about heat prostration from working in 130°F (54°C) temperatures, poor food and drink, and the lack of safety precautions. The "muckers," who did the most dangerous job of shoveling up dynamite-loosened rock to be hauled away, got the lowest pay.

Great Depression

Legalized gambling returned to Nevada in 1931 during the Great Depression, legitimizing a small but lucrative industry. Phil Tobin, a northern Nevada rancher who had never visited Las Vegas, persuaded the Nevada Legislature to pass a gambling bill whose pro-

truck driver's suit brought against the Six Companies, the contractors who had won the construction contract with a bid of $48,890,955. The driver claimed he'd lost his sexual powers from exposure to the carbon monoxide fumes in the dam's bypass tunnels, but his suit failed. Undoubtedly there were fumes. Murl Emery, a boat operator who took many of the men to work on the dam, said that at one time "They were hauling men out of those tunnels like cord wood. They had been gassed. I laid them on the bottom of the boat, on the seats and what not… They were real sick from being gassed working in the tunnel along with the running trucks."

ceeds would raise taxes for public schools, an idea so durable that today nearly one-third of Nevada's current $1.8 billion annual state budget comes from the 6.25 percent tax on casino winnings.

Local businessmen had been operating most of the original gambling halls, with enforcement handled by the sheriff. The city relied on their lawman to rid the town of undesirables – vagrants, card cheats, suspected thieves, moonshiners, drug dealers and the like – usually by giving them a "floater," meaning they had to leave town – and soon – or face incarceration. Later came the realization, born out of the Prohibition era when bootleggers bribed local authorities and politicians, that bribes could be converted into legitimate revenue, and the state legislature set up the Nevada Tax Commission.

Originally, Las Vegas had been visualized as a resort city, serving visitors who came to see Boulder Dam (later renamed Hoover Dam) and go boating on Lake Mead, but the nationwide crackdown on illegal gambling unexpectedly benefited the state. One man in particular, an ex-carnival barker named Harold Smith, spread the message around the world with no less than 2,300 signs advertising his Lake Tahoe Harold's Club in places as far afield as Casablanca and the Antarctic.

SHALL WE PLAY CARDS?

When Tom Hull, owner of a chain of motor inns, built El Rancho Vegas, he concentrated on the swimming pool. The casino was an afterthought.

Ernie Cragin, a former insurance salesman, was the mayor. An unashamed racist, his policemen rigidly enforced segregation in a town where most of the casinos and nightclubs refused to serve blacks.

During WWII, when black military officers guarding the dam came to town, there were gun battles with the local police. Matters did not improve for blacks until two decades later,

Boulder City was a federally run enclave, created to house the workers in a place where liquor, gambling, and prostitution could be banned. Cars were searched and impounded if liquor was found. Naturally, its off-duty residents flooded into Vegas to enjoy themselves. This created problems with black people in particular, and sometimes pitched battles occurred *(see below)*. Today, Boulder City is still the only town in Nevada that outlaws any form of gaming, including slot machines.

LEFT: conditions during the construction of the Hoover Dam were primitive and damaging to the health.
ABOVE: opening ceremonies for the Hoover Dam.

when NAACP lawyer Charles Kellar instigated protest marches on the Strip, and civil rights lawyer Ralph Denton helped to get Governor Grant Sawyer elected.

El Rancho

By 1941, with a population of about 8,000 people, a group of local businessmen invited Tom Hull, owner of a chain of El Rancho motor inns, to town. Hull chose a site just outside town where Highway 91 intersected San Francisco (now Sahara) Avenue for El Rancho Vegas. With cheap land taxes and water, he built a 65-room motor inn with a swimming pool; the casino was an afterthought.

Later expanded to 125 rooms, El Rancho Vegas became popular for banquets and wedding parties. It was the headquarters of the valley's first radio station, an ABC affiliate named KENO. The station's owner Maxwell Kelch, a major Vegas promoter, sold the town like a product. He never ran for office or invested in a casino. As he told his son, "there's two businesses you don't get involved in. One's liquor and the other's gambling." El Rancho Vegas was destroyed by fire in 1960.

In 1948, the El Cortez Hotel was built at Fremont and 6th streets. Among its partners were Meyer (real name: *Suchowljansky*) Lansky and Benjamin "Bugsy" Siegel. Lansky

invested $60,000 for his 10 percent stake, and left it to Siegel to run. In their youth the pair had worked a New York protection racket, beating up and killing bootleggers. Siegel traveled to Los Angeles to consolidate the rackets there, and later came to Las Vegas to handle the Mob's race book wires and gambling business. In Manhattan, Siegel lived at the Waldorf Astoria and traveled with bodyguards in a bullet-proof limousine. Out west, he soon made friends with Clark Gable, Jean Harlow, Cary Grant, and other members of Hollywood's movie colony.

"He was a frustrated actor who secretly wanted a movie career," actor George Raft said, "but he never quite had nerve enough to ask for a part in one of my pictures." Siegel muscled his way into illegal gambling, including Tijuana's Agua Caliente racetrack in Mexico. He also helped to import narcotics from Mexico, and took a cut from a huge prostitution ring.

His big break in Vegas came soon after, with the arrival of a colorful Hollywood entrepreneur named W.R. Wilkerson. Wilkerson had begun betting on the World Series and at the track while he was at college. He founded the influential *Hollywood Reporter* in 1930, and played regularly with $20,000 chips at movie mogul Sam Goldwyn's weekly poker game. An obsessive gambler, he would charter a plane to fly from Los Angeles to Las Vegas, and soon thought of owning his own hotel in the desert resort in order to entertain his movie-star friends. That was the genesis of the Flamingo Hotel which – through amply documented chicanery – came to be known as Siegel's place.

In December 1942, movie chain mogul R.E. Griffith introduced a western motif at the Last Frontier. The casino had Pony Express lanterns hanging from wagon wheels, Texas cattle horns, leather bar stools in the shape of saddles, and a bullet-riddled mahogany bar. The hotel, later renamed the Frontier, offered horseback and stagecoach rides into the desert terrain. Frontier Village was established with ancient buildings rehabilitated from old Nevada ghost towns. The Last Frontier also started the idea of "the junket," gaming tours arranged by the operator of a small airline called Kirk Kerkorian.

Downtown thrives

The late 1940s and early 1950s saw the growth of the Fremont Street area with a whole clutch of clubs springing up. The Golden Nugget was built, then the Monte Carlo Club. Then came Benny Binion, a colorful Texas gambler who sported big, white cowboy hats and a buffalo-hide overcoat. In his early career Binion had been twice convicted for bootlegging and once, after getting a jailor drunk and using a key, stole a truckload of liquor right out of the jail.

In the late 1930s in Dallas he operated craps games out of hotel rooms by taking the tables in and out disguised as beds. In 1947, with his partner, Binion opened the Las Vegas Club on Fremont Street. Four years later, he opened the Horseshoe and set the town on its ear by offering a $500 limit on craps games – ten times the other casinos' limit. A cherished principle of Benny Binion's was "giving a lot of gamble for the money."

In 1946, "Bugsy" Siegel took over the part-completed Flamingo Hotel when the *Hollywood Reporter* publisher's initial investment of $1.5 million ran out. By the time the Flamingo opened, Siegel was heavily in debt. Costs escalated massively because Siegel took his eye off the business. Expensive construc-

dreadful weather to attend went across the street to El Rancho Vegas or the Last Frontier to stay over and bet.

Siegel closed the place to get it finished, reopening in early 1947, but the Mob was displeased by the venture's losses. Meyer Lansky discovered that Siegel had been skimming the Flamingo building fund, sending his girlfriend Virginia Hill to deposit large sums in a

tion materials hiked the costs, though maybe not as much as the freight that was driven in through the front gates and out the back gates over and over again without ever being unloaded. Palm trees kept appearing, disappearing, and then reappearing again. By the opening night on December 26,1946, the still-unfinished Flamingo had already cost $6 million, and because the hotel rooms weren't ready, the few celebrities that braved the

LEFT: the "Dancing Dice" of El Rancho, one of the first influential casinos in Vegas.
ABOVE: ex-president and showman Ronald Reagan at the Last Frontier, another early club.

Swiss bank account. In June, as the hoodlum sat reading in the window of Miss Hill's Beverly Hills home, a single shot blasted through the glass. Bugsy Siegel was dead.

"In death he became a legend taller than any Las Vegas resort," said *Review-Journal* columnist John L. Smith. Virginia "Flamingo" Hill was in Europe at the time of the murder, probably on the advice of his killers.

A few years later, Hill appeared before a commission on organized crime. Asked why she had associated with mobsters like Frank Costello and Joseph Epstein, an Al Capone underboss, Flamingo replied, "Senator, I'm the best goddammed cocksucker in the world." ❏

PLAYERS AND DESERT PALACES

Mobsters and mincing showgirls, wire-taps
and wild publicity stunts – in 1950s Vegas,
this was all in a day's take

On a New York spring morning in 1957, Frank Costello, the "Prime Minister of the Mob," was cut down by a volley of gunshots in the paneled lobby of his apartment building in Central Park West. The injured mobster was rushed to the hospital and in the ensuing bustle, a quick-thinking cop checked the pockets of Costello's beautifully cut suit. A hand-written note was among the contents. It read, "Gross Casino Win as of 4-26-57… $651,284," which tallied the first 24 days' takings from the Las Vegas gaming house, the Tropicana Hotel.

Memo from the Mob

The Costello memo was the first solid evidence of Mob ties to Vegas casinos since a series of ground-breaking hearings into organized crime headed by Tennessee senator Estes Kefauver in 1950 and 1951. This was also the year that Alan Dorfman, son of one of Al Capone's soldiers, first started to get loans to finance casino construction from the Teamsters Union's western states pension fund.

During the proceedings, Nevada's Lieutenant Governor Cliff Jones was asked about "undesirable characters with bad police records" who had earlier been engaged in gambling in the state. He conceded that there had, indeed, been such occasions. But Jones – himself a part owner of the Thunderbird casino – elaborated further: "…people who came here when the state started to grow –

they weren't particularly school teachers or anything like that. They were gamblers."

After Kefauver concluded his hearings into Mob connections, he proposed a 10 percent federal gaming tax which was averted only through persistent efforts by Nevada senator Pat McCarran. A defense lawyer and later district attorney, McCarran had lost many races before being elected senator in 1932, and had served for 20 years when he halted a move to tax gaming.

"It isn't a very laudable position for one to have to defend gambling," he conceded. "One doesn't feel very lofty when his feet are resting on the argument that gambling must pre-

LEFT: showgirl and friend at the opening of the Dunes.
RIGHT: Frank Costello, "Prime Minister of the Mob."

vail in the state that he represents. The rest of the world looks upon him with disdain."

McCarran, a popular politician in his native state, fought for the retention of silver in US coins – Nevada is "the silver state." He also wrote much civil aviation legislation, and McCarran airport was named for him, but his reputation was marred by a friendship with the Communist-baiting senator Joseph McCarthy. On this he had faced considerable opposition from Hank Greenspun, until his death in 1989 the publisher of the *Las Vegas Sun* newspaper, the only rival to the dominant *Review-Journal*. Greenspun arrived in Vegas in 1946, acted as publicity manager for Bugsy Siegel's

Flamingo, and founded KLAS-TV, a CBS outlet, which he sold to the reclusive tycoon Howard Hughes in the 1960s.

Four years after Estes Kefauver's exposures of Mob involvement in Vegas, a Gaming Control Board was established to regulate and legitimize the industry. Gambling had already become the state's greatest source of income.

The whole southern Nevada region was on a roll by the early 1950s, largely due to the efforts of publicity man Steve Hannagan, who had promoted the Indianapolis Raceway and Miami Beach before he was hired to promote the city of Las Vegas. It was a bright Hannagan protegeé, Harvey Diederich, who gained

massive coverage from a stunt in the 1956 US presidential election. He posed a scantily clad showgirl named "Miss Bea Sure 'N Vote" with a campaign poster for Dwight D. Eisenhower in her right hand and one for Adlai Stevenson in her left. "Cold Turkey" was the caption for another girl, posed astride an ice turkey, carved by the Topicana Hotel chef. "Publicity far exceeds the value of advertising," said Diederich. "It's more believable."

Downtown began its rapid growth when Texan Benny Binion opened the legendary Binion's Horseshoe, the first off-the-Strip casino with a carpet, as well as being the first to offer free drinks not just to high rollers but also to slot- machine players. He also arranged for customers to be collected at the airport in limousines. "If you wanna get rich," Binion said, "make little people feel like big people."

Around that time, the Atomic Energy Commission started conducting above-ground nuclear test explosions at test sites about 100 miles (160 km) northwest of Las Vegas. President Harry Truman declared the valley "a critical defense area," which did wonders for Las Vegas' economic well-being. In 1951, the first year of testing, the Commission's construction payroll topped $4 million.

The idea for the Desert Inn, with its lavish golf course, came from a former San Diego bellboy named Wilbur Clark. "It was Wilbur's dream… he worked hard to get the hotel together," his widow Toni said years later. "He always said the bubble would never burst in Las Vegas and he was right. It was all class then. People used to dress every night. It was a very glamorous place, a winner from the day it opened. Everybody loved being there." Frank Sinatra's first singing engagement in Vegas was at the Desert Inn on September 4, 1951, when he was still getting over his break up with actress Ava Gardner.

Moe Dalitz

Along with his Cleveland partners, Moe Dalitz, "a smart, brilliant man," according to some, owned three quarters of the Desert Inn. During prohibition Dalitz had bootlegged liquor with Meyer Lansky across the lake from Canada, and in 1958 kept his chain of Midwestern laundries free from union interference with hoodlum strong-arms. In a dazzling display of business acumen, Dalitz raised $8 million from the Teamsters Union's pension fund to finish the Stardust Hotel.

Government investigations showed that the Teamsters Union's investments in Nevada casinos eventually exceeded $238 million. Dalitz got out, but years later the mobsters who still owned it were jailed for skimming the profits, or "conspiracy to defraud the government of taxes through illegal and unreported income," as the rap sheet put it.

A mobster and a gentleman

In his book, *Gamblers' Money*, Wallace Turner wrote, "In Cleveland, Moe Dalitz was a boot-

THOSE WERE THE DAYS

According to the *New York Times*, in 1953 a first-class hotel in Vegas charged $7.50 a day, while a motel charged $3.

in the tailored suit of corporate citizenship."

Dalitz himself told an interviewer in 1975, "I was never a member of any gang. I never considered myself a gangster or a mobster. I was always in a business that threw me into meeting all kinds of people."

When he died in 1989, the foundation that he had set up distributed $1.3 million to charities, and the 300 mourners at his funeral

legger but in Las Vegas he stands as an elder statesman of what they call the gaming industry," and *Las Vegas Review-Journal* columnist John L. Smith rhetorically asked, "How did a former bootlegger and illegal casino operator… go about gaining respectability? Dalitz took the same approach that many other American capitalists did. He donated generously to political causes and wrapped himself

LEFT: Estes Kefauver's investigation into organized crime in 1950–51 exposed Mob connections.
ABOVE: singer Phyllis McGuire, seen here with Desert Inn owner Moe Dalitz, was a girlfriend of Mafia boss Sam Giancana.

included politicians, judges, and other influential figures.

The Stardust was the first to break from what had already become casino star policy by bringing from France the *Lido de Paris* stage show, which ran for 31 years. The topless revue was produced by legendary showman Donn Arden. Arden, a one-time tap dancer, went on in the 1990s to produce the on-stage *Sinking of the Titanic* in one of the current Strip revues, which – by the end of the 20th century – had sunk 15,000 times and looks likely to continue to sink indefinitely. The Dunes had brought topless revues to the Strip with *Minsky's Follies* in 1957, but it was

THE SHOWGIRL WALK

"If you twist right and swing that torso, you get a revolve going in there that's just right. It isn't the way a woman should walk necessarily – unless she's a hooker." – promoter Donn Arden

Arden who was most associated with the statuesque, bare-breasted showgirl who became such an emblem of Vegas.

"There's a certain way a girl can walk, particularly when crossing a stage," he once explained, somewhat painstakingly. "By simply twisting the foot it swings the pelvis forward, which is suggestive and sensual. If you

Sahara's Casbah Lounge. In 1955, Miller shifted to the Dunes and introduced the first of what became known as "production shows," a revue called *Smart Affairs*.

Until 1955, the Desert Inn had offered guests the highest unobstructed panoramic view of the Las Vegas Valley from the resort's third-floor Skyroom – cocktail and dancing favorite of visitors, residents, and celebrities. Soon after, the Riviera Hotel rose to nine stories and took the towering title to become the city's first high-rise building.

That same year, the Moulin Rouge opened across the city, at a time when blacks were still unwelcome guests at Strip casinos and black

twist right and swing that torso, you get a revolve going in there that's just right. It isn't the way a woman should walk necessarily unless she's a hooker. You're selling the pelvis. That's the Arden walk."

Talent agent Bill Miller, former partner in a dance act, is credited with originating Las Vegas' famous lounge shows. The lounges became major entertainment attractions in their own right, spawning the names of comedians Don Rickles and Buddy Hackett among others. As entertainment manager of the Sahara in which he had bought a 10 percent stake, Miller hired bandleader Louis Prima and his wife Keely Smith to play the

entertainers were required to live off-premises while entertaining. The hip, interracial crowd that filled the Moulin Rouge's club after midnight attracted so many showgirls and performers from other casinos that some threatened to dismiss cast members who were seen there.

The Moulin Rouge starred former world heavyweight boxing champion Joe Louis as owner-host, and singer Bob Bailey from the Count Basie Orchestra as producer of the stage show. The club had a stormy existence, closing and re-opening many, many times, and when Bailey moved his show onto KLAS-TV, he had to go back to using the service entrance. Bailey himself worked to get Grant Sawyer elected governor in 1958. "He indicated that if he was elected governor, certain changes would be made. He struck me as a man you could believe."

Three years later, the legislature established a commission to examine the subject of discrimination. Joe Louis moved on to become a much-loved casino host at Caesars Palace. The Moulin Rouge was declared a national historic site in 1992. But in 2003, the boarded-up casino was tragically and permanently damaged by arson. Although the unsafe remains still stand, its future as a protected landmark remains uncertain.

In 1955, casinos were going up right and left, and the city's population was on the verge of a huge increase, from 45,000 to 65,000 residents. But Governor Sawyer abhorred the fact that so much of the industry was under the sway of hoodlums, and helped to set up the Nevada Gaming Commission and the Nevada Gaming Control Board to license and police the scene. At the time, there were hundreds of hidden investors, constantly changing names and faces and holding different percentage points in different operations, an ever-shifting mosaic of fronts and corporations.

The Black Book

Then, and for a decade afterwards, Nevada law required all casino owners to be individually licensed, making it impossible for public companies with multiple stockholders to be owners. The law was changed in the late 1960s, allowing small investors to own less than 10 percent of a casino's stock without the need for individual licenses.

Sawyer also promoted the idea of the board publishing a list of disreputable characters to be barred from casinos. To his surprise, the US Federal Court upheld the state's right to a List of Excluded Persons known since as "the Black Book."

Some of the "disreputable characters" were, of course, already established in management *inside* the casinos. The hidden FBI micro-

phones at the Fremont Hotel in 1961 picked up one of the owners, Ed Levinson, discussing what seemed to be a skimming operation involving Meyer Lansky and casinos. Las Vegas telephone records show that from 1961 to 1963, they had leased 25 lines to the FBI, leading from the local office to concealed listening devices in various hotels including the Desert Inn, the Stardust, the Fremont, the Sands, the Dunes and the Riviera.

Later, the FBI uncovered evidence of skimming at the Flamingo; apparently the New York office was the beneficiary of gambling debts which had somehow been omitted from the casino's books in Las Vegas.

The hotel owners pleaded guilty, and admitted skimming a total of $36 million of untaxed income during the decade.

In the late 1950s, community leaders realized the need for a convention facility to help fill the hotel rooms during slack tourist months. Commissioner George Albright was no fan of gambling, and he lobbied hard for the building of the convention center. A site was chosen one block east of the Strip, and in April 1959 a 6,300-seat, silver-domed rotunda with an adjoining exhibition hall opened on the site of the present-day Las Vegas Convention Center. The silver dome was demolished in 1990 to expand the center further. ❑

LEFT: Marlene Dietrich, seen here in 1953, was a frequent guest and performer in Vegas.

RIGHT: the silver-domed convention center opened in April 1959 with the World Congress of Flight.

THE RAT PACK, THE KING AND THE RICHEST MAN IN THE WORLD

The first and second kings of Las Vegas,
along with the reclusive lord of the valley,
left distinctive impressions on the city

hree men cast such long shimmering visions over Las Vegas that the town will never be quite the same again. Sinatra brought high-society elegance into the lounges. Elvis brought the mass market to the Strip. And Howard Hughes brought the appearance, at least, of respectability to the business of owning and running casinos.

A crooner called Frank

Jack Entratter had been the general manager of New York's Copacabana Club and later brought entertainers like Lena Horne, Danny Thomas and others to the Sahara. In 1952, Entratter's attention turned to a crooner named Frank Sinatra, and soon, Frank was on a roll. He won an Oscar for the movie *From Here to Eternity*, and released an album, *Songs For Young Lovers*, that became a bestseller.

Veteran lounge singer Sammy King said, "He was actually the king of Las Vegas because the minute he stepped in town, money was here. He drew all the big-money people. Every celebrity in Hollywood would come to Las Vegas to see him."

Sinatra bought 2 percent of the Sands for $54,000 and within a decade owned 9 percent, by which time the Rat Pack – a loose conglomerate of singers, actors, and comedians – was the hottest thing in town. One night, as a version of the story goes, actress Lauren Bacall was at the Sahara watching Noel Coward perform. Across the table were Humphrey

Bogart, Frank Sinatra, Judy Garland, David Niven, Angie Dickenson, and agent Swifty Lazar. Glancing across their faces she said, "You look like a goddam rat pack," and the name was born. In true Vegas style, it was heisted by Sinatra, Dean Martin, Sammy Davis Jr, actor Peter Lawford, and comedian Joey Bishop as the moniker for their gang.

The Pack's era began when Sinatra joined Dean Martin on stage at the Sands in January 1959, and loosely came and went through 1963. Together the group performed two shows a night in the Copa Room, followed by a friendly and less formal gathering in the lounge, getting together in the daytime for

LEFT AND RIGHT: the Rat Pack were "the greatest, cool, hippest entertainers around."

filming. When they were scheduled to perform, there wasn't a hotel room to be had anywhere which, according to some estimates, benefited Sin City to the tune of an extra $20 to 30 million a week. As a group, the Rat Pack never recorded an album or released a single, although informal live recordings survive.

Sinatra and the broads

Tony Badillo, a long-time dealer at the Sands, said, "Back in those days we used to let Frank and Sammy and those guys deal the game. Of course, with the Gaming Control Board you couldn't do that now. Frank was a pretty good gambler (but) sometimes he'd get angry. Like

mit at the Sands," and was as loose as the Pack's image. Veteran director Lewis Milestone, an Oscar winner for *All Quiet on the Western Front* (1930), was only once able to assemble the entire cast during the five-week shoot. Sinatra turned up, usually late in the afternoon, on only nine days. The others also turned up late, restricting Milestone to a day's shoot of about three hours. "Frank would tear handfuls of pages out of the script and allow (Milestone) only one take," Lawford recalled.

"Some people think Frank is arrogant and overbearing and something of a bully," Milestone said in *The Rat Pack,* a 1998 book written by Lawrence J. Quirk and William

if a woman at the table didn't laugh at his jokes he'd say, 'Tony, get that broad off my table...'"

In 1959, Peter Lawford, Pack member and brother-in-law to John F. Kennedy, discovered a movie script about a group of World War II veterans who rob several Vegas casinos simultaneously. When Jack Warner gave the green light to what was to become *Ocean's 11*, Sinatra said, "We're not setting out to make *Hamlet* or *Gone With the Wind*." Warner himself is claimed to have said, "Let's not make the movie. Let's pull the job."

Filming on *Ocean's 11* was scheduled to coincide with the group's January 1960 "Sum-

Schoell. "Well, he isn't really; he just won't take crap from people." Everybody who could turned up for the star-studded premiere at Las Vegas' Fremont Theater on August 3, 1960. In the next day's *New York Times* strait-laced reviewer Bosley Crowther criticized the film's "surprisingly nonchalant and flippant attitudes towards crime."

Taking a look back at the movie 41 years later – during the filming of the George Clooney remake – *Las Vegas Life* called it "a time capsule of a Las Vegas that no longer exists," and said that Milestone "would have been better off shooting the Rat Pack's nightly performances."

Ocean's 11 certainly was no *Hamlet*, and was trashed by most critics. But *Variety*'s assessment that it "would rake in the chips," was right on the money. According to the *Hollywood Reporter*, the movie went on to become one of the five biggest box-office attractions in the history of Warner Bros. It spawned two Rat Pack celluloid reunions, *Sergeants 3* and *Robin and the 7 Hoods*.

Sinatra and the Mob

Joseph Kennedy asked Peter Lawford, his actor son-in-law and Rat Pack member, to throw his support behind his son John F. Kennedy's 1960 presidential bid. In the

thing for him, especially seeing to it that his privacy would be respected."

Some of the million bucks' donation was funneled to Frank's friend Skinny D'Amato, owner of an Atlantic City club where the singer returned to perform faithfully year after year. That money was used to ensure that JFK won the West Virginia Democratic primary.

In the Chicago primary, Kennedy was facing defeat and Giancana again came to the rescue. Exerting the kind of juice available only to high-ranking mobsters, the Chicago primary was fixed – resulting in a 100,000 vote plurality for JFK, the smallest margin in history. Giancana, who boasted to associates that he

process, Lawford got Sinatra involved in what became a murky political campaign. Two weeks after announcing his race for the presidency JFK picked up a $1 million donation from Sinatra's friend, Mafia boss Sam Giancana, during a trip to the Sands. "(Jack) loved his brief visits to Las Vegas," reported Michael Herr in the book *The Money and the Power: the Making of Las Vegas and Its Hold on America*. "He was the most star-struck of stars... and his Vegas friends arranged every-

had elected a president, had been promised by Sinatra that in return for his help he would have Bobby Kennedy's investigation into organized crime called off. Understandably, Frank felt betrayed when the new Attorney General resumed his attacks, Giancana topping the list.

Worse was to come. Shortly after his election, President Kennedy was scheduled to stay at Sinatra's lavish mansion in Palm Springs, but a few days beforehand the FBI uncovered evidence of a two-year affair JFK had with a woman named Judith Campbell. Surveillance tapes showed her also to be the mistress of Sam Giancana. FBI director J. Edgar Hoover delivered the tapes to Bobby Kennedy in per-

LEFT: Pack members Frank Sinatra and Peter Lawford with Lawford's brother-in-law, Robert Kennedy.
ABOVE: the Sultan of Swing, with harem, in 1955.

son, and JFK's Palm Springs vacation was abruptly canceled. The president had been introduced to Campbell by Sinatra.

In 1963, two months before President Kennedy was assassinated, Sinatra did battle with the Gaming Control Board. The FBI discovered Sam Giancana's presence at Sinatra's Cal-Neva Lodge in Lake Tahoe. (Cal-Neva was where Marilyn Monroe had spent the week before her suicide, distraught from her affairs with both Kennedy brothers.)

Hoodlum Jimmy Hoffa was suspected by the FBI of providing a loan from the Teamsters Union's pension fund for improvements to the lodge. The subsequent investigation

cent language in a tone that was menacing in the extreme and constituted a threat." Sinatra was ordered to appear and defend himself, but instead decided to divest himself of his casino interests and let the license go.

Four years later in 1967, intemperate language and tone occurred again after Howard Hughes bought the Sands Hotel. Sinatra had continued to play there since unloading his stock, but there was animosity between the singer and his new boss. Hughes had once invited actress Ava Gardner to a Lake Tahoe cruise, where he made an unsuccessful play for her. Sinatra was furious, as he was wooing Gardner at the time. When the new owner

showed that Sinatra's loan had, in fact, been turned down by Hoffa. Nevertheless, when the FBI reported their findings to the Nevada Gaming Commission, Sinatra's gaming license was suspended. He had been one of the public partners, Giancana a secret partner. A girlfriend of Giancana's, singer Phyllis McGuire, spoke of Sinatra's relationship to the mobster: "He'd been friends with the boys for years, ever since he needed to get out of his contract with (band leader) Tommy Dorsey."

Gaming Control Board chairman Ed Olsen said that he received a call from Sinatra who had "used vile, intemperate, obscene and inde-

stopped Sinatra's credit at the tables, the singer lost his temper and started rearranging the furniture in a rage which ended when a burly casino manager knocked out two of "Ol' Blue Eyes's" teeth. Sinatra promptly took his show across the street to Caesars Palace.

The boy from Mississippi

Elvis Presley's first Las Vegas gig was in April 1956 at the Frontier. He was 21, billed as "the atomic-powered singer," and opened a show for comic Shecky Greene. *Newsweek* magazine reported that the audience were "underwhelmed," and made comparisons to "a jug of corn liquor at a champagne party."

Recalling the date, Shecky said, "The presentation was terrible. He wasn't ready. He walked out with three or four guys. It looked like a rehearsal hall." After that, "Colonel" Tom Parker steered Elvis away from live performance and into Hollywood for a 12-year series of high-yield movies, most of which the singer loathed. The move did wonders for the Colonel, however, and made some money for the boy from Mississippi.

In 1969, Kirk Kerkorian, owner of the Flamingo, put the finishing touches on the International (now the Las Vegas Hilton) and talent agent Bill Miller contacted Parker about getting Elvis to perform. Elvis had married Priscilla Beaulieu at the Aladdin two years earlier and been a long-time Vegas fan. "Parker didn't want him to open in that big 2,000-seat theater. He said we'd have to put somebody else in to open and Elvis would follow." Miller booked Barbra Streisand.

Parker is said to have signed Elvis for a four-week engagement at $100,000 a week. Having been a long time off the stage, the singer was nervous. He studied other performers in showrooms, and took Tom Jones as his model, particularly for the way the Welsh singer aroused a female audience.

Elvis was a sensation on opening night. He delivered a relaxed show, rated by many among the best of his career. He referred to his time in Hollywood as, "ten years with my top lip curled." Colonel Parker sat down with the International's general manager and wrote a contract the following day, according to the late Kenneth Evans, a Nevada newspaper writer and later, media relations manager for the Nevada Tourist Commission. Elvis was to appear at the International for four-week gigs twice a year, and he was to be paid $125,000 a week. By the end of the singer's first four-week stint, the hotel's showroom had generated more than $2 million in revenue. Evans wrote that Elvis' contract was for a "piddling sum," and speculated that it was due to Parker wanting to settle in Vegas, where he became one of the highest rollers, often losing $50,000 a night. Evans called Parker a "degenerate

gambler," a phrase used by others at the time. *(For more Elvis, see pages 166 and 171.)*

Howard Hughes

Early in the morning on or around Thanksgiving Day in 1966, the eccentric tycoon Howard Hughes arrived in the parking lot of the Desert Inn and was carried on a stretcher to the hotel's ninth-floor penthouse. The windows were blacked out with drapes, armed guards were stationed by the elevator, and seven Mormon personal aides worked shifts around the clock, catering to his every need. He checked in for 10 days, and, during the four years he was there, never left his far-from

THE AUTOBIOGRAPHY THAT WASN'T

In 1972, novelist Clifford Irving made publishing deals with McGraw Hill and *Life* magazine for what he claimed was billionaire Howard Hughes' autobiography. Mike Wallace inteviewed Irving about the book on CBS's show *60 Minutes*. Hughes was so reclusive that it took months for the manuscript to be exposed as a fake, Hughes himself finally giving a telephone press conference. *60 Minutes* called Irving "Con Man of the Year," and he admitted, "I was filled with the success of my fairy tale." He repaid the $765,000 advance to McGraw Hill, was convicted of fraud, and served 14 months in jail. Years later, Irving published the whole story in *The Hoax*.

LEFT: Milton Berle, part-time Rat Packer and card-spinner at the Sahara.

RIGHT: Howard Hughes "changed Las Vegas forever."

lavish bedroom. He took daily codeine injections for spinal injuries he'd sustained in an airplane crash, and subsisted, it's said, on Campbell's chicken soup and banana-nut ice cream. He stored his urine in sealed glass jars and, despite his phobia about germs, the room was never cleaned during the whole of the four years.

Hughes hired Robert Maheu to act as his personal liaison to the outside world. Maheu did not meet Hughes when he was hired, nor during his four-year employment, or ever afterwards, but during his tenure, he was as close as anyone outside would get to Hughes.

When the reclusive tycoon hadn't initially

checked out in time to make room for the high rollers booked in for the Christmas season, the owners of the Desert Inn were furious. So was Hughes. Hughes' man, Maheu, contacted John Rosselli, the Mob's liaison with Vegas. Maheu and Rosselli had known each other allegedly from their having collaborated on an abortive CIA plot to murder Fidel Castro. Maheu also called on Jimmy Hoffa for help as the resort's owner, Moe Dalitz, had been partly financed from the Teamsters Union's pension fund which was under Hoffa's control. Dalitz succumbed and agreed to sell the resort to Hughes. After a lot of quibbling Hughes took possession of the Desert Inn on April 1, 1967 for $13.2 million.

"Just by showing up, Hughes changed Las Vegas forever," Kenneth Evans said in *The First Hundred*, a book about the men and women who shaped Las Vegas. "If one of the richest men in the world, one of the nation's largest defense contractors, was willing to invest in Las Vegas, it must not be such a sordid, evil place after all."

Lord of the valley

Hughes had seen Las Vegas's potential, and was attracted by the fact that it would take only money for him to become lord of the valley. Nevada had no income tax, inheritance tax, or state corporate tax. "We can make a really super environmental city of the future here," he wrote. "No smog, no contamination, efficient local government where the taxpayers pay as little as possible and get something for their money." He sold his TWA stock and went on a buying spree. He acquired the Frontier for $14 million, and the land now occupied by the Mirage and Treasure Island, which he never developed. He also bought the lot now occupied by the Fashion Show Mall, then the Silver Slipper, adjoining the Frontier, although he was denied the right to buy the Stardust Hotel. Then Hughes bought the Sands. Together with the Landmark, large lots on the Strip, the North Las Vegas airport, a TV station, and a small airline, Hughes spent a total of $300 million.

Predictably, he declined to emerge from his hideaway to fill out application forms or be fingerprinted, and Governor Paul Laxalt waived all requirements. About him not appearing personally, Control Board chairman Alan Abner stated, "Hughes' life and background are well known to this board and he is highly qualified." Shortly before, Hughes had written to the governor pledging money for a medical school at the University of Nevada. On November 5, 1970, Howard Hughes was carried from the Desert Inn, still on a stretcher, and put on a plane to the Bahamas. He died five years later, aged 70. ❑

LEFT: Jimmy Hoffa was president of the Teamsters Union and helped friends like Moe Dalitz purchase casinos by embezzling from the union's pension fund.
RIGHT: Elvis Aaron Presley ties the knot with Priscilla Beaulieu at the Aladdin Hotel in May, 1967.

MODERN LAS VEGAS

The opening of Caesars Palace heralded the
current era of fantasy writ large. And larger.
And then as large as it could get

Jay Sarno's visions were studies in excess.
It's rumored that he wanted to stock the
fountain pool of a restaurant at Caesars
Palace with piranhas, which would be fed a
pig at mealtimes. The Health Department
banned the stunt. His deputy at the Circus Circus casino, Don Williams, said, "His insights
all came from his own appetites. Get prettier
girls. Build bigger buildings, get better restaurants, have bigger gamblers around. All those
things came from his loins, not his brain."

Hail Caesar

The opening of Sarno's Caesars Palace in
August 1966 heralded the modern Las Vegas
era of fantasy writ large. The towering white
palace of illusion with Greek- and Roman-
style edifices set the tone for the giant spectacles which now line the Strip. Jay Sarno,
owner of a chain of theme hotels, was a visitor
to Vegas in the 1960s to play craps, at which
he was a consistent loser. He later admitted
that he lost $1 million gambling over two
years. Although Sarno may have been a lousy
gambler, he was a visionary. He felt that the
hotel casinos were commonplace.

His daughter September says, "He was
building slick, gorgeous hotels and making a
living. Then he saw modest hotels here making money hand over fist. He realized he was-
n't building the wrong kind of hotels, he was
building them in the wrong place." Former

LEFT: the implosion of the Sands Hotel in 1966
marked the beginning of the Venetian Hotel.
RIGHT: Steve Wynn, architect of Las Vegas.

Nevada Journal editor A.D. Hopkins said that
Sarno's radical philosophy was for casinos to
be "an island of fantasy in a mundane world."
Sarno traveled to Europe, photographing
columns, pilasters, and flying buttresses.

So was born Caesars Palace, a new kind of
gambling resort that shifted the style of the
city. Inspired by Italian baroque, its approach
dotted with fountains and its staff dressed as
gladiators, Caesars Palace was a sensation.
The restaurant was called Bacchanal, and
wine goddesses massaged diners as they ate.
"People would travel from faraway places just
to get a shoulder and neck massage from these
goddesses," September told an interviewer.

Three years later Sarno sold Caesars Palace for $60 million, double what it had cost, and planned an even more ambitious casino, Circus Circus, targeted exclusively at the high-rollers. For Sarno, though, Circus Circus was a bust. Money was wasted trying to fly a pink-painted elephant on an overhead track. Patrons descended by fireman's pole or a waterslide into the casino, but too many drunks were nearly injured. Some concessionaires on the midway operated crooked rackets, and serious gamblers were distracted by the overhead show. There were no hotel rooms to keep customers on the premises, but the fatal flaw was probably the notion of an admission charge.

After five years of losses, Sarno sold out to new owners, who turned Circus Circus around. It was successfully marketed to a middle-class audience. *Las Vegas Life* writer Greg Blake Miller called Jay Sarno, "The Freud and Ford of Las Vegas. The first in town to fully realize the link between our dreams and our appetites. The central assumption of his career was that we wanted the same things he did."

Howard Hughes' stay from the 1960s to 1970 brought change to the casino business. His acquisition of six casinos, generating about a quarter of Vegas' gaming revenues, marked the shift to corporate ownership, and the influence of the Mob is said to have virtu-

A MODERN TALE OF SEX, DRUGS, DEATH, AND BURIED TREASURE

On September 17, 1998, Sandy Murphy, 26, called for an ambulance at Ted Binion's Las Vegas ranch. Paramedics found Binion lifeless in his den, surrounded by drugs and drug paraphernalia. Police quickly concluded that death was by a self-inflicted overdose.

Ted had succeeded his father Benny in running the family businesses, including Binion's Horseshoe, the casino in downtown Vegas. He always kept cash handy, and buried silver worth $6 million in a desert vault. Ted had drug problems and a stormy affair with Sandy, a lap-dancer. Ted's lawyer, James J. Brown, told police of a call from Binion the previous day. "Take Sandy out of the will

if she doesn't kill me tonight," Binion said. "If I'm dead, you'll know what happened." Ted's associates were amazed no cash or items of value were discovered when the ranch was searched. The next night, police found Murphy's "companion," Rick Tabbish, unearthing Binion's silver stash in the desert with a truck and a digger.

Following a lengthy trial, Murphy and Tabbish were found guilty of Binion's murder by "Burking" (smothering the victim with a pillow, named after William Burke, a 19th-century Scottish murderer). Top-notch attorneys, however, successfully appealed the convictions and won a new trial for the pair.

ally disappeared. Today, vigilantly monitored by the state gaming authority and tax watchdogs, the gambling business seems financially respectable. As usual, this paid off. The 1970s and 80s saw Vegas continue in its role as playground to the stars – whether they were appearing on stage, gambling in the casinos, or working it off on the golf courses. Everyone who was anyone made a pilgrimage to Sin City: Liz Taylor and Richard Burton, Sonny and Cher, the Beatles.

Steve Wynn became a familiar face to US television viewers when the youthful casino boss appeared in the 1980s in a series of TV commercials with Frank Sinatra. The world's most famous crooner had signed a three-year contract to appear at the Golden Nugget, of which Wynn was president.

Wynn's winners

In 1989, Wynn built the Mirage. With a waterfall, an active "volcano," and white tigers, it made a $44 million profit in the first quarter, and profits of 17 or 18 percent in its first year, at a time when Caesars Palace, its next-door neighbor, declined by 43 percent. Ever the self-publicizing showman, Wynn conducted a video tour of the hotel in all 3,044 guest rooms. He followed this in 1993 with Treasure Island, and filled the sidewalk with spectators who gawked at its nightly "naval battle."

At the time, Wynn's annual salary of $34.2 million made him the highest-paid executive in the USA. In 1992 he paid $75 million for the Dunes, then spent another million blowing it up, accompanied by a huge fireworks display for an audience of 200,000 people on the Strip. He promised that its replacement, Bellagio, would be "the single most extravagant hotel ever built on earth." With choreographed colored fountains jetting water 160 feet (49 meters) into the air and a lobby dominated by Dale Chiluly's glass chandelier (see box, page 130), it fulfilled his boast.

Wynn sold all of his holdings in March 2000 to Kirk Kerkorian's MGM Grand Inc. for $6.4 billion to plan a new spectacle: Wynn Las Vegas. For a location, Wynn bought and

demolished the 50-year-old Desert Inn. Speaking to a convention in 2001, Wynn said "My new hotel has been the most wonderful experience of my life. It's about our desert and the southwestern United States."

The MGM Grand was the biggest hotel in town, and both incarnations of this casino were owned by Kirk Kerkorian, a former charter airline operator. In 1967, as owner of the Flamingo Hotel, he was able to start work on the International. This was so successful that his $16.6 million investment was soon worth $180 million. After selling the International and the Flamingo to the Hilton hotel group, Kerkorian became a majority stockholder in

both MGM and United Artists Studios. The first MGM Grand was opened in December, 1973 with 2,100 rooms. It suffered a disastrous fire on November 23, 1980, in which 83 people died and 700 were injured. When the hotel was sold to the Bally Corporation in 1985, one fifth of the price – $110 million – was reserved for outstanding settlements arising from the fire.

Kerkorian has always craved privacy. "I think it's better to keep your business private," he told writer Dave Palermo during an interview in which he expressed his admiration for his former rival Howard Hughes. "I liked him. He was a helluva guy. If you take him early in

LEFT: Jay Sarno was, according to a local writer, the "Freud and Ford of Las Vegas."
RIGHT: Kirk Kerkorian, money-maker *extraordinaire*.

his career he didn't get the credit he deserves." Of Kerkorian himself, a stock analyst said, "Every shareholder who has participated with him has doubled or tripled his money. That's a record few men have."

In 1994, plans were announced for the 1,500 room hotel-casino New York-New York. When it opened three years later, 100,000 visitors a day came. One satisfied customer was Sue Henley, a Vegas construction inspector who won $12.5 million from a slot machine, the biggest jackpot up to then.

Downtown casinos were regarding their competitors on the Strip with both awe and envy and in 1994 began to fight back by

breaking ground for the Fremont Street Experience, a six-block section of the main street topped with an elaborate canopy onto which were presented giant animation shows.

Costing millions of dollars both to build and to operate, it drew tourists but ultimately proved to be a financial disappointment and by 2002 there were signs that the whole idea might need to undergo a reappraisal.

The closing years of the century were marked by even greater expansion on the Strip. The first tunnel under the Strip was completed, the Desert Inn Road arterial; the Monte Carlo and the Stratosphere Tower both opened; and in quick succession came Steve

Wynn's Bellagio, the even larger Venetian – on the site of the former Sands Hotel – Paris Las Vegas with its replica of the Eiffel Tower; and the Mandalay Bay Resort, where the owners, Circus Circus Enterprises, went so far as to change their name to the Mandalay Resort Group. MGM Grand's acquisition of Mirage Resorts Inc. from Steve Wynn created the largest corporate buyout in gaming history. By now, Las Vegas had 19 of the world's 20 biggest hotels and was attracting 32 million visitors per year.

But all was not well. Urban growth brought with it familiar problems. Police reports show an influx of the kind of street gangs seen in almost every major city. A *Washington Post* story suggested that some citizens yearned for the bad old days. "Those punks wouldn't have dared show their faces when Bugsy was around," one old-timer groused.

Trouble in paradise

But not all of this is new. Throughout the last three decades, the Strip has had its share of labor problems. Unions voted for strike action on March 11, 1970, known locally as Black Wednesday. The Desert Inn, Las Vegas Hilton, and Caesars Palace were hit. The strike was said to have cost the casinos $600,000, and the state lost $500,000 in tax revenue. The Frontier was hit by a strike for 75 days in 1985, and again on September 21, 1991 in action that lasted six years and four months. The unions vowed they would be out "one day longer than the Elardi family's ownership," and they achieved it. There was talk of strike action again in April 2002, when unions representing staff in 36 casinos complained of lay-offs after a downturn in trade following September 11, 2001, and increased burdens in working conditions. That same year, a bartenders' strike was called in the downtown area.

About one quarter of the visitors to Vegas each year are coming for the first time, and they were among the first block of trade to fall off after September 11. To lure them back, along with as many veterans as possible, a $13 million eight-week campaign was centered around a rediscovered and never-before-released Sinatra song, *It's Time for You,* licensed by Tina Sinatra.

An important part of the city's – and particularly the Strip's – plans for the future is the Las Vegas monorail. Significantly, the monorail is a rare example of a public transportation system substantially funded by the private sector. It is claimed to be the first such project "in the world," but that's just Vegas.

Travel by monorail

The existing link between the MGM Grand in the south and Bally's/Paris was opened in 1995 at a cost of $25 million. The current system uses two trains which were purchased from Walt Disney World. The project extends the route to the Sahara in the north along a 4-mile (6.5-km) route, with stops serving the

reduce traffic around the Strip by 4.4 million journeys per year, cutting annual carbon monoxide emissions by 135 tons. Ultimately, the monorail is hoped to be extended as far as Downtown, although the fortunes of the downtown area may need a fillip in some form well before then.

Although the US government stopped exploding nuclear bombs at its Nevada test site in 1992, its actions continued to arouse passions when, six years later, it announced that Yucca Mountain, 90 miles (144 km) northwest of Vegas, was to be the site where the entire nation's nuclear waste was to be entombed. Congress decided that the moun-

Flamingo Hilton, Harrah's/Imperial Palace, and the Convention Center. The nine automated four-car trains are capable of carrying up to 5,000 passengers per hour in both directions. The monorail design is built to be upgraded to 20,000 passengers per hour by the addition of further trains, considerably more than current projections of demand. An automated fare-collection system is also incorporated. The monorail opened in early 2004.

Present estimates are that the railway will

LEFT: Vegas has suffered from strike action.
ABOVE: although Vegas already had private monorails like this, 2004 saw the opening of a public monorail.

tain was the best place to hide 77,000 tons of radioactive rubbish that would theoretically remain deadly for hundreds of thousands of years. The plan, furiously opposed by Nevadans, would be for the site to begin storing the nuclear waste in 2010. Nevada governor Kenny Guin vetoed the plan, claiming that the nuclear industry had spent $120 million in support of the proposal. The veto was overridden by simple majorities in the House and Senate, but the battle goes on. The license for the US Energy Authority is not due to be presented until December 2004, and between now and then many Nevadans will be looking for ways to prevent the scheme. ❑

Decisive Dates

300 BC The Anasazi tribe are thought to have inhabited the territory about 60 miles (96 km) north of present-day Las Vegas.

1829 Mexican trader Antonio Armijo's party discovers the area and names it Las Vegas, Spanish for "the meadows," or the fertile plains.

1830 Caravans of traders begin trekking along the Old Spanish Trail through native Paiute land, camping without permission.

1844 Noted explorer John C. Fremont, leading an overland expedition, camps at a site that as a tribute to him years later becomes known as

Fremont Street, in downtown Las Vegas.

1848 The US acquires the region by treaty after winning the Mexican War.

1855 Mormons build an adobe fort in what is today the downtown area of Las Vegas to protect the mail route from Los Angeles to Utah. They abandon it three years later.

1859 Three white men are killed by Paiutes. An expedition from Fort Tejon, California, kills five Paiutes and leaves bodies hung from the gallows "as a warning."

1864 Nevada is admitted into the Union during the American Civil War.

1866–68 US troops suppress the Paiutes in the "Snake Wars." In the end, 1,000 Native

Americans are force-marched across the desert to Fort Tejon.

1905 The San Pedro, Los Angeles, and Salt Lake Railroad (later to be known as the Union Pacific) makes an inaugural run, and lots are auctioned locally.

1908 Phone lines and water lines are established in the region.

1910 In the first of what were to become many policy changes, gambling is outlawed throughout the state of Nevada.

1911 The city of Las Vegas is incorporated. Noted ranch owner Mrs Helen Stewart deeds 10 acres (4 hectares) of her land "for the use of Paiute Indians."

1920 Mayme Stocker opens the first Las Vegas gaming hall, the Northern Club, in Downtown's Fremont Street.

1922 Westside School is built in Mission style for the education of the children of Old Town, the original town site on Washington Avenue along the railroad tracks.

1923 The Hitching Post wedding chapel is built at 228 Las Vegas Boulevard South.

1926 Western Airlines lands its first commercial flight in Las Vegas.

1928 Herbert Hoover, as Secretary of Commerce, steers the enactment of the Boulder Canyon Project Act, making way for the Boulder – later Hoover – Dam.

1931 The Legislature passes a gambling bill by rancher Phil Tobin to raise taxes for public schools. Construction begins on Hoover Dam.

1935 President Franklin Roosevelt dedicates Hoover Dam.

1941 Tommy Hull builds El Rancho Vegas on land opposite today's Sahara Hotel. El Cortez Hotel opens Downtown.

1942 The Last Frontier Hotel opens, later to be called the Frontier. The Basic Magnesium plant, employing 3,000 workers, opens at Basic, a community south of today's town of Henderson.

1946 The state levies gaming taxes for the first time. The handsome mobster Benjamin "Bugsy" Siegel, a member of the Meyer Lansky crime organization, opens the Flamingo Hotel. He is murdered six months later, allegedly for "skimming the take."

1949 The *Las Vegas Review-Journal*, incorporating earlier newspapers, is born, followed the next year by the *Las Vegas Sun*.

1950 Vegas's population reaches 24,624.

1951 Vegas Vic, the huge Downtown neon icon, is erected on Fremont Street.

1955 The 9-story Riviera Hotel is the city's first high rise. Former heavyweight champion Joe Louis is co-owner of the Moulin Rouge, but black entertainers are told to live off the premises. Nevada legislature creates the Gaming Control Board.

1959 In an attempt to control gambling in Las Vegas, the state legislature creates the Nevada Gaming Commission.

1960 The El Rancho Vegas burns down. Las Vegas's population reaches 64,405.

1966 Howard Hughes arrives to buy casinos and live reclusively in a penthouse on top of the Desert Inn.

1967 Nevada's state legislature decides to allow publicly traded corporations to obtain gambling licenses legally.

1970 Las Vegas's population doubles.

1977 The gaming revenues in Clark County – in which the city of Las Vegas is situated – exceed $1 billion.

1989 The Mirage casino and hotel opens with 3,039 rooms.

1990 Las Vegas's population doubles again in just a decade to reach 258,295. Car saleswoman Jan Jones is elected mayor of Las Vegas, unusual in US politics.

1992 The success of Warren Beatty's movie *Bugsy* prompts the Flamingo Hilton to open the Bugsy Celebrity Theater.

1993 The Dunes' owner, Steve Wynn, demolishes Bugsy Siegel's office to make way for a new resort. Treasure Island and the Luxor casinos open. The MGM Grand opens as the world's biggest resort.

1994 Fremont Street is closed as work begins on the Fremont Street Experience.

1995 Clark County population tops 1 million. Clark County casino gaming revenues are $5.7 billion – 78 percent of the US total. The extravagant Fremont Street Experience opens to woo visitors to Downtown.

1996 Siegfried & Roy celebrate their 15,000th Las Vegas performance. A tunnel under the Strip is finally completed: the Desert Inn Road arterial. The Monte Carlo and the Stratosphere Tower

open on the Strip. The Sands Hotel is imploded to clear the way for the Venetian Hotel and Resort with 6,000 suites, the largest hotel to date.

1997 New York-New York opens, initially welcoming 100,000 visitors a day.

1998 Bellagio opens, billed as the most expensive hotel in the world. A 66-year-old Las Vegas resident wins $27 million at the Palace Station Hotel Casino.

1999 Paris Las Vegas opens. Barbra Streisand is reputedly paid $1 million to perform at a millennium celebration.

2000 The Venetian Hotel opens. Las Vegas now has 19 of the world's 20 biggest hotels and attracts 36 million visitors per year.

2002 Nevada is the fastest-growing state in the US. Meeting with local opposition, the US government gets approval to ship nuclear waste to a permanent burial site in Yucca Mountain, 100 miles (160 km) north of Vegas. The US Energy Authority License application is due in late 2004.

2003 The boarded-up Moulin Rouge casino is damaged in an arson attack. Roy of Siegfried & Roy is mauled on stage by one of the magicians' tigers. Treasure Island rebrands itself as "T.I."

2004 Monorail opens to run from the MGM Grand to the Sahara. Elton John booked for Colosseum dates when Celine Dion is resting. ❑

LEFT: Vegas's Old Mormon Fort, built in 1855.
RIGHT: the Venetian, less than 150 years later.

VIVA LAS VEGAS

The city is built on illusion and dreams.
In many ways, this is reflected by the people
who live and work here

Las Vegas is truly a 24-hour city. Most modern cities make that claim, but it is almost impossible to get served a decent meal at 4am at any of them. Here, night and day really are almost indistinguishable. At any hour of the day or night you may need to and you can, without difficulty: buy clothes and jewelery, get married, hire an attorney, get divorced, or engage an Elvis impersonator.

Just ordinary stars

But in other ways Vegas is a city just like any other – ordinary folks live here and go about their business, albeit with a larger percentage of people associated with entertainment, nightlife, and the *demi monde*. Between them, the casinos and hotels employ a total of 166,000 Las Vegas residents. For many, Vegas is their last stop – a place to work at that final job before retiring. But it's not just the aging butchers, bakers, or cabinet-makers who will settle in Sin City. For many others it just seems to become a natural home. These include musicians, comics, dancers, and other performers who have spent a part of their working lives here and developed an abiding affinity with the place.

Professional athletes – tennis players, golfers, football and baseball stars – may also have earned some of their living here, and for many of them, gambling may not be an unfa-

miliar pastime. Wild-haired Don King and his fellow-promoter Bob Arum have chosen residence in this city where boxing plays such a large part. The defeated heavyweight and ex-convict Mike Tyson keeps a home here, too.

World-champion basketball star Shaquille O'Neal, who plays center for the Los Angeles Lakers, has a home, reputed to be a mere five minutes from the Strip. The multiple Grand-Slam winner Andre Agassi, still ranked as a world-class tennis player, enjoys family life here with wife Steffi Graf and their son Jaden Gil.

Basketball star Greg Anthony, who got his start playing on the Las Vegas campus of the University of Nevada, has played for a num-

PRECEDING PAGES: Blue Hawaiian Room of Viva Las Vegas; smoking is allowed and eating encouraged.
LEFT: Elvis lives, on almost every Vegas stage.
RIGHT: Cirque du Soleil have three permanent shows.

MAN POWER

The Las Vegas area has the second-highest man-to-woman ratio in the United States, exceeded only by far-flung Alaska.

ber of professional teams during his 11-year career, and is now with the Milwaukee Bucks but still maintains a home locally, as does Las Vegas-born Marty Cordova, currently a left fielder for the Baltimore Orioles. Former Boston Red Sox second baseman Marty Barrett ended his career with the San Diego Padres in 1991. He has supported local youth baseball players and provided TV commen-

Performers Debbie Reynolds and Wayne Newton have made businesses here, much like magicians Lance Burton, Penn and Teller, and Siegfried & Roy. Celine Dion seems to be following the trend in the opposite direction. Impressed by Cirque du Soleil having a theatre custom designed and built around a single show, she wanted one of her own. Now she has it, designed by the same outfit.

"Trying to identify all the celebrities who live here is difficult," said Sonya Padgett, who compiled a list for the *Review-Journal*, "because many prefer to keep a low profile… (and) while we think our hospitality and favorable weather are selling points, it's just as

tary for the Las Vegas 51s. Kevin Elster settled here after spending most of his career with the New York Mets, and former city councilman Frank Hawkins had once been a professional footballer with the Oakland Raiders.

Stage and television stars who have chosen Las Vegas to set up home include the former teen heart throb David Cassidy, actor and artist Tony Curtis, and singers La Toya Jackson, Clint Holmes, Gladys Knight, Steve Lawrence and Eydie Gorme, Tony Orlando, and Sheena Easton. Comics Marty Allen, David Brenner, Rich Little, and Jerry Lewis have settled in the Las Vegas Valley, as have musicians Sam Butera and Carl Fontana.

likely celebrities decide to move to southern Nevada for the tax advantages."

One of the disadvantages, however, might be the commuting problems. Nevertheless, it's not every town where Meals on Wheels might be delivered by a nationally known racing-car driver in his souped-up speedster, which is what happened the day that NASCAR Busch Series driver Larry Foyt kicked off the casino Harrah's sponsorship of the famous program that feeds needy seniors. Often praised for its community outreach, Harrah's donated a refrigerated Meals on Wheels delivery van to the Catholic Charities of Southern Nevada and, through its 25 casinos in 12 states, is a national corporate sponsor of the program.

Like anywhere else, but maybe for different reasons, people arrive in Las Vegas for a visit and then never leave. What's more, the city is a perfect man-trap. After Alaska – which has a ratio of 107 men to every 100 women, Las Vegas has the second highest man-to-woman ratio, 103.9 men to 100 women. Nationally there are said to be 143.4 women to every 100 men.

Although Las Vegas is a city dedicated to tourism, there is a surprisingly rich local social and cultural life including two active theater companies, concerts, a winter season by the Las Vegas Philharmonic, and a community

---

PEAK POPULATION

A local study concluded that the population of the Las Vegas Valley had increased 194 percent over the past 20 years.

---

the arts," commented Jody Johnson, who used its stage for productions by the Rainbow Company, a children's theater she started with local playwright Brian Strom.

Almost immediately the troupe won recognition from the Children's Theater Association of America as best in the United States. Many of its graduates, now grown up, have gone on to successful theater careers.

center which screens art-house movies and stages both jazz and classical concerts.

The university's Performing Arts Center hosts ballet, chamber orchestra and jazz concerts, and the city turned over an old Mormon facility which it had been using as a city hall while a new one was built. This old building, renamed the Reed Whipple Center after one of the commissioners who brokered the deal, was designated for recreational and cultural affairs. "It's rare that a municipality seeks out

The City Council chose local artist Patricia Marchese to run the town's highly active cultural affairs program. Las Vegas's "Queen of Culture," as one of the local papers called her, takes enormous pleasure in the increasing privatization of the arts. "The arts are not going to make it in this town till the casinos get into the business. And now they have. You have top Broadway shows here. Cézanne here, Russian jewels here, all in casinos.

"I would hope that this would turn into an enlightenment that will lead people to greater support of the local arts. Any time people are exposed to high-level arts, it engenders a desire for more," she said.

LEFT: the glamorous life of a showgirl.
ABOVE: Oscar Goodman, ebullient high-profile politician, at the Golden Nugget casino.

Locals live here, too

A few years ago, Syl Cheney-Coker moved to Las Vegas from Sierra Leone with her husband. At first she was frustrated, trying to find the "city." She wrote in *Las Vegas Life* that the initial impression was surreal.

"I kept asking people, 'Where is it? Show me the center, its soul, its rhythm (besides the awful traffic), the complex social atmosphere of happily interacting souls.' But drive away from the Strip and half a dozen blocks later you are in a different world, less magical – something I believe Fellini would have found absurd; a vast, disconnected suburban sprawl howling of empty hours, loneliness, family-

inheritance plots of Dallas-like magnitude and, yes, people angry and suspicious."

"The architectural madness," she said, "sometimes reminds me of bad opera in which the libretto and the music do not harmonize… try to imagine what this place would be like if only more poets, painters, writers and other artists moved in to create the right atmosphere… It is crying out to be an artist area like Soho or the Village in New York. All it needs are the cafés, bookstores, studios and art galleries." "The city has something like this in mind," Anthony Curtis wrote in the *Las Vegas Advisor* – a six-block area on Fremont and Carson streets east of Las Vegas Boulevard,

where it aims to create an entertainment area with bars, nightclubs and restaurants. "But," he concluded, "nerves are still raw after the city's last land grab (the Fremont Street Experience) so don't count on such a development any time soon. What we are likely to see for a while is more expansion and renovation as the most profitable casinos grow bigger and the rest do what they have to do to keep pace."

Because of the sale in 2001 of 1,900 acres (769 hectares) by the US Bureau of Land Management, a further 5,000 homes are projected in North Las Vegas which abuts the downtown area. There has also been an increase in upscale development in the city itself. Four 40-story towers comprise Turnberry Place, a luxury high-rise at the corner of Paradise Road across from the Hilton.

"In the past few years, Las Vegas's homeless population has doubled to 12,000, but for many, Las Vegas is the American dream come true – affordable housing, no state income tax, and well-paying jobs that don't require much education," said an Associated Press story in 2002. "Only three states have fewer college graduates, but the average household income of $24,177 is the nation's 19th highest. Valet car attendants can easily bring in $50,000. Card dealers on the Strip can make more than that and don't need a high school diploma."

Between 1990 and 2000 the Las Vegas Valley had the country's biggest metropolitan area increase, even in an area known for population growth. "The city has become a glamorous getaway for visitors but also attracts the desperate, people who couldn't make it anywhere else and came here as a last resort."

A stripper in a local bar might make $300 on a good night, and one just off the Strip could more than triple that. Barbara Brent, a sociologist at the University of Nevada Las Vegas said that the city "is built on illusion and dreams. Its whole goal to tourists is to sell fantasy. In some ways that spills over into people who see it as a place where they can fulfill things that they couldn't do elsewhere."

Maybe it's the glamour of the 24-hour twilight zone, in this town with no sense of time. ❑

LEFT: moving walkways keep pedestrians on the move.
RIGHT: bride, groom, and the Venetian.

DICING WITH LADY LUCK

Hope springs eternal in the human breast, and nowhere is this more evident than on the floor of a gaming hall

Alan Wykes once said in a book on the subject, "Gambling is a way of buying hope on credit." Or, as Alexander Pope said, "hope springs eternal in the human breast." Everybody dreams of leaving this town a lot richer than they arrived.

The 2003 Las Vegas Visitor Profile reported that 65 percent of the city's tourists citing the primary purpose for their visit was other than gambling, but closer examination reveals that 87 percent actually had a little flutter. For some it was no more than quarters in a slot machine, but the average number of hours spent gambling was four, and the average spent on gaming $480.

A Godfather speaks

Mario Puzo, author of *The Godfather*, wrote from his own experience. "A gambler should never write a check or sign a chit," he said, "gambling only with the money he brought with him, if he wants to stay out of trouble." He discussed what he calls the "ruin factor," less important when you have nothing to lose, but, "now I have too much to lose, and the ruin factor is decisive. Of course, I had to lose a great deal of money… before I could figure this out. Gambling education is not cheap."

Once upon a time in America, government policy was to discourage or even prohibit gambling, but that was another age. Today,

more and more states not only allow, but encourage, gaming. Politicians seem to have fallen under the spell of easy revenue, almost as much as the casinos and the punters.

The most significant change on the green baize map in recent years has been the growth of gambling on Native American reservations. As semi-autonomous regions, indigenous nations are able to run casinos even in states which otherwise prohibit it. Of America's 561 tribes recognized by the Federal government, 108 are in California. Las Vegas casino owners were alarmed by the competition so nearby, and spent $20 million fighting to prevent Native American gambling businesses, until a Cali-

LEFT: more than $1 million in chips at Bellagio.
RIGHT: casinos are very careful about dice: cheats have been known to substitute their own weighted dice so that they always roll to a given number.

fornian legal decision allowed it in 1988. Forty tribes already have bingo parlors and 50 more are demanding recognition from the government and the right to reservations of their own. Las Vegas claims that Native American casinos in California, from where up to one-third of their 36 million visitors come each year, are taking 10 percent of their business – a whopping $1 billion a year. In what looks like an acceptance of the new reality, however, Harrah's partnered with the Rincon Reservation near Escondito in California for a co-managed casino resort. Nevertheless, Las Vegas continues to hold sway because, according to *The Wine Spectator* "Nowhere on earth will serious

bettors find more games and fairer odds… more diversions and greater spectacles… a city as wonderfully warped and slick as this incongruously lush outpost in the desert."

Compulsive gambling

From high rollers like radio host Howard Stern, who tried to place a $1 million bet on a blackjack hand, to the nickel-slots players, gambling cuts across social and economic classes. Gambling has been studied from just about every angle, and in minute detail, and in almost every way the statistics go up and up. According to the *Las Vegas Review-Journal*, Nevada gaming revenues for 2001 were around $9.67 billion. The average gambler is in the $48,000 a year income bracket and the troubled ones had gaming debts of $37,000, based on 3,000 calls to New Jersey's Council on Compulsive Gambling. More than 80 percent of callers were male, white, and between the ages of 21 and 55.

The percentage of women gamblers has also soared, as reported by the Connecticut Council on Problem Gambling, with a huge increase in calls to its hotline. Statistically, men and women carry similar gambling debts, about $21,000 according to the council, but men have a greater average lifetime loss: $74,000 against $54,000. Independent studies suggest that compulsive gambling may be higher among teens than adults. For teenagers, gambling may begin with friendly wagers on sports events, penny-ante card games, or the lucky "gift" of a lottery ticket from an adult family member.

To their credit, the casinos do not sweep the problem of compulsive gambling under the rug. Eight gaming companies are represented on the Council on Problem Gambling, which develops treatment resources and displays large posters exhorting, "Know when to stop." The posters also give a 24-hour-a-day help line number to call (1-800-522-4700).

Compulsive gambling is described as "an emotional illness that remains hidden until the consequences begin to affect the financial and emotional security of the gambler and his family." Early warning signs, according to the leaflet, include: losing time from work or family, borrowing money to gamble, gambling to escape worry, selling personal possessions to

CITY OF SLOTS

There are a few non-gambling oases in Vegas, but slot machines seem to pop up in more places all the time. In 2000, the Gaming Commission allowed drugstores and grocers to install slots if they were walled off from the rest of the store, but they also made specific exceptions: new liquor stores, gas stations, no-booze restaurants, car dealerships, motels, car washes, fast fooderies, and sandwich shops. Tourists at McCarran airport find slot machines as much of a lure as the shops. Contrary to the myth that machines outside the casinos seldom pay off, within a two-week period in 2002, there were two million-dollar winners on McCarran's slots.

get gambling money, and lying about the time and money spent on gambling.

Harrah's, a member of the council, is more forthcoming than some gaming companies on the subject. Their director of community relations, Mary Jane Fuller, says that Harrah's has invested $250,000 a year in compulsive gambling programs. "In a gambling addiction," said writer Joseph Epstein, "one tends to bet on anything – from the gestation period of a gerbil to different lengths of two paper clips."

One thing that might help is the Innovative Gaming Corporation of America's technology, which allows gamblers to program a set limit on their ATM cards at a casino kiosk, then use

got its modern name from the frontier practice of paying out extra on a hand of an ace with the jack of spades, i.e. "blackjack." The natural house edge is around 3.5 percent, but a skilled player can reduce it to 1 percent or less, among the best odds in the casino.

Avery Cardoza, a gambling author and publisher said, "Blackjack is a game of skill that can be beat. However, to win, you must learn the game properly." The game is played against the house, the object being to beat the dealer. This can be by drawing a higher hand than the dealer without going over 21 – "busting" – or by not busting when the dealer does. The top hand, an ace and either a 10 or a pic-

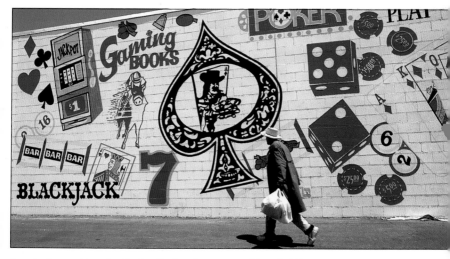

them in slot machines that "lock up" when the limit is reached. The gambler is not allowed to use the card again for five to 10 days.

The history of blackjack

Also known as "Twenty-One" or *vingt-et-un*, blackjack is a descendant from the French game of *chemin de fer*, as is baccarat. There are stories of the game having been played in casinos in France as far back as the early 1700s. It arrived in the US in the 1800s, and

LEFT AND ABOVE: statistically, men and women carry similar gambling debts, but men have a greater average lifetime loss.

ture card is called blackjack. The house pays evens (1-1) to a winner, and 3-2 for blackjack.

There are innumerable systems for blackjack which all promise to tip the odds in favor of the player. The system known as "card counting," however, is still treated as cheating by Nevada casinos. Widely regarded as the world's greatest blackjack player, Ken Uston gave up his post as a senior vice-president of the Pacific Stock Exchange in order to organize teams of card counters.

He also developed a tiny computer, worn in the user's shoe, which aimed to predict the fall of the cards with 80 percent accuracy. When the Atlantic City casinos tried to bar him from playing, he mounted a successful challenge in the Supreme Court.

Poker ploys

Regardless of status, motive, or method, most people make unconscious revelations through body language. In poker, this can be the difference between winning or losing. Tics, twitches, nervous laughs, or facial expressions can be crucial giveaways. Andy Bellin discussed these "tells," as they are called, in an article in *Atlantic* magazine.

"Pop psychologists theorize that tells are unintended actions birthed in the subconscious," he writes. "Having a poker tell can be

disastrous (although) overcoming a tell is as difficult as changing any other habitual aspect of your personality." Often, he says, a player will react to a called bet, slumping in his chair when he has nothing, jumping to flip the cards over when he has a good hand. "The more attention you pay to the body language of your opponents, the less money you'll leave on the table when you walk away."

New Yorker reviewer Joseph Epstein says that poker is not a game for delicate souls. "Good players always beat less-good players over the long haul, but in poker the short haul can kill you." He identifies aggression as the main dividing line between poker players –

"the instinct for the jugular." Newer games such as Let It Ride, Caribbean Stud, Casino War, and Spanish 21 are played against the dealer. "The intimidation factor has been diminished a lot," says Barney Vinson, casino floor supervisor at Caesars Palace. "In a poker room, you don't know who you are playing against, and it can be expensive if you turn up against the wrong person."

However, the odds of winning in these specialty games are lower than in standard casino games. The house edge on craps and blackjack can be 1 percent or less, but it's about 3.5 percent in Let It Ride and around 5 percent in Caribbean Stud. Casinos claim that it takes longer for the house to make a profit, and there's truth in that. The games are popular in part because the hands take longer to play out.

The noisiest, rowdiest places in a casino are usually the craps tables. Play is fast and generates a great deal of excitement. The stickman calls the shots like a carnival barker, and two dealers handle the bets, with a boxman who supervises the game and settles disputes. The dice move from one player to another, and bets can be made either for or against the "shooter" making his target, or "point."

Dice games date back to the Bible, and craps is traced back to before the 1700s, when it is thought to have come to the USA from Europe. Benny Binion introduced craps to casino gaming in Texas, and he brought it to Vegas with him when he opened Binion's Horseshoe, the Downtown casino.

Kirk Kerkorian, founder of the MGM Grand, was known as the "Perry Como of the craps table" for his style and equanimity in regularly winning – or more often losing – from $50,000 to $80,000 in an evening. Legend has it that he and a buddy were down to their last $5, and the buddy suggested they buy breakfast. Kerkorian snatched the $5 bill and took it to the craps table, returning half an hour later with $700. After establishing his own casinos, Kerkorian reputedly stopped playing craps.

Granddaddy of all slots

The century-long history of the slot machine began with the original three-reel machine which emerged from Charles Frey's San Francisco workshop in 1898. The German-born inventor pioneered many kinds of coin-operated gaming devices, most of which found a place in the gambling clubs of San Francisco's Barbary Coast district.

The basic design of "Liberty Bell," the granddaddy of all American slot machines, is still used today, although the simple trio of reels have evolved into microprocessor-controled machines, with up to five spinning reels holding hundreds of symbols. By the time Bugsy Siegel added slot machines to his Flamingo Hotel in the late 1940s, they had already spread across the USA as a way to entertain the wives and girlfriends of high rollers. Soon they were making more revenue

the next. Reuters reported that in 2002, casinos on the Strip kept 6.67 percent of the slot receipts, as against 6.3 percent in 2001. The average take for all games on the Strip has also risen from 5.53 percent in 1996 to 6.03 percent in 2002. Nickel slots pay out significantly less than the higher-stake machines, though Gary Thompson, speaking for Harrah's, said this was not the reason for the ever-increasing nickel slots. "We're not tightening the slots," he said, "It's the customers who are opting to go for the nickel games."

The phenomenal popularity of slot machines is doubtless because they require no skill and the pace can be set by the player.

than the table games. Slot machines now generate two-thirds of Nevada casinos' take, with the nickel slots producing $1 billion annually. Slots take up 60 percent of casino floor space and generate more profits than all the table games combined. The machines are programmed for a jackpot rare enough to make a big pay off, but still allow a tidy profit for the casino. Pay outs are somewhere between 83 and 98 percent, but vary from one casino to another. Pay offs also vary from one year to

LEFT AND ABOVE: slot machines were introduced to entertain the wives and girlfriends of high rollers. Now they generate more revenue than table games.

Players are driven by the illusion that a machine will be ready to pay off after a certain amount of play. The machines are driven by random generators that make new selections every 1,000th of a second, with no reference to what went before, so in reality the machines are never "ready to hit."

Phenomenal popularity

These days, some machines don't even pay a jackpot on one single coin, but the three-coin jackpot often pays 150 percent of a two-coin win. Theoretically costing a quarter or a dollar, they only pay out substantial sums if two or three coins are deposited instead of one. But less than half of slot players play more than one coin at a time, says Crevelt in his book *Video Poker Mania*. He advises, "You should always play the maximum number of coins because there is a bonus when you win (which) can be up to 5 percent of the payback, which doesn't apply if you are not playing to the full extent." Playing only a single coin at a time leaves the casino an extra advantage.

Multiple-coin slot machines were soon followed in the USA by video machines, which substituted screens for the old-fashioned reels. This enabled other games like poker, keno, blackjack, and craps to be played on them instead of just at the table. William Silas "Si"

other games. "A lot of people have learned to play poker on the video poker machines," says Alan Abrams of the El Cortez casino. "Now they enjoy the camaraderie of a table game where people interact with each other."

The 3,000-year-old game

Keno evolved from a Chinese game which is at least 3,000 years old. The modern game makes a slightly inclined bow in China's direction in the "Yin-Yang" symbols on most tickets. Keno runners, like many casino workers in Vegas, count on tips for most of their income, so they're usually easy to find and eager to help. The idea is to predict as many

Redd developed video poker machines when he bought Fortune Coin Co. and converted the early Pong machines for poker.

Casinos were quick to capitalize on the explosive growth of video poker, and in a short time they were taking the place of the original slots. More than 15 percent of Harrah's 1,760 slots are now devoted to video poker, and the percentage is increasing. The video poker machines far outrank the table games in popularity, especially among women; almost three quarters of visitors to Las Vegas play slots as opposed to the 29 percent of players who opt for table games such as blackjack or craps. But playing the slots can also lead to

numbers as possible of the 20 picked in a random draw. There are about half a dozen combination tickets, the bets tend to be small, and pay outs can be up to $50,000. The probability of winning is too low for serious gamblers, but for a frivolous flutter, there is a game about every 20 minutes in most casino hotels, often in the bars or coffee shops.

Super Bowl and other sports

Every January, the handful of men known as the Las Vegas Sports Consultants meet in a three-story building near McCarran airport to establish the "line," (i.e. set the gaming odds) on the USA's Super Bowl American football game. The Sports Books in Las Vegas, plus some in other casinos around the country, are among the clients who await the official word, the yardstick from which bets can be figured. Betting during Super Bowl weekend is about three times that of an average weekend in the National Football League season and includes not only low-wagering tourists, but the high rollers – who tend to stick around town for a while, and the "wise guys" – professional sports gamblers who stay only long enough to win or lose big.

Georgia-born Billy Baxter, a wise guy and three times winner of the World Series of Poker, wagers about $1 million that weekend,

trol Board, casinos pulled in $2 billion in sports wagers but pocketed only $118 million, a winning margin of 6.5 percent.

Cards, chips, and cheats

The accoutrements of games – dice, cards, and chips – have to be as tamper-proof as human skills can make them. Early dice were made from the knucklebones of sheep; today those used for craps are crafted to a tolerance of one ten-thousandth of an inch.

Most of the thousands of decks of cards used annually in Las Vegas are supplied by the US Playing Card Company of Cincinnati, Ohio, whose Bicycle brand – and the Bee

half on college football games on Saturday, the rest on pro football on Sunday.

LVSC has 14 odds-makers for sports, all of whom are licensed by the Nevada Gaming Control Board. After the Super Bowl, the NCAA basketball tournament is the single biggest gambling event. "Blink at the wrong time," says the Stardust's Sports Book manager, "and you can easily lose six figures." In 2001, according to the Nevada Gaming Con-

---

LEFT: dealer at *pai gow* in Caesars Palace, a form of poker adapted from a Chinese domino game and growing in popularity.
ABOVE: a craps game at the Venetian.

brand for casinos – are the most widely used cards in the country. The Bee, first introduced a century ago, uses the highest percentage of rag content. This gives the card a good "memory," the term for how well a card snaps back after being bent.

Gemaco is number one in that other gambling town, Atlantic City, partly because their cards stand up well to the coastal city's notorious humidity. The company has also patented a special design called Safety Peek Faces which enables a dealer to identify his face card without turning it over entirely. Commemorative chips are always a winning move for casinos because many gamblers take the chips home without redeeming them. Chipco International Ltd of Windham, Maine, specializes in colorful, designer graphics with what is termed a high "walk factor," meaning that many people do take them home. Its SmartChip, however, can be tracked by computer and trips a sensor-activated alarm if it is taken from the casino.

Paul-Son is among the growing number of

$5 chips in the betting circle and angle the chips slightly towards the dealer... an attempt to block the dealer's view of the bottom chip," says George Joseph. And then, "if the cheater gets a good hand he will slide a higher value chip underneath."

Magic skills

The sleight-of-hand evidenced by most magicians are much the same as those employed by casino cheats. "They're magicians, too," says writer Deke Castleman. "They're expert at diverting attention while they pull off their scam. The quickness of the hand deceives the eye." Because it plays the highest odds (35-1

security-conscious companies manufacturing casino gambling chips which are, after all, as good as cash. Casino officials are trained to check all chips for a dot no bigger than a speck of pepper. This is an anti-counterfeiting device which, under magnification, yields encoded symbols. The other big Las Vegas chip manufacturer, the Bud Jones company, makes chips with embedded metals, three-dimensional, and holographic chips which they claim are almost impossible to counterfeit.

Since in one way or another the house nearly always wins, some determined casino customers are constantly devising new ways to cheat. "Some cheaters will place a stack of

if betting on a single number), roulette is a popular target for cheats. Sometimes one of a team will blatantly try to place a late bet and, while the dealer is distracted and arguing about it, a confederate executes the ploy. In London in 2004, an East European group were suspected of successfully using a concealed laser device to predict where the ball would land. They were caught when they unwisely returned for a second night's play.

Craps cheats surreptitiously slip their own dice, "loaded" with tiny weights behind the dots, into a game. Magnetic dice have been manipulated by canny players in wheelchairs that are equipped with powerful hidden electromagnets. For table games, cards can be bent or marked with sharp fingernails. "Sanding" is done with a piece of sandpaper glued to the underside of the finger, which can scratch off some of the print on the card. Oils, waxes, and "daub," a substance like eye shadow, are used to mark cards.

Blackjack gives good odds to the gambler, and some players, like Ken Uston *(see page 65)* have improved the odds still further with a technique known as "card counting." This involves mentally logging the high-value cards (10 or above) and low-value cards (6 or below) as they are dealt, to calculate the probable turn of the cards remaining. When

Since the margin between the house and the player is close already, this gives a skilled "counter" a strong chance of beating the house over a long sequence of games. Casinos consider this to be "cheating," and are vigilant for the tell-tale signs. Miniature technology is now enabling cards to be produced with transmitters, allowing automatic detection of card-counters' patterns of play. Suspects are likely to be greeted by large gentlemen offering firm invitations to leave the establishment.

Even slots are not proof against illicit intervention. On the old machines, there'd always be one bettor playing around with wire and magnets. Once Bally's casino introduced

there are a large number of high-value cards left in the deck, the odds are with the player, and he increases his bet.

Gambling for Jesus

The late Jesuit minister Joseph R. Fahey was a mathematical genius and a skillful card-counter. Fahey was eventually banned from casinos after winning tens of thousands of dollars, all of which he donated to the church to uphold his vow of poverty. He died in Boston in 2002, aged 65.

LEFT: betting is fast and furious for most gamblers.
ABOVE: a private game in Bellagio's baccarat room.

electrical slots, a new type of tech wizard appeared. Most electronic slots have a light-optic reader which counts the number of coins being paid out. It didn't take long to discover that a "light device" can be inserted into the machine through the same opening and "blind" it so that it keeps paying.

So, do the casinos do their own cheating? Apparently not, at least in the view of Mario Puzo, who said, "after 15 years of watching and trying to figure out how they cheat, I reluctantly came to the conclusion that Vegas has honest casino gambling, and it may be the first time in the history of civilization that gaming houses have been run straight." ❑

How to Win

There is one sure-fire way to make money from a casino – buy one. If you play the slots, the tables, or the Sports Book in Las Vegas, do it to have fun. You may have Lady Luck at your shoulder and win a fortune at the tables. Then again, you may not. The golden rule for happy gambling is setting a limit beforehand and not exceeding it. If you can manage that, the other motto is "quit while you're ahead." Serious players pre-calculate a stake range – highest to lowest bet – by multiplying the

number of hours they intend to play by the number of games per hour, and dividing their "bankroll" by the result, to set a maximum stake. A low stake is then set at around 20 percent of the maximum, or less. Low bets are made until a winning streak is hit, then stakes are progressively raised. This way, losses are kept small and winnings are maximized.

It's a good idea to ride a winning streak. If you strike it lucky, put a profit to one side, then raise your stakes and go for it. If you start to lose, cut back or – better still – walk away. Playing comfortably low stakes offers more fun in the long run. Betting $5

a hundred times and winning some of the time gives more hours of entertainment than playing $500 and maybe losing, once.

Blackjack

Blackjack offers some of the best odds in the casino. The house's natural edge is between 3 and 5 percent, and skilled players can narrow that to 0.5 percent with betting and playing combinations.

The object is to get a hand of cards closer to 21 than the dealer. Cards take their face value, except for pictures counting as 10, and aces, which the player can value as 1 or 11. The top hand, an ace with a 10 or a picture, makes 21 – "blackjack."

Blackjack deals are from a six or eight-deck plastic "shoe." Some casinos, mostly Downtown, play with a single deck, giving the player much better chances to predict the remaining cards.

Craps

A craps game may look daunting, but is really fairly simple. It also offers good odds to players; the house edge on a simple "pass line" bet is only 1.4 percent. Bets are made for and against a dice roll, called "right" or "wrong" bets. The dice pass around the table. No-one has to roll, but the thrower must bet on his own game.

At the first, or "come out" roll, a throw of 2, 3, or 12 is known as craps. This is a win for bets on the "don't pass" line, or wrong bets. The numbers 7 or 11 are automatic winners for "pass-line" right bets. Any other number rolled establishes the shooter's "point." The aim then is to roll the point again before hitting a 7.

Keno

Keno is hugely popular because it is so simple to play, and a $50,000 payout is possible on a $1 bet. All you need do is pick some numbers on a ticket and wait. It's easy, and it's fun. It's also among the lowest player odds in the house, with a casino edge of 20 to 30 percent.

Due to a mystery of Nevada gaming regulation, keno is not, technically, a lottery. Pay outs must be collected immediately after each game, and before the next game starts, or they are forfeited. Take a place at the bar or café and call a keno runner over, pick your lucky numbers and wait for the draw. Any number of tickets can be bought for each game, and there are endless combinations to mark the numbers, which the runner will happily show you. If the runner returns with winnings, it is polite to tip.

Roulette

The wheel spins, the ball spins against it. The ball drops, and clatters. It bounces once, twice, and comes to rest in number 7. The dealer places the white marker next to your chip on the 7, and your $100 bet is joined by $3,500 in chips.

Or not. Pay out can be a dizzying 35 to 1, but the 0 and 00 make the odds 38 to 1 against you predicting the correct number. If the ball falls on 0 or 00, all bets lose, save for those predicting that exact outcome. This makes the overall house edge 5.26 percent, and about the poorest table odds in town. The safest bets on the wheel are the outsiders; the "dozens" (first 12, second 12, third 12, or one of the three "columns"), which pay out 2 to 1. Otherwise, 1 to 1 payouts are offered by "red or black," "odd or even," or "first or last 18."

Sports Books

In the Sports Book, players back their expertise in predicting sports events. Odds are offered on football, baseball, Indy car races, and championship boxing. But the main event in the book is horse racing, still the largest spectator sport in the US. A horse's previous performance, or "form," is a guide, and the simple bets – "win" or "place" – are the most profitable.

The Sports Book is the one place in a casino you are guaranteed to find a clock.

Poker

A tip from one professional poker player is this: sit down at the table and spot the sucker. If you haven't made them within five minutes, get up and leave. It's you. The

ability to read other players at the table can be as important in poker as getting the best cards. In the betting rounds, the players who think they have the strongest hand will try to lure money into the "pot." But players who believe they have weaker cards may bluff, to scare others out of the game. Poker is the only game where play is against other gamblers and not against the house. Instead, the house makes its living from a cut – usually around 5 percent – off the top of each pot.

A common form of poker in Las Vegas is "Texas Hold 'em." Each player is dealt two cards, face down. Through progressive bet-

ting rounds, five "community cards" are dealt, face up. Each player then makes the highest five-card hand they can from the seven cards available.

Advice from the pros

Serious and professional players consider whatever is in front of them as their own money – not the house's – and safeguard their chips accordingly.

The house plays most games with what seem like relatively small odds. Over time, though, the odds will most likely attract your bankroll across the table. The main thing your skill can do is to slow the roll.❑

LEFT: the best way to win – own a casino.
RIGHT: the surest bets on a roulette wheel are the outside numbers.

BEHIND THE SPECTACLE

Surveillance in the sky, sex that sells, transporting
tigers through rush-hour traffic – keeping Vegas
running to schedule is big-time business

Of the apparent paradoxes in quantum physics, Albert Einstein said, "God does not play dice." Maybe he does, maybe he doesn't, but if he did, Las Vegas wouldn't be a bad place to check the table action. Paradox is deeply embedded in every aspect of this most modern of cities, and nowhere more than in the built-up landscape of illusion, facade, and *trompe l'oeil*. Indoor rivers, canals, and sunsets, erupting volcanoes – nothing here is presented without a sprinkle of star-dust.

The zany architecture, of course, is the first thing visitors tell their friends back home about, but being Las Vegas even something so obvious is hardly ever what it seems. In the words of one commentator, "it's the only place in the world where they try to make buildings look smaller." Writing in *The Atlantic*, Richard Todd said it was hard to believe people who visited such casinos really thought they were having a New York or Paris or Venetian experience. "We like this architecture, if we do, for its ingenuity, not its realism. We are gratified that someone has gone to such lengths to entertain us: it's performance architecture."

Illusion by effort

Bellagio, by any standard, is spectacular, but its executive vice president Alan L. Feldman said its theme, unlike, for instance, the theme of the Luxor, is understated.

"The theme we had in mind was just 'romance.' We had thought of classical French styling but we had also thought of something very modern. In fact, we had a design and announced a hotel built in the shape of a great wave. But then Steve Wynn went to Italy and he was sailing on Lake Como and he looked back at the shore and said, 'This is the most romantic place I've ever seen. Let's build this.'"

What visitors are blissfully unaware of is how much behind-the-scenes activity must be generated to create such "effortless illusion."

Spectators who fill the street to watch Treasure Island's daily battles between a pirate ship and a British Navy frigate have no idea

---

LEFT: primping a private Pompeiian Fantasy Suite in the Forum Tower at Caesars Palace.
RIGHT: it takes thousands of people many days, and long hot hours, to maintain the city's illusions.

how widely designers Jon Jerde and Roger Thomas scoured the world to find the shutters, window grilles, cannons, and cauldrons to create the 18th-century pirate village's fake authenticity. Craftsmen and designers from Hollywood said they were delighted to create something that wouldn't be destroyed when the film ended.

Craig Dunbar, 50, a former Shakespearean actor, is one of the 10 original cast members, sometimes portraying a pirate and sometimes a British officer. None of the 30 actors knows from one day to the next what part they'll be assigned to. But Dunbar loves it anyway: "It plays to the child in us" he says. "What child

didn't want to play buccaneer, pirate, cowboy?" Treasure Island gets hundreds of applications for jobs but there is very little turnover.

New recruits, whether actors or not, start on the British ship working their way through all the parts except captain before transferring for more training to the *Hispaniola*. The pirate ship is more popular because the British sailors get dunked in the water when their ship is sunk – five times every day.

Operations personnel usually come from amusement parks or theaters where they have learned technical skills like pyrotechnics, hydraulics, audio, and lighting. Every step is well-rehearsed, with remote switches to stop the action in the hands of both captains and two overhead observers. "We've done everything humanly possible to make this as safe and exciting a show as possible," Dunbar says. "It looks spectacular and dangerous but it is well orchestrated and safer than it looks. But it is still live, and danger is there."

Horticulturists are taught rappelling and climbing so they can reach plants in the rocks and lagoons of the pirate-village waterfront. Less visible are the scuba-diving plumbers who maintain the waterfalls at the neighboring Mirage, while 17 florists work round-the-clock shifts pampering the 60-foot (18-meter) palms, banana trees, and orchids.

Stars at Mandalay Bay's Shark Reef are the diver-aquarists, most with biology degrees, who plunge into the tank with headsets, which allows them to answer visitors' questions. Sea turtles like to nibble on the divers' ears but sharks usually keep their distance. Brine shrimp are served to the jellyfish, and crocodiles are fed with long poles.

Tigers take a trip

Animals can play a surprisingly large role in everyday Las Vegas life. Rick Thomas is one local who uses tigers in his magic act in the Tropicana's Tiffany Theatre. Thomas and his family live with tawny tigers Zeus, Maximilian, Morpheus, Rocky, and white tigers Samson and Kira on a 2-acre (1-hectare) property north of town, and the trainer has to drive in and out of Las Vegas every day. "People don't see the work that goes into this," he says. "They're animals; they're not potty trained."

Up at 11am for bathing and primping, an air-conditioned trip into town, a nap in the dressing room adjoining the showroom, then two 10-minute afternoon shows are on the agenda before Rick drives all of them home to a dinner of 5 lb (2 kg) of steak tartare. "The cats are not just a prop," said Thomas. "The moment I make a cat appear on stage, I'm no longer a magician. I'm a trainer."

The most extravagant show in Las Vegas must surely be the Cirque du Soleil's *O* at Bellagio. Founded in Quebec, Canada in 1984, Cirque du Soleil tours the world with shows combining spectacle with circus arts, gymnastics, and choreography. With *O* they added water ballet, swimming, and diving, made possible only by the theatre which was designed and built around the massive water production. The performers have to combine a dazzling array of skills to bring off the show. A team of 15 divers work every show, 12 of them underwater the whole time, and all the cast have to be scuba-certified.

Kirsty Powell was a nationally known US gymnast before auditioning for the company, but she still found the mix of disciplines challenging. Speaking to *Las Vegas Life* she said, "When I'd been an athlete, it felt like if I was (playing games), it was goofing off. I know that's what they were asking for, but I hadn't much practice and experience."

hotel staff, and being Las Vegas, they employ them in huge numbers. At the MGM Grand, the business of hospitality takes 740 maids and 62 telephone operators singing the corporate mantra, "Thank you for calling the MGM Grand, have a Grand day," thousands of times a day. Fifty waiters and waitresses at a time handle room service, and the restaurants serve 30,000 meals every day.

Stage-door Johnnies

Backstage of certain shows, usually the ones featuring showgirls, have always held a certain attraction for what were once known as "Stage Door Johnnies." John F. Kennedy, both

Fabrice Becker, Cirque du Soleil's acrobatics scout said, "We are looking for three main aspects. A basic evaluation that includes abilities and strength, after that are the technical parts on the different aparatuses and disciplines, and the third part, which is the most important, is the artistic evaluation." Of Kirsty he said, "We know that she is a great gymnast; I had to find out if she was ready to dance and play some acting games." Did she make the cut? You'll have to check the show to find out.

Casino hotels on the Strip naturally employ

before and during his presidency, loved to watch the girls perform, and Frank Sinatra sometimes courted the leggy beauties by sending flowers backstage with amorous notes. Rich gamblers who made extravagant promises were occasionally hooked into marriage but officially, dancers and showgirls are no longer permitted to fraternize with the audience or in the casino.

After more than half a century, however, the mystique of the showgirls remains, and misconceptions abound. To help put them straight, the Tropicana offers a backstage tour of its *Folies Bergère* show *(see page 112)*. The classic showgirl, tall, stoic, slim, and poised,

LEFT: around 150 staff groom the gardens at Bellagio.
ABOVE: snatching phone calls home between shifts.

must not be so overly endowed as to offend wives and girlfriends, and these days topless shows are usually confined to the late performances. Dancers, who rarely appear topless in production shows, tend to be shorter and originally were "saloon girls," hired to spruce up a casino. Then legendary producer Donn Arden brought in a group of dancers to the Desert Inn's Painted Desert Room which began the tradition of runway models.

One of the first showgirls was Dorothy Dandridge, whose beauty and dancing skills made her a headliner at the famed Club Bingo in the late 1940s. Dandridge won a Best Actress nomination in 1954 for her part in

many entertainments for children and a number of hotel casinos have been themed around family-friendly motifs, the resort is turning back to its earlier market.

The *Las Vegas Review-Journal*'s Dave Berns wrote, "Marketeers of the desert city, *circa* 2000, have made an aggressive push to reposition the town as an adult getaway." He said it is "a hip place Frank Sinatra would have enjoyed, a setting where people can leave their day-to-day lives behind in Des Moines, Iowa, or Des Plaines, Illinois and chase drink, song, money and sex." Casino executives are attracted to the demographic of the middle-aged baby boomer because their

Carmen Jones. Minsky's Follies, which opened at the Dunes in 1957, was the first topless production show. The *Follies* ran for more than four years, and set show attendance records. The Sands never went topless. The "Texas Copa Girls" or "Pony Girls" were a line of 16 beauty queens from Texas brought specifically to entertain the big Texas moneymen (and therefore big spenders) in the late 1950s. The women were not trained dancers nor did they have any show experience.

In the 1980s and 1990s, Las Vegas was marketed as a resort for young families and seemed to see an important part of it's future in family vacations. Though there are still

average age is 49 and up. As the Mandalay Resort's president Glenn Schaeffer clarified, "For the next decade, one American will turn 50 every 11 seconds."

Sex

Sex is a major component in the Las Vegas spectacle, and the part on display is barely the tip of an iceberg. In a city whose very essence is promise and enticement, the sex trade flourishes. Some visitors find themselves victimized by sex-tease clip joints where women hustlers extort huge sums for drinks with the promise of future action later. "Later" never comes. These operators prey mercilessly on the unwary and the mistaken belief that prostitution is legal in Las Vegas. Reputedly, they will charge anything up to $6,000 for a bottle of non-alcoholic "champagne," and the "non-alcoholic" part is the giveaway.

Although sex-tease clubs are tolerated, they aren't granted liquor licenses, so if you find yourself, for any reason, in a bar with no beer, you may want to leave smartly.

Legalize the liaison?

Prostitution is illegal in the city, but nobody pretends it doesn't happen. Out on the Strip are countless freesheets and flyers, with phone numbers for women who offer a wide range

dealer and bootlegger who went on to become chairman of the state's Republican Party in the 1950s said, "They're trying to lay all this crime we have today on hookers and pimps. Well, if that's the problem, why the hell don't they legalize (prostitution) so they can regulate it? Regulating it is all you can hope to do because they have never succeeded in eliminating it in a thousand years of trying."

Stocker made his remarks in 1982, the year before he died, still advocating the legalization of all "victimless" crimes, especially prostitution, a lesson that he said should have been learned from gambling's history. Nevada state law prohibits brothels in any county with

of exotic services in your hotel room. Like any city in the world but Las Vegas style – more overt, with a lot of glitz and show.

Expectations are high because of the apparently endless population of glamorous women, anxious to make a living by any means necessary. This goes for men, too; a growing market in Sin City is the number of full-time male striptease revues. Pressure to legalize prostitution dates back almost as far as the city itself. Harold Stocker, a former

more than 400,000 inhabitants. The closest legal brothels to Las Vegas are in Nye County, particularly in the desert town of Pahrump about 60 miles (96 km) away.

The very existence of a place tagged as Sin City attracts all kind of people with all kinds of motives. It's not surprising that the euphemistically styled "adult entertainment" industry holds its annual trade show – the Adult Video News Expo – at the convention center in Las Vegas. That, in turn, is all part of the attraction for Mike Foster and Craig Cross of xxxchurch.com, a Vegas-based crusade against the porn and flesh trade. "If Jesus were walking the earth today," said Cross, 26, "he'd

LEFT: Anthony, Caesar, and Cleo take the weight off their sandals.

ABOVE: dinner with the Tropicana's Rick Thomas.

be here, too. After all, he hung out with prostitutes and stuff." They work with a church, whose pastor said, "It is very near to our hearts to help people overcome sexual addiction and to help them have healthy sexual boundaries with other people."

And surely, God would love Las Vegas as much as any of us. Referring to Einstein's quote, Stephen Hawking, the modern cosmologist said, "God plays dice all the time."

Security and surveillance

Not many gamblers glance upwards as they navigate the aisles but most of them are well aware that their every move is watched

Review-Journal columnist John L. Smith wrote about the time when the MGM Grand hired a former hotel burglar and jewelry fence, now dead, for its surveillance team. He "made a small fortune turning in people who not long ago would have qualified as his running mates," Smith wrote, reminding readers of the old adage, "set a thief to catch a thief."

Gaming establishments, he explained, "have a long tradition of employing convicted card and slot cheaters to catch those still practicing the racket."

The plastic bubbles in the casino ceiling house flexible cameras which can rapidly shift to any angle, and zoom in instantly. They are

through the ubiquitous one-way mirrors and cameras that the casino has mounted along the walls and catwalks and in the ceiling.

The video cameras are programed to zoom in automatically at the earliest sign of unusual activity. They are silent because recording audio contravenes the Federal laws against wire-tapping, but surveillance goes on around the clock with particular attention, sometimes with the aid of binoculars, on games where illicit activity is suspected. This is often on the part of the customers, although dealers and pit bosses are not above suspicion, and casinos also have to keep an eye on their own security staff.

part of a system mandated by the enforcement division of the Nevada Gaming Control Board, whose agents have full access at all times, and the power to demand any videotape they want. Officials are unwilling to give details, but all the videotape of both play and players is said to be collected daily and stored in a warehouse, ready for replaying if necessary. Tapes are usually saved for seven days but in certain areas, the law mandates 30-days' retention. Cameras are equipped with infrared and ultraviolet imaging to detect concealed devices, as well as face-recognition.

George Joseph, formerly the director of surveillance at the Dunes, reveals some things about surveillance techniques in his book *Why Shouldn't a Woman Wear Red in a Casino*, subtitled *The 101 Most Asked Questions About Las Vegas and Casino Gambling*. Dyes can be applied to clothes for concealment or camouflage, so surveillance equipment is tuned to detect dyes on clothing. Cheats conceal devices under hairpieces, so the cameras also exaggerate the color tone between real hair and a wig or toupée – an uncomfortable discovery for rug-wearers.

Surveillance cameras have been known to pick up almost invisible beams of infra-red light from a hidden miniature video camera. In one instance, it was in the purse of a woman

TAKE THE STAIRS

Surveillance cameras pick up more than just casino cheats. Apparently, videotapes of people having sex in the elevators are particularly popular.

Magazine writer Sergio Lalli says that five people are likely to be in the count room at one time, and each of them has to be authorized by the Gaming Control Board. They are not subject to casino authority.

Nevertheless, new methods of skimming keep turning up which manage to bypass all the best-laid plans. An ingenious scheme at the Stardust some time ago involved a change

sitting by a blackjack dealer, and it transmitted a picture of his hole card as he peeked at it before taking players' bets.

Back in the days when microphones were allowed, Joseph says that some customers used to "audition for the lounge shows," by singing into the mics mounted at gaming tables. Today, though, the only microphones allowed in casinos are those that monitor audio in the count rooms, where the sound of money can be as important as the actual sight of it.

LEFT: sex is a big component in the Sin City spectacle.
ABOVE: in most casinos, someone, somewhere is always watching.

booth which operated with "surplus" coins from a miscalibrated scale. The bills received by the girls who dispensed change were deposited back into the rogue booth, whose takings never went to the count room.

In his book *Loaded Dice,* self-confessed "casino cheat" John Soares recounts his years working with a team adept at switching the dice in craps games with custom-crafted dice of their own. Soares repeatedly points out the risks inherent in cheating – when failure might have resulted in sudden death and an unmarked burial in the desert – but he claims that he and his canny team ripped off millions without any serious setbacks.   ❏

VEGAS IN THE MOVIES

The fantasy facades of Sin City offer endless opportunities for movie-makers. The fact that Vegas is just a short hop on a Lear jet from Hollywood doesn't hurt

Las Vegas magic is the magic of illusion, and many of its spectacular displays are the work of designers, set builders, and special effects experts from the movie business. The puffy clouds and sunsets inside shopping arcades like the Forum Shops, the millions of megawatts of artificial light outdoors, the pyramids and volcanoes, and the sea battles of Treasure Island make the town like a Hollywood blockbuster set. The gold and the glitter, the instant flips of fortune, and the fantasy facades also offer endlessly rich plot potential. All this has kept Sin City in the movies and in the business of movies. The fact that Vegas is just a short hop in a Lear jet from Hollywood helps, too.

Made in Vegas

From the days of the silents, Las Vegas had starring roles in movies like *The Hazards of Helen* and John Ford's 1932 film *Airmail*. Edwin L. Mann's 1946 film *Lady Luck* was a moral tale about the irresistible lure of gambling. In 1960, both Marilyn Monroe and Clark Gable played their last movie roles in John Huston's *The Misfits*, much of it filmed in the Nevada desert. Arthur Miller's script about a disillusioned divorcée was uncannily prophetic of the Monroe-Miller marriage.

Ocean's 11, also made in 1960, was the famous Rat Pack saga, directed by Lewis

Milestone when Frank Sinatra, Dean Martin, Sammy Davis Jr, and Peter Lawford could spare time from carousing. Though the film wasn't highly rated by critics, it made respectable enough ticket sales for a follow-up, *Robin and the Seven Hoods*. *Ocean's 11* was remade in 2001 with George Clooney, Matt Damon, Andy Garcia, and Julia Roberts topping a stellar bill, and featured several interiors that were shot in Bellagio.

Elvis Presley wooed Ann-Margret from the Sahara in the Strip all the way to Lake Mead and Mount Charleston in *Viva Las Vegas* (1964), a famous pairing rumored to be mirrored off screen, too.

LEFT: Sean Connery as James Bond makes Fremont Street safe for the world in *Diamonds are Forever*.
RIGHT: Sarah Jessica Parker and Nicholas Cage in *Honeymoon in Vegas*, featuring the flying Elvi.

In 1971, Sean Connery went Downtown to Fremont Street as James Bond in *Diamonds Are Forever*, which critic Leonard Maltin described as a "colorful comic book adventure." Dustin Hoffman won an Oscar for his role in *Rain Man* in 1988, which co-starred fresh-faced Tom Cruise, and featured a scene filmed in the Pompeiian Fantasy Suite of Caesars Palace. Actor Nicolas Cage is a virtual Vegas veteran, having starred in three local movies: the 1992 comedy *Honeymoon in Vegas*; the 1995 dark drama *Leaving Las Vegas*; and two years later, *Con Air*.

Lavish high-roller suites and turns of the tables provided the setting for Adrian Lynn's

dinary cameo from Tom Jones, and no fewer than two roles for Jack Nicholson. In that film, the Las Vegas Strip was spectacularly demolished by creatures that now have small-screen lives of their own as *Butt Ugly Martians*.

In the same year, the special effects were about the only stars of *Independence Day* to survive with reputations intact. Some feel that *Independence Day* is easily as funny as *Mars Attacks* but not, alas, intentionally. In 1998, Klingons visited Sin City in a dastardly plot to kidnap guests from the Las Vegas Hilton, foiled by the time-traveling crew of the Starship Enterprise in *Star Trek: The Experience*.

Rick Moranis reprised his goofy scientist

Indecent Proposal (1993), where Woody Harrelson rashly encouraged screen wife Demi Moore to spend a night with tycoon Robert Redford for a million dollars, and lived to regret it – until the last reel, of course.

Sci-Fi on the Strip

In *The Amazing Colossal Man* (1957) Las Vegas came under attack from an Army officer who grew 60 feet (18 meters) tall after surviving an atomic explosion, but the assault came from elsewhere in *Mars Attacks*.

Tim Burton's wild 1996 sci-fi fantasy brought to town a galaxy of stars including Pierce Brosnan, Annette Bening, an extraor-

role from *Honey I Shrunk the Kids* in *Honey I Blew Up the Kid* (1992) where his two-year-old son becomes 150 feet (46 meters) high and grows even larger when he comes near electricity. In Las Vegas – well, you can imagine.

Gangsters and godfathers

In 1972 and 1974, parts 1 and 2 of Francis Ford Coppola's *The Godfather* trilogy were partly filmed and set locally. Between them, the two films won 13 Oscars and 11 Golden Globe awards for their stars and the mercurial director. The saga of the Corleone family includes references to the Mob's attempts at legitimacy in the Nevada gaming business.

The movie also features the now-legendary tale of a Hollywood producer who finds the head of his favorite horse tucked up under his silk sheets as a timely reminder to employ a certain skinny, Italian-American crooner.

Warren Beatty played a highly romanticized Benjamin "Bugsy" Siegel while conducting an on-screen romance with his soon-to-be wife Annette Bening in Barry Levinson's *Bugsy* in 1991. Until then, the owners of the Flamingo Hotel had been a little coy about the casino's associations with Mr Siegel, but interest in the movie persuaded them to open the Bugsy Celebrity Theater.

Martin Scorsese's *Casino* (1995), starring

gush of television documentaries with Las Vegas as the backdrop. Barely a week goes by without one of the networks shooting in town, a bonanza that brought $135 million in production work in 2001, bringing the total to more than $1 billion since the Nevada Film Office was first set up.

The Nevada Film Office assists hundreds of films, music videos, and multimedia productions every day of the week. Mimosa Jones heads the Entertainment Development Corporation, in striving for its share of the $16 billion budget that Hollywood loses annually to "runaway productions." Jones said that the city's 36 million tourists also "provide a

Robert de Niro and Sharon Stone, is a brutally comic tale of mobsters hustling their way into the casino business, much of it filmed in the Strip's Riviera casino. *Get Carter* was a classic British gangster movie made in 1971, and it confirmed Michael Caine's status as a powerful screen actor. The movie was remade in 2000, set in Vegas and Seattle, and starred Sylvester Stallone killing lots of people.

The 2001 remake of *Ocean's 11*, the caper about casino robberies, unleashed a veritable

steady audience for game shows and audience-based TV shows." Feature films bring between $35,000 and $100,000 a day in goods, services, and local talent, while documentaries, corporate and industrial productions all sweeten the pot. Sometimes movie money gets spread around unexpectedly: a scene in *Rush Hour 2* involved scattering millions of dollars of fake money, some of which was collected by bystanders and allegedly passed off as real currency. In this Tinsel Town, it's not even unusual for a group of tourists to discover that their local waiter or shop manager had a "starring" role in a movie they have seen (*see photo on page 138*). ❑

LEFT: Warren Beatty as a largely fictional but good-looking Bugsy Siegal in the 1991 film, *Bugsy*.
ABOVE: Sharon Stone and Robert de Niro in *Casino*.

GOING TO THE CHAPEL

Britney Spears did it; Mickey Rooney did it
eight times in the very same chapel.
The neon nirvana is a mecca of matrimony

Las Vegas is a favorite destination not only for gambling and conventions, but also as a mecca of matrimony, a paradise of promises, a Valhalla for vows. Over 174,000 troths are pledged here every single year.

In 1943 when the Little Church of the West was located at the New Frontier, Betty Grable and trumpeter and band leader Harry James exchanged their vows. The *Las Vegas Review-Journal* reported that more than 100 locals left their beds in the middle of the night to make a trip to the train station, hoping to get a glimpse of Grable as she waited for James to return from Mexico with his divorce papers. The wedding took place not long before dawn and after the ceremony the couple drove right back to Los Angeles.

Here come the brides

Celebrity weddings have always been fashionable in Sin City. Zsa Zsa Gabor married actor George Sanders in 1949 at the Little Church of the West. Zsa Zsa purred through another seven marriages, but she didn't try her luck at love in Vegas again. In 1949, Rita Hayworth married singer Dick Haymes at the Sands. Hayworth had been married to Prince Ali Khan, and to Orson Welles, and her partnership with Haymes lasted only two years. On July 19, 1966 Ol' Blue Eyes married Mia Farrow at the Sands, Sinatra's second home for nearly a decade.

LEFT: Tom kisses Kelly.
RIGHT: weddings can be cheap – one reason over 174,000 troths are plighted each year.

Mickey Rooney married Ava Gardner at the Little Church of the West in January, 1942. Over the next three decades he made seven return trips to the same chapel, concluding with a marriage to January Chamberlin in 1978. Rooney is definitely in line for frequent-matrimony miles.

More recently, in January 2004, singer Britney Spears married hometown honey Jason Allen Alexander at the Little White Chapel; the marriage was annulled 50 hours later. The Little White Chapel was also chosen for the happy day for Michael Jordan and Juanita Vanoy in 1989. Bruce Willis and Demi Moore were married there, and the chapel beams a live wedding over the Web every few minutes via its Wedding Cam onto the Discovery Channel's Internet site. The chapel displays Joan Collins' and Michael Jordan's name in lights. Owner Charlene Richards said, "Joan Collins told me, 'Charlotte, when I leave this place you can tell the world if you like.'"

Billy Bob Thornton was married to Angelina Jolie at the Little Church of the West on May 5, 2000. According to Greg Smith, owner of the Little Church of the West, the oldest wedding chapel in Vegas, and now opposite Mandalay Bay, most big-name stars want their weddings quiet and unpublicized. When Richard Gere and Cindy Crawford

of former boxing champion Ingemar Johansson. Of the public appetite for celebrity splicings, he said, "I think basically people have a latent voyeuristic streak in them and they like to peek in on other people's lives."

Invitation to impulsiveness

Vegas has about 50 wedding chapels which are open daily from 8am to midnight, and stay open 24 hours on legal holidays. The invitation to impulsiveness is taken advantage of by an average of 337 couples every day, with Valentine's Day weekend understandably the busiest time of the year, when as many as 2,000 licenses are issued. The chapels issue at

arranged their nuptials in 1991 he didn't know who the bride and groom were to be until they arrived. "They said it would be a celebrity wedding and if they saw any press hanging around outside they wouldn't come in," said Smith. Both stars were dressed casually and told him they had been having dinner in Los Angeles when they got talking about it.

"Then, they just got on one of Disney's planes and came here and did it." The couple asked that photos be taken but made sure to take the negatives with them when they left.

Las Vegas has hosted 500 celebrity weddings or more, according to Dan Newburn who officiated at the Treasure Island wedding

least 87,000 marriage licenses per year, each for a $50 license fee. Some legal identification is required, like a driver's license, passport, or birth certificate, as well as divorce papers if either party has previously wed. Betrothed couples fly friends, well-wishers, and families to Vegas just as a starting point for the adventure. The inexpensive 32-room motel behind the Viva Las Vegas Wedding Chapel at the northern end of the Strip offers a Blue Hawaiian room named and modeled after the Elvis movie, rooms themed with headstone headboards and a coffin bathtub, and an Al Capone room with an image of a bound-and-gagged bellboy inside a closet.

The Excalibur provides a medieval-themed ceremony, the MGM Grand offers Merlin the wizard to officiate while a fire-breathing dragon attempts to thwart the nuptials. The Las Vegas Hilton provides Intergalactic Federation regalia and hires several of the *Star Trek* characters as witnesses. Betrothals can be made by, with, or even to the Phantom of the Opera. Other settings include a beach party, a Wild West wedding on horseback, an ancient Egyptian theme, on a pirate ship, at the Las Vegas Motor Speedway, at the bottom of the Grand Canyon, and a wedding under water. Ceremonies can be arranged at the top of Paris Las Vegas's Eiffel Tower.

marry on a bungee jump, during a roller-coaster ride or, for even whiter knuckles, parachute-jump or sky-dive during a wedding. Ceremonies can be officiated in a helicopter hovering over the Strip, the Grand Canyon, or the Hoover Dam. For more serene mid-air marriages, a hot-air balloon is available with a basket large enough for bride, groom, and the assembled company.

The 3-millionth wedding in Las Vegas was celebrated at the Imperial Palace's We've Only Just Begun Wedding Chapel in July 2001, and coincided with the 92nd anniversary of the first recorded wedding in Clark County in 1909. The couple, Alberto and Mar-

Drive-thru venue

One wedding chapel provides a convenient drive-thru venue, so the bride and groom don't even need to leave their car. For the more up-market autophile, you can have a limo drive to the scenic backdrop of your choice – and get married in the back of the stretch. In fact, a few limos come equipped with whirlpools and hot tubs, so the happy couple can bubble and betroth simultaneously.

Those with a taste for the extreme can

LEFT AND ABOVE: you can choose to be married by a wizard or a medieval minstrel, on a bungee jump or under water. Elvis may participate or even officiate.

ian Recio of Miami, Florida, renewed their vows in Spanish, serenaded by Elton John, Elvis, and Wayne Newton lookalikes from the hotel's *Legends in Concert* show.

The Clark County Recorder's office has made marriage records available on the Internet, and certified copies can be bought for around $7 apiece. Requests for duplicate certificates come in from around the world.

If the marriage doesn't go quite as planned, however, a solution is close to hand. About 446 miles (718 km) north of Las Vegas in Reno, Nevada, divorces can be arranged almost as spontaneously as weddings, and in just as many interesting ways. ❑

SPECTACULAR SPORTS

Tennis aces, golf pros, maniacal motorcycle riders,
heavyweight boxers – everybody wants to
flaunt their physicality in Vegas

Hundreds of years before the Las Vegas Valley was discovered by non-Native Americans, members of the indigenous Southern Paiute tribes had been playing and wagering on a game involving several small sticks. The game, which is still played by the local tribes around the Las Vegas area, takes skill, courage and, of course, luck.

Crowds of spectators gather to watch as the players use finesse and daring to outwit their opponents. Fortunes, relative to the era and values of the time, are won and lost by players and spectators alike.

Although the game, whose exact rules are still closely guarded by the Southern Paiutes, bears little similarity to the games of chance played in the big casinos of today, it could be said that this was the beginning of the history of sports and sports-betting in Las Vegas, which is now a multi-million dollar industry.

Headline sports

In terms of money, Las Vegas is truly a modern-day sports capital, yet surprisingly the city has so far been unable to support a professional sports team of any kind – hockey, basketball, football, soccer, or baseball. Attempts have been made to seed professional franchises in southern Nevada, but no professional team has yet inspired Clark County's 1.5 million inhabitants.

In spite, or perhaps because of this, the city's sports are guaranteed to make headlines.

LEFT: NASCAR racing at Las Vegas Motor Speedway.
RIGHT: golfers of all types love Vegas's 50 fairways.

There was, for instance, Evel Knievel's 1967 attempt to jump over the fountains of Caesars Palace, a stunt that landed him in the hospital for 31 days. Or his failed jump over Snake River Canyon in the desert in a souped-up rocket bike called the "Skycycle."

Twenty-two years later, son Robbie Knievel drew equally large crowds when he effortlessly sailed over Caesars' fountains (with no hands on the handlebars), and later, when he made a successful jump in the Grand Canyon. (Papa Knievel, meanwhile, is rumored to be bored with retirement, and might be opening an Evel Knievel Xperience Cafe in the desert town of Primm.) And who can forget the Flying Elvi, those Elvises in pompadours and white catsuits who parachute out of airplanes on a regular basis and played a stirring role in the movie *Honeymoon in Vegas*?

Spectacular sports, live-action sports, sports in general, and sports betting in particular are prime draws for visitors to Sin City. On Super Bowl weekend (usually late January), Vegas swells to capacity as more than 200,000 sports fans converge for raucous parties, and bet millions of dollars on America's football championship. Resorts host lavish invitation-only bashes to lure the highest of high-rollers, to the casinos to drink, party and put up as much of their money as they dare.

Probably the best-known live sport in Las Vegas is boxing. The city hosts many world championship boxing matches, bringing in millions of dollars for both the city and the contenders. The big-ticket ringside seats are coveted by the social, entertainment, and sports elite, male fans often in black tie and tuxedo, their female consorts in long evening gowns and sparkling with jewelry.

Las Vegas was world-renowned as a boxing venue long before defeated and disgraced heavyweight boxing champ Mike Tyson chewed Evander Holyfield's ear (literally) in 1997. Most, if not all, of the great fighters in the modern boxing world have fought in Las

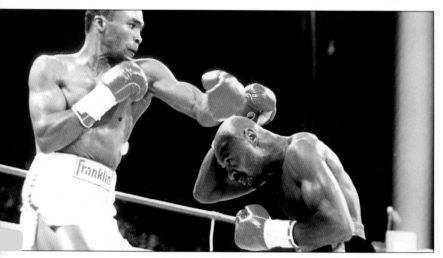

HEAVYWEIGHT CHAMPIONSHIP BOXING

Below are some of the momentous Las Vegas fights in which the world heavyweight title has changed hands:

Sonny Liston vs Floyd Patterson July 22, 1963
Liston landed a knockout punch in the first round.
Cassius Clay vs Floyd Patterson November 22, 1965
Clay won with a technical knockout in 12 rounds.
Muhammad Ali vs Ron Lyles May 16, 1975
Ali (formerly Clay) won, but Lyles held him to 11 rounds.
Muhammad Ali vs Leon Spinks February 15, 1978
Olympic champ Spinks won only his 7th professional bout.
Larry Holmes vs Muhammad Ali October 2, 1980

Muhammad Ali was knocked out in the 11th round.
Larry Holmes vs Tim Weatherspoon May 20, 1983
After 12 long, hard rounds, Holmes won a split decision.
Larry Holmes vs Mike Spinks September 22, 1985
Leon Spinks' brother Mike took Holmes' title.
Michael Moorer vs George Foreman November 5, 1994
Foreman wasn't deemed a suitable opponent due to his advanced years, but knocked out Moorer in the 10th round.
Evander Holyfield vs Mike Tyson November 9, 1996
The fight was stopped in the 11th round, with Holyfield the clear winner. A year later Tyson couldn't win the title back, but took some of Holyfield's earlobe instead.

Vegas rings, including Sugar Ray Leonard, George Foreman, Oscar de la Hoya, Riddick Bowe, Lennox Lewis, and Muhammad Ali. Heavyweight champion Joe Louis became a casino "greeter" at Caesars Palace after his long and illustrious boxing career ended, and he called Las Vegas home for many years.

Mike Tyson currently keeps a multimillion-dollar house in the southern part of the valley. Tyson's 2002 fight with heavyweight champion Lennox Lewis, in which Tyson was knocked out cold by Lewis, was originally scheduled for Las Vegas. The Nevada Athletic Commission, however, refused Tyson's license to fight in the state, decreeing that

rational game, a sport for those a cut above the common man. Nearly every casino on the Strip sported acres of posh green fairways, kept vibrant with wells deep in the Las Vegas Valley aquifer, below the Mojave Desert.

The Tropicana, the Dunes, the Sahara, and the Desert Inn all maintained lavish courses, often with fairways right outside the casinos. Many of the legendary performers who played Las Vegas showrooms at night enjoyed clearing their heads of cobwebs with a stylish daily round on a Las Vegas course. The roster of legendary drivers and putters included Dean Martin, Bob Hope, Bing Crosby, Debbie Reynolds, the McGuire Sisters, Willie Nelson,

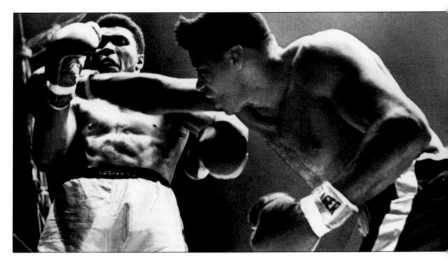

Tyson's image wasn't what Nevada boxing is all about. They had some cause. Before the two ever met in the ring, Tyson bit Lewis on the leg in front of the cameras during a pre-fight news conference in New York City.

Singers and swingers

Golf is another sport long associated with Las Vegas. In the early years – the 1940s, 50s, and 60s – the casino builders saw golf as an aspi-

LEFT: Sugar Ray Leonard defeats Marvin Haglar for the World Middleweight title, April 6, 1967.
ABOVE: Floyd Patterson and Cassius Clay in the World Heavyweight title bout, November 22, 1965.

Joe DiMaggio, Burt Bacharach, and others too numerous to mention.

In the early 1990s, however, the landscape began to change for Las Vegas golfers. Strip-resort entrepreneurs realized that the land around their casinos covered by grass and sand-traps for golf would be far more valuable covered by a casino, a parking lot, or an amusement arcade. Their fate was sealed, and the first of many courses began to sink beneath the creeping spread of concrete.

The Tropicana hotel's golf course, which was on the northeast corner of Tropicana Avenue and Las Vegas Boulevard South, was purchased by Kirk Kerkorian and annexed into a major part of the MGM Grand Hotel, Casino and Theme Park.

The same year the MGM opened, Steve Wynn purchased and blew up the Dunes Hotel. Out of the Dunes' lush green fairways rose Bellagio, with its massive dancing fountains – fountains supplied with the water from wells that had formerly watered the Dunes Golf and Country Club. In June 2002, Wynn closed the Desert Inn golf course, the last course on the Strip. Wynn has promised a new course with his most recent hotel, currently being built on the site of the old Desert Inn.

Despite the loss of the Strip courses, golf remains a huge business in Las Vegas for courses with long-time coach Butch Harmon, who has a home in southern Nevada. Former president Bill Clinton was known to play golf every time he visited Las Vegas, and was one of the first to play Southern Highlands Golf Club when it opened in April 2000.

At least a dozen PGA Tour players live in Las Vegas or have close ties to the city, and often seen on local courses are stars of the green Jeff Gallagher, Craig Barlow, Chad Campbell, Bob May, Edward Fryatt, Robert Gamez, Skip Kendall, Stephanie Keever, John Riegger, Chris Riley, and Eric Meeks. Entertainers still flock to Las Vegas courses and are regularly spotted by fans: Celine Dion, George

everyday golfers as well as for the rich and famous. There are more than 50 courses nearby *(check the discerning list in Travel Tips in the back of this book, pages 233–4)*, including Steve Wynn's Shadow Creek Course, rated by many to be among the best in the world. And private trips to private golf clubs – usually in a private limo or helicopter – are a regular perk offered by casinos to high rollers.

Las Vegas courses are still celebrity-packed, and it's not unusual to run into the elite from the world's of sports, politics, or entertainment. Golfing phenomenon Tiger Woods won his first major tournament in Las Vegas in 1996, and he still works out on local

Clooney, Eddie Van Halen, Smokey Robinson, Will Smith, Lou Rawls, and Joe Pesci are often seen on the links.

Cowboy get-together

Every December, Las Vegas's western roots show proudly when the city plays host to the National Finals Rodeo (NFR), the final event in the exciting ProRodeo Cowboys Association rodeo calendar. Broncos are ridden and steers are broken in pursuit of the hotly contested cowboy title, World Champ All-Around Cowboy. Only the top 15 cowboys from the national rankings in each event are invited into the competition.

NASCAR action

One of the fastest-growing spectator sports in the US is NASCAR Winston Cup car racing. About 10 miles (16 km) north of the city, Las Vegas has one of the USA's largest and best racing tracks. Every year the city plays host to the Sam's Town 300 and the UAW-Daimler Chrysler 400 NASCAR race at the Las Vegas Motor Speedway. Tens of thousands of supporters flock to the track to cheer – and place bets on – their favorite drivers. In 2002, 137,500 fans turned out for a 3-hour, 400-mile (640-km) NASCAR race, the largest single crowd for a sporting event in Nevada. More than 5,000 people who came to the track in

longest-running off-road vehicle races in the country, offering valuable purses to both the winners and the losers. Desert enthusiasts race anything from big-wheeled motorcycles to huge custom-built trucks costing hundreds of thousands of dollars; the vehicles scream, scramble and slide around a track of 50 miles (80 km) in length. Modern racers who compete in the SCORE Henderson's Terrible 250 have five laps of a desert course to complete, starting and ending at Black Mountain.

Tennis aces among the dice

Tennis is another sport with southern Nevada connections. Andre Agassi, the tennis phe-

recreational vehicles established a virtual city in one of the speedway's massive parking lots.

Since the early 1970s, southern Nevada has also become the home of an off-road vehicle race sponsored by the Los Angeles-based SCORE International. The USA's oldest established major desert-racing organization, SCORE's roots in Las Vegas go back to the heyday of the Mint Hotel and Casino located Downtown. The Mint 400 is one of the

LEFT: Rachel Sproul in the demanding barrel-racing round, National Finals Rodeo, December 16, 2001.
ABOVE: Evel Knievel's "Skycycle," used in a failed attempt to jump Snake River Canyon in 1974.

nomenon of the 1980s and 1990s, was born and raised in Las Vegas. Agassi is one of only a handful of players ever to have won each Grand Slam tournament at least once. For years, Las Vegas has hosted tournaments showcasing great names of the game like Arthur Ashe, Rod Laver, Chris Evert, and Martina Navratilova.

The Nevada desert has served as a sports ground for as long as man has lived here. From the stick games played by the Native American inhabitants to the world-title boxing matches, and the roar and scream of the NASCAR vehicles, its popularity shows no sign of declining yet. ❏

PLACES

A detailed guide to Las Vegas and its
surroundings with the main sites clearly
cross-referenced by number to the maps

L as Vegas is a twinkling, flashing, glittering, lop-sided crown, jutting
irregularly out of the desert. It soars and scrambles upwards, stranded
in an arid dust-bowl. When approached at night from the air, it beckons like a seafront arcade from the wilder edges of science fiction. Arriving after dark on the road, it pulsates and looms ever larger, defying belief. Closer up, the giant neon glare evolves into shapes, signs, and pictures, and the spectacle of the world's most lavish playground unfurls in the car windshield.

Disembarking at McCarran Airport, passengers are greeted by the Las Vegas theme tune – the continuous, tuneless chord of the slot machines, with percussion from jangling coins. Travelers pass through several aisles of gaming machines before reaching the luggage carousels, so there's no need to be bored if the bags are late. In any of the hotel casinos on the Strip, the carpet, the decor, and the dress of the staff tell you instantly where you are. Paris Las Vegas is all blue, a European classic; the Luxor is, well, Egyptian. But close your eyes, and the electronic music of the slots is identical everywhere – except perhaps for the frequency of the jackpots.

The casinos on the Strip are almost impossible fantasies made flesh; the town is a realization of innumerable show-business dreams. Inside, these pleasure domes take Kubla Khan's vision about as far as technology and invention will go. Expense has clearly been no object. The food and the entertainment are world-class. That is to say, world-class offerings are plentiful. For those who prefer simpler, earthier distractions, these too are only a short step away.

Downtown works hard to lure the Strip-bound gamblers away. The Fremont Street Experience is a spectacular technological marvel, still drawing long, spontaneous applause at every show. And Downtown competes with the Strip by giving the crowds something that they really want – better odds at the slots and tables.

Whatever your taste in post-millennial recreation, roll up, roll up, ladies and gentlemen, it's all here waiting right here for you. Step right in. ❏

PREVIOUS PAGES: Bellagio's fountains, choreographed to music; Luxor aims to capture "the essence of Egyptian architecture;" champagne and slots at Paris Las Vegas.
LEFT: a little bit of Italy in the desert sun: the Venetian.

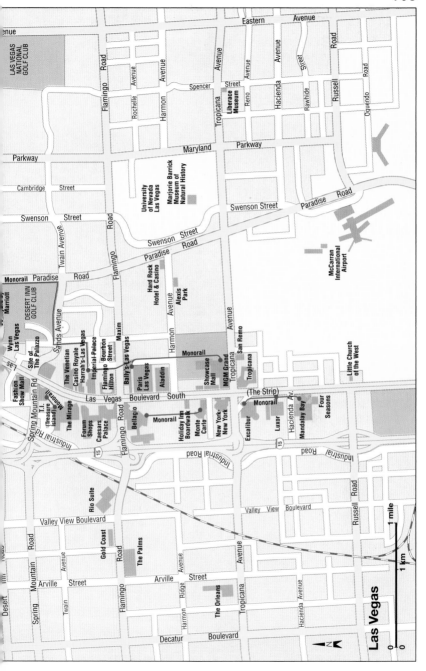

Las Vegas

CROSSROADS OF THE WORLD

All kinds of visitors from all over the globe converge on this busy intersection, and its collection of "performance architecture" reflects a surreal multi-culturalism

One of the busiest junctions in Las Vegas is where Tropicana Avenue crosses the Strip, connecting casino-hotels on all four corners. Everyday, thousands of pedestrians ride up and down elevators and escalators, and across the elevated pedestrian crossways. CBS Television calls this the "Crossroads of the World," and often recruits targeted audiences to test pilot shows at the junction.

As David Poltrack, CBS vice president for research and planning says, the location is perfect because, "It is the one place in the country where you can get a socio-economic cross section of America, with great geographic diversion."

In other words, you can find all kinds of people from all over the USA – and lots of other countries, too – right here. The themes of the adjacent casinos are also – at least outwardly – multi-cultural. In the short stretch of the Strip covered in the next two chapters, the hotels evoke France, olde England, Egypt, the Far East, the Caribbean, and the East Coast of the United States.

I love New York

Opened in January 1997, towering, 47-story **New York-New York ❶** (3790 Las Vegas Boulevard South, tel: 740-6969 or 800-693-6763 was

Nevada's tallest casino at 529 feet (160 meters). Its 2,035 rooms were filled even before it opened, by previewers excited by the appeal of staying in the Big Apple without having to actually go there. Visitors can admire the world-famous skyline and visit replicas of landmarks such as the Statue of Liberty, a 47-story Empire State Building, and the Brooklyn Bridge.

The resort's towers include the 40-story replica **Chrysler building** and the 41-story Century building.

Map on page 108

LEFT AND BELOW: your poor, your weary – Las Vegas is not the place to bring them.

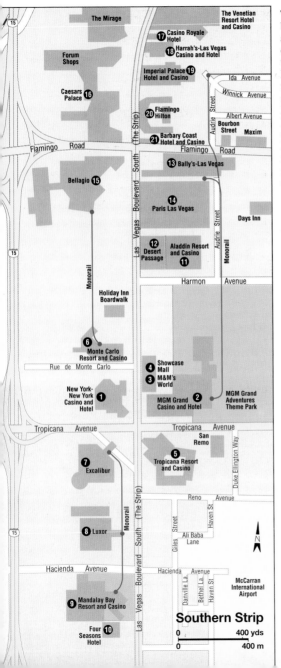

The large gaming area is surrounded by Park Avenue and Central Park, and adjoins **Times Square**, which offers perhaps the city's best selection of fast-food outlets, including Broadway Burger and Pizza. Visitors can cross the 300-foot (90-meter) **Brooklyn Bridge**, ride the **Manhattan Express** or a Coney Island-style roller coaster, and stroll along a prettily graffitied Lower East Side street of shops and eateries. Thousands of coins are thrown into the "lagoon." These numerous coins are fished out at a later date and donated to the charitable Make a Wish Foundation.

Successful

"The interesting thing to me about New York-New York," says University of Nevada professor Dave Hickey, "is that visually, externally it really is a successful building. It solves the facade problem by multiplying facades, which also solves the scale problem."

The facade problem Hickey refers to is the difficult trick of providing thousands of rooms in one complex, but giving all of them a desirable view. This is the reason that so many hotels on the Strip are built in an "X" or a "Y" shape. The "scale problem" is that visitors could easily be overwhelmed by the vastness of the buildings in Las Vegas. Bellagio's canny architect addressed this by making each "window" actually cover four rooms, making the hotel appear only one quarter of its size.

The exterior of New York-New York is esthetically better than the interior, but there's a Nathan's Coney Island hot-dog outlet and the ESPN Sports Bar with 12-foot (3-meter) screens and 160 TV monitors, of which a dozen are located in the washrooms (designated *Guys* and *Dolls*) so you need never lose track of the track, so to speak. The

Disney Company operates New York-New York along with six other casinos around the country. A Las Vegas construction inspector named Sue Henley won $12.5 million on a New York-New York slot machine in 1997, at the time the biggest jackpot ever.

In 2003, the owners of New York-New York decided to spice up the resort's wholesome image by staging the third Cirque du Soleil show on the Strip. Called *Zumanity*, and taking its cue from the adult-oriented accent that is part of Vegas's post-2001 redefinition, one of the main ingredients of the show is sex. *Zumanity* is, in fact, a circus of sexuality, from homoerotic to racy to kinky, offering g-strings, fetish wear, and nudity aplenty. The stage juts out suggestively into the audience, and there are scenes of naked people woven into the carpet.

The show should have been a winner. And although profits are acceptable, *Zumanity* has not reached the dizzy heights of popularity achieved by Soleil's other two shows, *O* and *Mystère*. As a result, on whether the adult-oriented theme is carried over into a proposed fourth Soleil show at the MGM Grand in a couple of years, the verdict is still out.

Map on page 108

MGM Grand

Currently, Las Vegas' biggest hotel is the 5,005-room **MGM Grand ❷** (3799 Las Vegas Boulevard South, tel: 891-1111 or 800-929-1111). Guests are greeted at 38 reception-desk windows and entertained as they wait by panoramic images of desert scenes, baseball stadiums, and advertisements on an 80-panel video screen. Opened in late 1993, the MGM Grand has enough rooms and suites to offer a restless guest a different room every day for almost 14 years.

As the world's biggest gambling operator, the MGM-Mirage company's assets include New York-New York across the street, Bellagio, Treasure Island, and the Mirage. Dot-com millionaires Tim Poster and Tom Breitling, and world tennis ace Andre Agassi also have shares in the company.

Las Vegas welcomes up to 36 million visitors a year.

BELOW: moonrise over the MGM Grand.

Gameworks, by the Showcase Mall, is jointly run by Sega and Universal Studios. It offers over 200 state-of-the-art arcade games.

BELOW: the Showcase Mall has M&Ms galore, plus a Coca-Cola bottle you can ascend.

The corporation is headed by Kirk Kerkorian. A high-school drop-out who is now over 80 years' old, Kerkorian began his Las Vegas career as a tour operator. He went on to build a series of hotels which were always the biggest in town. "He doesn't do it for the money, he has more money than he'll need in five lifetimes," said one of his friends. "He does it because he gets bug-eyed like a little kid when he goes through the place."

The MGM Grand's entrance is flanked by a 45-foot (14-meter) high lion, which is claimed to be the largest bronze statue in the United States. This is the second lion on door duty here, the first was thought by Asian gamblers (of whom there are many) to bring bad luck, as guests' entry to the casino was through the lion's open mouth. The doorway was promptly removed.

At the entrance on the Strip, a walkway from the Tropicana leads onto MGM's balcony over the casino floor. At the far side, live musicians and trailers from forthcoming movies are projected onto a giant screen. In the amusing Rainforest Café, simulated thunderstorms and animated monkeys and crocodiles distract diners as they eat surrounded by imitation birds, animals, and butterflies.

Lions sleep here, too

On the casino floor to the right, visitors walking through the glass entrance to the **Lion Habitat** find lions sleeping over their heads or beneath their feet. The 450-lb (204-kg) beasts frolic with their trainer among waterfalls in a rocky African Savannah enclosure. Metro, Goldie, and Louis B, three of the resident pride, are said to be descendants of the MGM signature lion whose yawn-like roar was the company's movie logo.

MGM's casino is the biggest in town at 171,500 square feet (16,000 square meters) and significantly has 3,500 slots. Slot-machine betting, the fastest-growing game over the past decade, increased at the rate of about 12 percent every year, producing $1 billion a year for casinos from nickel slots alone. MGM-

Mirage's patent on coinless slot machines using paper currency, pre-printed coupons, or "cash-out slips," has been licensed to Reno's International Game Technology, the world's largest manufacturer of slot machines with an 85 percent share of the market.

The special events area seats 17,157 and has a reputation as a world-class venue for superstar concerts and world championship sports events. A 15-minute walk from the hotel entrance leads to what used to be the 33-acre (13-hectare) **MGM Grand Adventures** theme park, now used only for special events.

Behind the time-share Polo Club, a monorail curves around connecting the MGM Grand with Bally's and Paris Las Vegas. The long-time ambition of Las Vegas authorities is to connect the Strip, Downtown, and McCarran airport by monorail. Investors have divvied up $600 million for the next phase of the extension, which runs from the MGM to the Sahara.

Outside the MGM Grand is

where visitors are recruited to attend the free screenings of CBS pilot TV shows, to give their opinions and help shape the coming schedules. In return they are offered $10 discount certificates that can be used in the adjoining Television City gift shop. Tests are conducted all day, and shows last about one hour, including the time to gather reactions. There is rarely a wait of longer than a few minutes.

Previewed shows sometimes offer good entertainment, and the venue has become CBS's most important test-market. "People come here for the nightlife and try to figure out what to do during the day," said one participant. "This is a place where people have time to spare."

M&Ms play here

Adjoining the MGM Grand are **M&M's World ❸** (3785 Las Vegas Boulevard South 2, tel: 736-7611) whose candy stores, Racing Cafe and interactive exhibits are especially attractive to children, and the **Showcase Mall ❹**, with a theme

Map on page 108

BELOW: the *Folies Bergère* first took the Vegas stage in 1959.

loosely based around the Grand Canyon, with the aid of 60 tons of textured "rock," rope bridges, and a hovering helicopter.

Climbers with harnesses can ascend the 75-foot (23-meter) studded concrete "tree" to the amusement of the crowd below, and lightning storms and flash floods feature in the hourly show. An elevator takes visitors up the 100-foot (31-meter) high Coca-Cola bottle so they can enjoy the view of the Strip from above.

The Tropicana

The **Tropicana** ❺ (3801 Las Vegas Boulevard South, tel: 739-2222 or 800-634-4000) is themed as "the island of Las Vegas." The concept began in 1986 when a 22-story tower opened on a 5-acre (2-hectare) landscaped island among flamingos, parrots, cockatoos, and swans. Over the years more wildlife, more towers, and a walkway link were added, and the pool area expanded. Another island fronts the hotel. Home to two 35-foot (11-meter) tall sculptures of Aku Aku

gods and a Polynesian house nestling in tropical landscaping, it gives nightly laser shows that are highly regarded.

The hotel's main attraction is the long-running *Folies Bergère* show. With its origins in Paris in 1869, the show was brought to the Tropicana in 1959 by Lou Walters, father of ABC-TV's Barbara Walters, and has now given more than 25,000 performances. On many nights there are two shows: the "classic" show is at 10pm, while a show "suitable for children," i.e. no nudity and no drinks, begins at 7pm. A Folies performance with no bare breasts seems a strange concept, since nudity is what the show was founded on originally.

Highlights of the show form a part of the afternoon tour, which goes backstage through dressing rooms that are strewn with sequined costumes, wigs, false eyelashes, and feathered fans. Personal items, flowers, and photographs adorn the dressing tables lined up in a row. Each dancer has at least half a dozen pairs of $150 shoes.

BELOW: Trop tattoo.

Entertainment abilities

Along with their entertainment abilities, performers must have minimum height qualifications to work here – 5 feet 3 inches (1.6 meters) for acrobats, 5 feet 6 inches (1.7 meters) for dancers, 5 feet 10 inches (1.8 meters) for showgirls – and the cast range in age from 18 to about 40. These glamorous girls make around $45,000 a year, but they also have plenty of opportunities for pay-per-hour jobs at conventions.

Topless showgirls first arrived on the Strip in 1957 at the Dunes Hotel show, *Minsky's Follies*. Early shows included a dance group produced by Donn Arden, the man credited with setting the style for modern showgirls, at the Desert Inn.

At that time, the hiring practice was for girls 5 feet 8 inches (1.75 meters) tall or above, and today the classic showgirl is still very tall, ultra-thin, and perfectly poised. Dancers can be shorter and sometimes perform clothed. The showgirl style was followed successfully at the Stardust Hotel, where the *Lido de Paris* show was imported from France for a run that lasted 31 years. Both the Dunes and the Desert Inn have been imploded.

The Tropicana sports a kind of funky, old-fashioned charm, promoting its Caribbean theme with flamingos, macaws, and toucans. A wooden bridge overlooking a waterfall offers a romantic backdrop to the many weddings that are conducted here. Labyrinths of corridors lead from the flower-filled garden to the casino.

The highly entertaining bird show features eagles, parrots, and macaws. Tiki the macaw swings from his beak, and Lolita, an Amazon parrot, sings operatic selections. It's a free show (three times daily, except Thursday) during which the birds perform unlikely tricks like riding scooters and flying through hoops.

Legends live here

The Tropicana's **Casino Legends Hall of Fame** is one of the most interesting museums in town, a museum of casinos and gaming. Colorful and mostly defunct gambling chips, autographed boxing

Map on page 108

BELOW: never let an opportunity go by at the Tropicana.

gloves, hotel security uniform patches, ancient slot machines and porcelain decanters shaped like slot machines, packets of Desert Inn cigarettes, vinyl album covers, and glittering costumes worn by performers are among the 15,000 items in the three crowded rooms.

The walls are lined with rarely seen historical documents and photographs. Exhibits are drawn from 738 casinos, of which 550 have passed into history themselves, and chart 70 years of Las Vegas gambling history.

A videotape showing the implosions of the Aladdin, Hacienda, and Sands hotels runs continually, near to a glass case of memorabilia from El Rancho Vegas, one of the first casinos *(see pages 27–29)*, and a catalog from the Sands' auction held in July, 1996. Other screens run scenes of the Sinatra-led Rat Pack antics, and inductees of a Hall of Fame. These range from Las Vegas veterans like Phil Tobin, who first arranged for gambling to be legalized, to stars like Sinatra himself.

There is an admission charge to the museum (open daily) but free tickets are often handed out – along with a free slot-machine pull – in the hotel's parking lot. One intriguing exhibit is a sample page from the secret "Black Book," which gives a glimpse of pictures and background notes on gamblers of "notorious or unsavory reputation" who are banned from the casinos. Between 1960 and 1995, 38 people were listed in the Black Book.

Adjoining the museum is the **Legends Deli** where customers enjoy their favorite stars in the form of sandwiches; the Joey Bishop (pastrami on rye with a pickle), the Liberace (grilled prime rib on a French roll), Jerry Lewis (baked ham on a wholewheat baguette) or, of course, "the King" (grilled banana, peanut butter, and grape jelly on white toast).

Monte Carlo

The **Monte Carlo** ❻ (3770 Las Vegas Boulevard South, tel: 730-7777 or 800-311-8999), from the outside low-key by Vagas standards, with arched domes, marble floors,

Lance Burton, Monte Carlo magician.

BELOW: kids outside the Monte Carlo.

ornate fountains, and gas-lit promenades, is modeled after Monaco's Place du Casino and is operated by the Mandalay Resorts Group, which runs almost a mile of Strip casinos to the south. The Monte Carlo's marble registration area overlooks the pool, which can produce 30-inch (75-cm) waves.

The hotel also has its own brewery, producing 8,000 gallons (250 barrels) of beer each month. Varieties of ale include Winner's Wheat, High Roller Red, and Jackpot Pale, the last checking in at 5.2 percent of alcohol by volume. Beer is brewed here every two or three days and aged from 14 to 60 days. Because it is not pasteurized and no artificial preservatives are used, the beer is best when kept refrigerated.

The giant copper tanks, each holding 620 gallons (2,350 liters), are visible through huge glass windows from the Medici Cigar Club. Stogies run from as little as $3.50 to as much as $25 each. Smokers can lounge around the brewery's floor where there is nightly entertainment, or on over-stuffed couches to view the scene from the floor above.

Street of Dreams

Outside, sharing space on the **Street of Dreams**, lit by old-fashioned gas lamps, is a Beer on Tap counter for those who want to drink standing up and then scoot. From a tram station at the end of the street, visitors take the (free) one-minute ride to Bellagio.

Both Bellagio and the Street of Dreams are the work of interior designer Terry Dougall, who was responsible for the much-lauded Forum Shops, and who also contributed to both the Venetian and Mandalay Bay hotel casinos.

Lance Burton is a long-time Vegas headliner who has been starring in his eponymously named theater at Monte Carlo since 1996. As a kid, Burton spent his money at the magic shop, getting some of it back by doing shows and charging 5¢ admission. The amiable Burton's act includes ducks, Elvis the parakeet, and a seemingly endless flight of white doves. ❏

Map on page 108

RESTAURANTS

America
New York-New York
Tel: 702-740-6451
Open: 24 hours daily. **$$**
Philly cheese-steak sandwiches from Pennsylvania and buffalo wings from New York are always favorites.

Coyote Café
MGM Grand
Tel: 702-891-7349
Open: L & D daily. **$$–$$$**
Spicy, modern southwestern cuisine. Specialties include salmon with pumpkin seeds.

Emeril's New Orleans Fish House
MGM Grand
Tel: 702-891-7374
Open: L & D daily. **$$$**
Celebrity chef Emeril Lagasse's creole-cajun seafood. Especially tasty is the BBQ shrimp.

Wolfgang Puck Café
MGM Grand
Tel: 702-891-3019
Open: L & D daily. **$$**
Circular restaurant surrounds an open kitchen dishing up high-class pizza and much more.

Mizuno's Japanese Steak House
Tropicana
Tel: 702-739-2713
Open: D daily. **$$$**
The Tropicana's finest dining experience: Teppan-style food with spe-cialties like tempura sand hibachi.

André's
Monte Carlo
Tel: 702-730-7955
Open: D daily. **$$$$**
Elegant dining in an up-scale setting, featuring award-winning chef André Rochat's gourmet cuisine and world-class wine cellar.

Monte Carlo Pub & Brewery
Monte Carlo
Tel: 702-730-7777
Open: L & D daily. **$–$$**
Food until 10pm; snacks until late. Good meals, great brews, and music from 9pm nightly in the first microbrewery in a Las Vegas resort. The casual atmosphere tends to attract a noisy but fun-loving crowd.

● ● ● ● ● ● ● ● ● ● ● ● ●
Price includes dinner and a glass of wine, excluding tip.
***$$$$** $40 and up, **$$$** under $40, **$$** under $30, **$** under $20*

EXCALIBUR TO MANDALAY BAY

Merry Olde England competes with tropical Eastern luxury, while the Sphinx next door shoots laser beams from its eyes. Where else could you be but Las Vegas?

Map on page 108

The multi-colored spires of the **Excalibur** ❼ (3850 Las Vegas Boulevard South, tel: 597-7777 or 800-937-7777) look just like a DisneyWorld castle. Alighting from the monorail, visitors are greeted by a sign setting the tone: "Welcome to the medieval time of your life." Across the moat and drawbridge, the resort itself is filled with heraldic motifs, plastic knights bearing battle-axes, Sir Galahad's Prime Rib House, and giggling couples with their heads in sets of wooden stocks, being photographed.

Through the endless, heavily carpeted corridors populated only by huge lamps, the first thing to reach is the Sherwood Forest Café, and then the casino itself. Few visitors look up to notice the colored-glass windows and intricate cornices decorated with statues. Inside, it really is as impressive as its startling exterior, assuming you have a liking for *faux* England.

Owned by the Mandalay Resort Group, which also owns the Luxor and Circus Circus casinos, this family-style resort was opened in 1990, covering 57 acres (23 hectares). With twin 28-story towers holding more than 4,000 rooms, it was, at the time, the world's largest hotel-casino. Some floors are given over to family-friendly non-gambling entertainment. Excalibur neverthe-less serves 1.2 million alcoholic drinks every month.

Medieval Village

The medieval fantasy continues in the **Renaissance Faire** on the second floor. Performers garbed in medieval costume play period arrangements on mandolin, flute, and harp, to accompany puppets, mimes and magicians. Performances are from 10am on the Court Jester's Stage at **Medieval Village**.

LEFT AND BELOW: Excalibur.

Costumed figures and strolling minstrels roam the area to provide entertainment. Of those who choose one of Excalibur's two wedding chapels for their nuptials, about one-quarter opt to do so in medieval attire.

Fantasy Faire

Fantasy Faire holds two motion simulator theaters. The Magic Motion Machines lure visitors into hydraulically activated seats for a rolling ride in either a runaway train or an outer-space demolition derby directed by Hollywood's George Lucas. Kitchen Table Poker, which is a series of free educational poker games, are conducted every morning for half an hour, after which participants put up $10 in real money and test their new-found skills.

The designer, Weldon Simpson, was also responsible for the Luxor and the MGM Grand. Simpson believes, "Las Vegas is better than virtual reality, because in virtual reality you have to trick your mind into thinking that you are someplace else – many other places."

Eventually, he believes, slot players will be enclosed in private virtual-reality environments, allowing 3-D interaction in a game based on the hotel medieval theme. The more the gambler plays, the further he advances in the virtual-reality game. "It will be like playing Nintendo. When you get enough points you will become one of the virtual reality characters yourself."

Charles L. Silverman, a designer of casino interiors for more than three decades, says that the customer base is not just the gambler any longer, "It is anyone who walks through our doors. If enough people come in, enough of them will gamble, so we are creating lavish palaces to attract them."

The Luxor

The huge atrium of the **Luxor** ❽ (3900 Las Vegas Boulevard South, tel: 262-4000 or 800-288-1000) is lined with reproductions from the Luxor and Karnak temples in Egypt, including portraits of Tutankhamen and Nefertiti. The 30-story, glass-paneled pyramid's atrium is said to be spacious enough to park nine

BELOW:
double jackpot:
in your dreams.

Map on page 108

Boeing 747s, and the beam of light from its summit shines 10 miles (16 km) into the sky, running up an electricity bill of $1 million per year. It's said the beam can be seen from outer space, but it's more likely to be just Vegas talk.

Local architect Dan Juba said that his aim was to replicate in the pyramid "the essence of Egyptian architecture," as faithfully as possible. "Using simple shapes and strict geometric organization about a central axis, the twin towers complement the dynamic pyramid, and they were designed to offer unimpeded views from most hotel rooms."

After two smaller pyramids, and low-rise villas with courtyards and terraces were added, the Luxor linked the pyramid to its sister property, the adjoining Excalibur, by a moving walkway (there's also a free monorail). Another walkway leads to the Mandalay Bay casino through a small shopping center.

The 100-foot (30-meter) Sphinx dominating the entrance can project a 55-ft-high (17-meter) hologram of King Tut's head on to a water screen using laser beams from its eyes, but the Federal Aviation Administration requested the lasers be switched off after complaints from airline pilots. In Egypt, the Sphinx, carved in the form of a lion with the head of a king, is seven stories tall, and a pyramid would typically take thousands of slaves 20 years to build.

Cairo Bazaar

Many of the Luxor's 4,008 guest rooms are accessed by elevators called "inclinators" which turn sideways and run horizontally along rollers at 39° at the upper floors, but only guests of the hotel are allowed to ride the inclinators. There are views down to the fourth floor. Here, in a thickly carpeted area reached by elevators from the lobby, are video arcades, a 3-D IMAX theater, and video Karaoke machines where you can make your own music video from a choice of 700 music tapes.

Elegant stone walkways lead to the **Giza Galleria** where, in the Cairo Bazaar, artisans and vendors offer themed wares. Also for sale are

The Luxor has real and reproduction treasures from Egypt.

BELOW: the beam of the Luxor cuts 10 miles (16 km) into the sky.

perfume bottles, papyrus art, carved statuary and small leather items imported from Egypt.

The sight of beautiful, or at least very bold women, is more or less guaranteed in the luxurious night-club Ra, thanks to its policy of giving free entrance all night to "female adult entertainers." The Luxor's lavish Sports Book area has individual television monitors for each seat, making it easy to bet in comfort.

The Sports Books date back to Bugsy Siegel's innovation of the Trans-America Wire Service, which had a monopoly on relaying all horse-race information in the US directly from the race track. No bookie could operate without this information, and so Siegel could charge pretty much what he liked. Today, the rates are set by a state commission.

Mandalay Bay

Elegant **Mandalay Bay** ❾ (3950 Las Vegas Boulevard South, tel: 632-7777 or 877-632-7000) is a luxurious, tropically themed resort on a lagoon, with its own rum distillery and a pool with a sandy beach. The beach is swept by waves from a giant machine that can generate 6-foot (2-meter) breakers for body surfing. Visitors can see the pool through windows near the entrance to Shark Reef, but only guests are allowed to swim.

In its evaluations of Strip pools, *Where Las Vegas* magazine gave top marks to the Mandalay Bay's sandy shore. The Luxor and the MGM Grand, each with five pools, received mentions, and also sited was Caesars' Garden of the Gods, inspired by Rome's Baths of Caracalla. The beach club at the Hard Rock Hotel is garnering accolades, too, as its extensive wave pool becomes better known.

Resorts are beginning to invest more in outdoor activities such as swimming pools, and indoor facilities such as spas. The owners have come to realize that anything that relaxes high rollers and their companions during the day is more likely to lead to a profitable time at the tables that night.

Shark Reef, an open 90,000-

BELOW: Mandalay Bay's "beach with surf" has won several awards.

square feet (8,350-square meter) aquarium holds 2,000 marine animals. It was installed after the hotel opened and has proven extremely popular. Sunken ancient temples, statues, old stone stairways and a ship are entombed in 1½ million gallons (5,676,000 liters) of water that is home to strange fish of all shapes and sizes.

The exhibit contains a dozen species of shark, ranging from a baby Port Jackson shark, only 10 inches (25 cm) long to a 12-foot (4-meter) long nurse shark which, in its coral-reef habitat, sucks its prey out of holes in the rocks. The exhibit points out that despite their fearsome reputation, millions of sharks are killed every year for every human killed by a shark.

Another exhibit is **Snakes & Dragons**, the former being pythons, and the latter fish. Visitors carry "narration wands" that describe the golden crocodiles from Thailand and the green-tree pythons. At the touch pool they can put their hands in the water to gingerly stroke the horseshoe crabs and baby stingrays.

Worth overdoing

Mandalay Resorts Group manages a total of 19,000 rooms, including the Excalibur and the Monte Carlo, and controls all the land on this side of the Strip for about a mile further south. They have constructed a three-level convention center on 17 adjoining acres (7 hectares), which the company hopes will tap into the $4.3 billion of business that conventions bring to the city each year.

With the city's own center now expanded to 3.2 million square feet (300,000 square meters) and a third center under construction by the Sahara, Las Vegas will have three of the country's seven largest convention centers. The widely read local columnist John Smith said that Las Vegans believe "if it's worth doing, it's worth overdoing."

State of the art

Mandalay Bay's restaurants *(see page 123)*, offer many cuisines and suit all pockets. The hotel's showroom offers state-of-the-art Show-Trans headsets providing plot developments in Spanish, German,

Map on page 108

Underwater god at Mandalay Bay's Shark Reef.

BELOW: Shark Reef has over 2,000 marine animals.

Map
on page
108

Italian, Japanese, and Mandarin.

The Mandalay Bay also has an extremely good gift shop, selling upscale crafts and clothes from around the world with a vaguely tropical theme. One timely buy is a parasol from Thailand, which comes in very useful when trawling the Strip during the 100°-plus (37° C) days in June, July, and August.

A Lazy River runs for ¾ mile (1 km) around the resort which comes third in casino size, after MGM and Bellagio. Like Harrah's, Mandalay Bay is experimenting with customer tracking, and awarding points for betting on its tables or buying from its shops or even eating in its restaurants.

The Four Seasons

Occupying the top five floors (36–39) of Mandalay Bay is the **Four Seasons** ⑩ (3960 Las Vegas Boulevard South, tel: 632-5000 or 877-632-5000), an opulent hideaway which is the only major hotel on the Strip not to offer gambling. In similar luxurious style to others in the chain, it is a peaceful sanctuary in shades of gold, green, amber, and purple. Furnished with antiques and a Renaissance painting, the Four Seasons has its own private driveway, three private elevators, and a separate lobby so that guests can avoid the casino in the Mandalay Bay altogether if they wish, a luxury many will pay for if only to avoid the ear-jangling, nerve-shattering, and ever-present sound of the slot machines.

Excellent service is guaranteed by a ratio of two staff members to each guest, and there are special little touches like Evian water in the bathrooms, and chilled grapes served at the poolside. Traditional Balinese and Javanese body rituals are a regular feature of the spa, where cucumber slices are dispensed to cover the eyes.

The concierge desk stands ready to book guests into any of the numerous golf courses in the area, or on trips into the Nevada wilderness or, in winter, they will find a slot for you to ski at the Las Vegas Ski and Snowboard Resort, 45 minutes away on Mount Charleston. ❑

BELOW:
pretty as a picture.

RESTAURANTS

Sir Galahad's Prime Rib House
Excalibur
Tel: 702-597-7448
Open: D daily. $$$
The house specialty is carved tableside of beef, offered with a choice of old-fashioned soups, or salad and delicious Yorkshire pudding.

Sacred Sea Room
The Luxor
Tel: 702-262-4000
Open: D Fri–Tues. $$$
Colorful tile mosaics, a ship's mast and a crow's-nest view of the casino gives this award-winning seafood house a unique look with cuisine to match.

Aureole
Mandalay Bay
Tel: 702-705-7133
Open: D daily. $$$$
Celebrity chef Charlie Palmer's version of his New York classic is architecturally arresting (a three-story wine tower and a pond with swans). The excellent food is complemented by an outstanding wine list.

The Burger Bar
Mandalay Bay
Tel: 702-632-7777
Open: L & D daily. $–$$$$
A burger to suit all tastes and pockets can be found here, from the $60 Kobe burger with foie gras and truffles, to the inexpensive dessert burgers with a donut base topped off with cheesecake, yummy chocolate or peanut butter and jelly. One dessert burger arrives with "lettuce" and "tomatoes" made entirely of sweet ingredients.

China Grill
Mandalay Bay
Tel: 702-632-7404
Open: D daily. $$$
Large portions intended for sharing. Mouthwatering favorites include the Shanghai lobster served with ginger, curry and spinach, or crispy duck with caramelized black-vinegar sauce and scallion pancakes. The architecture and décor are stunning.

House of Blues
Mandalay Bay
Tel: 702-632-7607
Open: B, L & D daily. $$
Creole and Cajun staples such as jambalaya and gumbo go down well here, as do the other Southern-style regional dishes. Fri and Sat blues band. For Sun brunch, tuck into grits and hickory-smoked bacon to the sound of live gospel music.

Red Square
Mandalay Bay
Tel: 702-632-7407
Open: D daily. $$$
A consistent winner in *Las Vegas Weekly*'s "dining with a scene" list, Red Square is the place to dress up, roll up to the ice bar, and partake of as many Russian-influenced cocktails as possible. Afterwards, it's only a short walk to a table to dine on dishes like Chicken Kiev.

Wolfgang Puck's Trattoria del Lupo
Mandalay Bay
Tel: 702-740-5522
Open: D daily. $$
Trattoria del Lupo means "restaurant of the wolf." This eatery is full of antiques and unique lighting fixtures and even includes an exhibition pizza station. Although known for pizzas, there are also delicious classic and contemporary Italian dishes on the menu.

Charlie Palmer Steakhouse
Four Seasons Hotel at Mandalay Bay
Tel: 702-362-5000
Open: D daily. $$$$
Celebrity chef Charlie Palmer presents most of his signature dishes here, like succulent wood-grilled filet mignon. Seafood or family-style side dishes are available to non-carnivores. Spacious premises with a clubby atmosphere.

RIGHT: outside Mandalay Bay's Red Square is a headless statue of Lenin.

ALADDIN TO BELLAGIO

Sensual, sumptuous, lavish, and outlandish,
the resort casinos along this section of the Strip
cater for the discerning sybarite

The 2,567-room **Aladdin** ⑪ (3667 Las Vegas Boulevard South, tel: 785-5555 or 800-582-2228) reopened in August 2000 on the site of its namesake, which was razed in 1998. Aladdin's greatest asset is its location, right in the middle of the Strip between casinos that clock in 200,000 visitors a week. Entry from the Strip was designed for convenience, past the 50-foot (15- meter) waterfall which cascades over sandstone cliffs. Unusually, the entrance leads directly into a shopping center, not the casino.

Once inside, the Arabian Nights theme is evoked between the minarets by genies in bottles and magic lanterns. Around the huge Aladdin's lamp centerpiece in the casino, cocktail waitresses waft between the tables in gauzy harem costumes. The 7,000-seat **Aladdin Theater for the Performing Arts** hosts headliner concerts and Broadway shows, and an Arabian Nights production runs every night in the smaller 1,000-seat theater.

Jewel in the crown

Planned as a music-themed hotel by Planet Hollywood, one of the original partners, Aladdin was financed by a New York developer and London Clubs International, a gaming entity seeking a foothold in the US market. Owners of The London Club, a private enclave with its own five-star restaurant inside the Aladdin, touted it as "the jewel in the crown" of their chain of clubs which included branches in the UK, the Bahamas, Egypt, and South Africa. It was fittingly flagged as "a cool oasis in a 100-plus degree desert," in a city visited by more Brits (254,000 in a recent year) than any other European nationals.

Aladdin has had a very checkered

Map on page 108

LEFT: Aladdin is built on the site of its namesake
BELOW: glittering in Glitter City.

history. It began life as the Tally-Ho casino in 1963, and was once owned by members of organized crime. To some, though, the site is still best known as the venue of Elvis Presley's marriage to Priscilla in 1967, in the private suite of the then-owner, Milton Prell.

Even with good restaurants, a spacious theater, and an attractive sixth-floor pool, there have been questions about the quality of management. The 116,000 square-foot (10,775 square-meter) casino was planned to contain 2,800 slots, but the owners gave in to pressure to cut out almost one quarter of them, ending up with 2,270, because the room was thought too cluttered.

The average daily revenue from individual slot machines dropped to $80, more than 25 percent below the industry average of $108 per machine. At its reopening, the 17-story hotel received a very unmusical welcome from the *Los Angeles Times* which slammed it for "miscalculations" like the lack of a grand, sweeping entrance and the need to climb stairs to reach the "underwhelming" doors. Having said that, guests seem to enjoy staying there, and single out the spaciousness of both their bedrooms and, especially, the bathrooms as real treats. Watch this space for new developments as they unfold, because in early 2004, Planet Hollywood, the Aladdin's original partner, made a bid for the premises.

Exotic opulence plus shops

The adjoining **Desert Passage** ⑫ (open 10am to 11pm daily) is an exotic complex of 135 opulent stores and restaurants. The publicity that described it as "extraordinary" was not exaggerated. Beneath a flawless blue-and-white sky are tiled benches and immense pottery jars. Occasional wall fountains line the smooth cobbled hallways plied by tricycle rickshaws (generous tips expected) for those too tired or too lazy to walk. Street merchants in Moroccan attire display their wares in stylish kiosks, and wedding parties accompanied by musicians and belly dancers thread their processions amid the throngs. The Endangered

BELOW: an elephant prowls the Desert Passage; indoor tropical storms occur here, too.

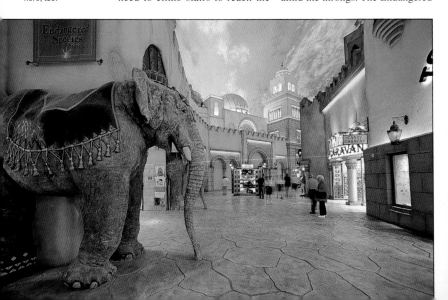

Species chain has a store, its entrance here guarded by life-size stone elephants. An indoor tropical "storm" with thunder and lightning rains down from time to time, but of course nobody ever gets wet.

A complaint from retailers has been that Desert Passage isn't making money fast enough. Despite annual sales well above the national average, the mall is far short of other casino shopping complexes. Its (usually successful) developers, TrizecHahn, may be planning to sell. Retailers say that tDesert Passage has become such a tourist attraction that many visitors are content to regard it as merely a spectacle and pass right through, with their wallets disturbingly undisturbed.

Bally's

What is now **Bally's** ⓭ (3645 Las Vegas Boulevard South, tel: 739-4111 or 800-634-3434) began life as Kirk Kerkorian's MGM Grand. The approach to Bally's is dramatic, via 200-foot (60-meter) long escalators flanked by cascading water, lighted pylons, and giant palm trees. Every 20 minutes the entry area erupts with a sound-and-water show involving a wave machine and blow-hole fountains. Water is very much in favor here, in the multi-million dollar show *Jubilee*, the *Titanic* sinks every night on stage.

Bally's has doubled the size of its baccarat room to target players willing to wager hundreds of thousands of dollars on a single hand, "whales" in gaming parlance. Liberal odds and high-bet limits make baccarat a favorite with high rollers, and in one recent year, the Strip's 55 baccarat tables generated $594 million, compared with the $482 million yielded by almost 900 blackjack tables.

Bally's was one of six Vegas casinos, along with the MGM Grand, New York-New York, the Monte Carlo, the Las Vegas Hilton, and the Riviera, which collectively voted against being represented by the Transport Workers Union, by 1,564 to 554. Since most dealers are paid only around $6 per hour, they rely heavily on tips or "tokes" to supplement their income.

Shannon Bybee, a casino indus-

Map on page 108

TIP

Unless otherwise stated, telephone numbers throughout this book are preceded by the code 702.

BELOW: backstage at Bally's.

This replica of the Montgolfier balloon glows with night-time neon, and is a significant Strip landmark.

BELOW: this bread-seller/opera singer will serenade you in one of five different languages.

try expert at the University of Nevada Las Vegas, said that most dealers probably didn't want to change the status quo, despite pressure from colleagues to unionize: "They make good money in tips and they don't want to risk losing that in contract negotiations."

When the old MGM Grand opened in 1973, it was the world's largest hotel, following a precedent Kerkorian had set in 1969 with his International Hotel, now the Las Vegas Hilton. "We opened that hotel with Barbra Streisand in the main showroom," he said. "The rock musical *Hair* was in the other showroom and the opening lounge act was Ike and Tina Turner."

But the Grand was the scene of a disastrous fire on November 21, 1980 that killed 84 people and injured 700. In 1993, Kerkorian opened the present MGM Grand further up the Strip.

Gay Paree

The monorail and **Le Boulevard**, a street of shops and French restaurants, connect Bally's to the $800

million **Paris Las Vegas** ⑭ (3655 Las Vegas Boulevard South, tel: 946-7000 or 888-266-5687). Both are owned by the group called Caesars Entertainment, whose empire includes 16 other gaming properties throughout the US, and in Australia and Uruguay.

The hotel casino is modeled on the 800-year-old Parisian Hotel de Ville, the Paris City Hall. It is distinguished by one of the city's more prominent landmarks, a 50-story replica of the **Eiffel Tower**, thrusting through the roof of the casino and rising 540 feet (165 meters) in the air, accompanied by a neon copy of the Montgolfier balloon.

A half-size scale model of the original, the tower offers panoramic views of the city from the 11th-story piano bar, one of eight restaurants at the casino specializing in regional French cuisine from Alsace, Burgundy, and Lorraine *(see page 133)*. Bastille Day (July 14) is celebrated at the ⅔ scale **Arc de Triomphe** in solidarity with ceremonies at the Parisian Arc. No special celebration is needed to indulge at Napoleon's

Champagne Bar, where a collection of featured quotations includes one from the blind French monk Dom Perignon who first concocted champagne, "Brothers, come quick! I am tasting stars!"

Eiffel Tower

The colossal legs of the Paris's Eiffel Tower are solidly planted inside the 85,000-square-foot (7,900-square-meter) casino which houses an attractive fountain and a plethora of signs saying things like "Le Salon des Tables," "Les Toilettes," "La Réception," "Le Bell Captain" and "Les Artistes Steak House." A romantic, lamp-lit bridge straddles the casino high above the room but access is available only to those with a ticket to climb the tower.

The Paris especially touts its classy spa: "Long ago the French recognized the healing benefits of massage, spa treatment and aromatherapy," offering "luxurious facilities and amenities," which include many styles of massage and body treatments. The larger suites – ranging from 1,000 to 4,180 square feet

(93 to 388 square meters), go under names like Napoleon, St Tropez, and Charlemagne.

Aware that many visitors will be familiar with Paris itself, the architects here aimed to duplicate its landmarks "with pinpoint accuracy," studying Gustav Eiffel's original 1889 drawings and covering interior facades with murals representing Parisian districts, before "aging" the buildings appropriately. Fronted at the Strip by the massive Academie National de Musique, Paris Las Vegas' other replicas include the Champs Elysées, the Louvre, the Paris Opéra, and the Palace of Versailles.

The *Notre Dame de Paris* show at the **Theater Paris Las Vegas** plays most days. Among the shops along a typical "Parisian" street is JJ's Boulangerie, where you might encounter "the singing breadman," a local opera singer named Lance Taubold who serenades visitors in any of five languages.

Shops offer ultra-chic Parisian fashion, and the casino has 2,200 slot machines. A knowledgeable but

Map on page 108

BELOW: Paris's Arc de Triomphe is two-thirds the size of the original.

rather stingy local suggests that lunch patrons of the excellent Paris buffet time their visits just before it switches to dinner (at 5:30pm), when more expensive dinner items such as king crab legs are added to the menu. This is a canny strategy at other buffets around town, although venues require a time break before introducing the more expensive dinner menu.

Bellagio

Superstar entrepreneur Steve Wynn's **Bellagio** ⓯ (3600 Las Vegas Boulevard South, tel: 693-7111 or 888-987-6667), now owned by MGM-Mirage, was admired from the outset for raising the level of local sumptuousness. It is said to have cost $1.8 billion to build, requires $2.5 million a day to break even and has almost 9,000 employees. But by the spring of 2001, Bellagio was posting an annual profit of $323.5 million, making it the world's most profitable casino.

Approaching from Bally's on the bridge over the Strip, visitors are greeted by operatic arias soaring

BELOW: Via Bellagio is one of Vegas's most elegant shopping arcades.

over the lake, where hundreds of fountains dance to music (ranging from Pavarotti to Gene Kelly), all perfectly programed to coordinate with jets as high as 240 feet (73 meters), fading to clouds of mist in quieter interludes. The water, all 1.5 million gallons (5.5 million liters) of it, emanates from an aquifer via the resort's own treatment plant, which also fills the lagoons in front of the Mirage and Treasure Island. It is a wonderful spectacle, but can get repetitive if staying at one of the classy rooms directly above.

The lake's design was conceived by Los Angeles' Universal City-based company Wet Dreams. Their staff of 90 designers, engineers, and support staff also created the glass cauldron which cradled the Olympic flame at the 2001 winter games in Salt Lake City, as well as the sidewalk fountains in which kids douse themselves at LA's CityWalk. "We work expressively with the water itself," notes Mark Fuller, the company's founder. "We don't do a traditional structure or something and then gush water over it."

Dale Chihuly: Man of Glass

Dale Chihuly, whose spectacular, glass-flower chandelier literally dominates Bellagio's lobby *(see photo on page 132)*, was the first person from the USA to be accepted by Venice's Murano community and his work truly merits the overworked adjective "gorgeous." When the Las Vegas Art Museum exhibited hundreds of his pieces, the show was described by *Where* magazine as "a vibrantly colored veil of glass." The sculptor's works can be found in 190 museums around the world, as well as his native Tacoma, Washington state, where the artist is contributing a pedestrian walkway with soaring crystal towers to the Museum of Glass.

Chihuly himself, blinded in one eye years ago by a studio accident, says "Glass inspires me. As I work it becomes magical… the only material you can blow human breath down. Sun and light come through it. Glass can't be carbon-dated so you can't tell how old it is, how hard it is – there are so many mysterious things about it. It has its own category: it's not a solid, and it's not a liquid. They don't even know quite what it is except that it's the cheapest material in the world."

Fountains and flowers

In desert climates, fountains are prized, and the water feature in the sweet-smelling **Conservatory** was imported from Italy. Fountains also had a religious significance for many ancient people, especially the Greeks and Romans. Brides who bathed in water from a *calirrhoe* – a fountain with nine pipes – could look forward to a long and prosperous life.

Bathing at birth, upon marriage, and after death was preparation for the journey to the afterlife. In Middle Eastern lore, wells with square enclosures can represent paradise. Fountains and water are the theme of the spectacular, and spectacularly expensive, *O*, the show by **Cirque du Soleil**. It takes 74 performers to mount this unique melange of acrobatics, theatrical effects, diving, and swimming which takes place on, in, and under an indoor lake. Tickets for the show are scarce since it gets booked as early as three or even six months ahead. If you want to see it, think as far in advance as you can. It's worth it.

From the Bellagio bridge, entrance to the resort is along a retail arcade, the **Via Bellagio**, which includes Tiffany, Chanel, Gucci, Armani, Prada, and Hermes. By the bank of reception desks inside is a wonderfully refreshing garden below an original, iridescent work of glass by the famed sculptor Dale Chihuly *(see box, page 130).*

Living plants and flowers, roses, anemones, peonies, birds of paradise, and cherry blossom, to name just a few, are distributed lavishly throughout the Bellagio's Italianate decor and what seem like miles of marble floors. Nowhere is the floral display more abundant than just beyond the lobby under the 50-foot (15-meter) high glass ceiling of the attractive Conservatory and botanical garden which changes with the seasons; its sweet-smelling displays are planned a full year in advance. The hotel employs 150 gardening and greenhouse staff alone.

Pathways lead to Café Bellagio, a 24-hour dining room, and to the Aqua restaurant, with Rauschenberg paintings. To one side of the lounge

Map on page 108

BELOW: Bellagio was modeled after a town on Italy's Lake Como.

Map on page 108

a pianist plays at the Petrossian café. This is only one of 17 different eating places in Bellagio, including a sister to New York's Le Cirque, and Picasso *(see page 133)* with furniture and carpet designed by Claude Picasso, son of Pablo, and papa's paintings on the walls.

Lake Como

Bellagio was inspired for Wynn by the charming village on the shores of Italy's Lake Como, and the promotional staff pulled out all the stops, lavishing the resort with phrases like "a place of special elegance, quality and distinction... (which) captures the romantic symbolism and classical imagery of Italian architecture. It represents the softer side of the human soul."

The **Gallery of Fine Art** was Wynn's inspiration, and he bought back three of the pictures for his personal collection when he sold the hotel. The gallery's multi-million dollar collection featured works by Renoir, Monet, Van Gogh, Rembrandt, Picasso, Roy Lichtenstein, and David Hockney. It welcomed

one million visitors from the time it opened in October 1998 to when it closed for renovations, despite a $12 admission fee for all, which some guests of the very expensive hotel described as "rather cheesy" behavior, given the exorbitant price of their hotel room.

The gallery reopened with a policy of exhibiting high-quality touring exhibitions from both domestic and foreign museums. Director Kathy Clewell says that they plan to bring in at least two exhibitions per year, "I think that art is here for the long haul."

Ocean's 11

The successful 2001 remake of *Ocean's 11*, based on the earlier caper movie with the original Rat Pack, was filmed partly on Bellagio's casino floor. "I was able to build a quarter of a million dollar set," says designer Philip Messina. "We cleared out slot machines and gaming machines and built a casino cage set. It was built and painted in LA, trucked out to Vegas and assembled on location."

After the MGM Grand, Bellagio has the second-largest casino in Vegas, but *The Wine Spectator* magazine rated it as "positively demure, the kind of place where a gent can feel comfortable in a dinner jacket." Many Bellagio guests play the offsite **Shadow Creek** golf course, lined with 21,000 fragrant pine trees from California and Arizona, along with Vegas high rollers who don't mind the $1,000 greens fee (limo transportation, golf cart, and caddie included). The course, known for the natural beauty of its rolling terrain, ponds, and waterfalls, was designed by architect Tom Fazio.

In December 2004, Bellagio elevated its splendor to even greater heights with the opening of the new Spa Tower, providing 928 additional rooms and suites. ❑

BELOW: Chihuly check-in desk.

RESTAURANTS

Zanzibar Café
Aladdin
Tel: 702-785-9001
Open: 24 hours daily. Late-night menu 1–6am. **$**
Specializes in food from the Middle and Far East, plus a few north American dishes for anyone longing for home.

Seasons
Bally's
Tel: 702-739-4651
Open: D Tues–Sat. **$$$$**
There's filet mignon and fresh Maine lobster as well as more exotic delicacies. The extensive menu changes with the seasons.

La Chine
Paris Las Vegas
Tel: 702-946-4663
Open: D daily. **$$$**
La Chine puts a French twist on Hong Kong-style cuisine, served in an up-scale atmosphere.

Eiffel Tower Restaurant
Paris Las Vegas
Tel: 702-948-6937
Open: D daily. **$$$$**
Gourmet Gallic entrées in an elegant atmosphere with a romantic view of the illuminated Strip from the 11th floor.

Mon Ami Gabi
Paris Las Vegas
Tel: 702-944-GABI
Open: L & D daily. **$$–$$$**
Enjoy the passing crowds or the Bellagio dancing fountains from this charming French restau-

rant. The best dishes on *le menu* are classic steak frites or excellent fruits de mer.

Ortanique
Paris Las Vegas
Tel: 702-946-3908
Open: D daily. **$$$**
Award-winning chef Cindy Hutson calls her style "Cuisine of the Sun: an eclectic fusion of different nations and their natural bounties prepared and placed creatively on one plate." So there.

Aqua
Bellagio
Tel: 702-693-7223
Open: D daily. **$$$$**
Aqua is an upscale seafood house from San Francisco where chef Michael Mina's creations are exquisitely prepared.

Café Bellagio
Bellagio
Tel: 702-693-7223
Open: 24 hours daily. **$$$**
Located in the ever-changing Conservatory, this café has a light and airy atmosphere with a gorgeous pool and botanical garden views.

Le Cirque
Bellagio
Tel: 702-693-8100
Open: D daily. **$$$$**
Coat and tie are mandatory for men. Le Cirque has creative gourmet entrées such as black-tie scallops (tied with black

truffles), consommé de boeuf with foie gras ravioli, roasted duck with a honey-spice fig glaze, and roasted lobster in a port-wine sauce. After all this culinary splendor, enjoy luscious desserts.

Olives
Bellagio
Tel: 702-693-7223
Open: L & D daily. **$$$**
Tasty Mediterranean food with a wonderful view of Paris Las Vegas's Eiffel Tower.

Osteria del Circo
Bellagio
Tel: 702-693-8150
Open: L & D daily. **$$$$**
The younger and more casual sibling of Le Cirque, there's a light-hearted feel to this fine restaurant. Nevertheless, it's an idea to leave

the kids at home, for the casual elegance and Tuscan dishes are best sampled without distraction.

Picasso
Bellagio
Tel: 702-693-7223
Open: D Thur–Tues. **$$$**
A feast for the eyes and the stomach: French food is served in a room designed by Pablo Picasso's son, Claude, with paintings on the walls by papa estimated to be worth $50 million.

PRICE CATEGORIES

Price includes dinner and a glass of wine, excluding tip.

$$$$ = $40 and up
$$$ = under $40
$$ = under $30
$ = under $20

RIGHT: Osteria del Circo is one of 22 places to eat or drink in Bellagio alone.

CAESARS PALACE TO CASINO ROYALE

The Garden of the Gods, Marilyn Monroe's convertible,
Bugsy Siegel's hotel, and live penguins in a tropical
garden are just a few of the attractions here

Map
on page
108

Caesars Palace ⑯ (3570 Las Vegas Boulevard South, tel: 731-7110 or 800-634-6661) has been the setting for more than a dozen movies and 80 television shows. The fabulous and venerable facade dominates the western side of this portion of the Strip with 50-foot (15-meter) cypresses imported from Italy, and a trio of eye-catching fountains spraying columns of water 35 feet (10.5 meters) into the air. It is claimed that due to ingenious recycling, water usage is about the same as that used on an average-sized lawn.

Beside the reflecting pool into which pours 10,000 gallons (38,000 liters) of water is a copy of Giovanni's 16th-century sculpture *The Rape of the Sabine Women* while nearer to the street is another famous statue, a good replica of the *Winged Victory* (300 BC) from Samothrace in the Louvre.

The approach is dominated by four gold-leaf horses and a charioteer, the fine Quadriga statue. The casino's entrance doors are flanked by more replicas of classical statues, including the Venus de Milo. Most famous of all, an 18-foot (6-meter) high David dominates the **Appian Way** inside the casino. Carved from the same Carrara marble as the Michelangelo original but at twice

the height, the replica weighs 9 tons.

Caesars Palace has had several owners since Jay Sarno completed it in 1966. It cost him $24 million, and he sold it three years later for $60 million. By the time ITT purchased the casino in 1995, the price was $1.7 billion. They spent almost another billion dollars increasing its rooms to 2,471. In 1998, the resort was acquired by Starwood Hotels and sold again for $3 billion to Park Place Entertainment Corporation (now Caesars Entertainment).

LEFT AND BELOW:
Caesars Palace.

Lucky numbers play an important part in Las Vegas life.

BELOW: Caesars is known for its high-profile sports events.

Garden of the Gods

The look of the casino owes much to Sarno's belief in the magically relaxing properties of the oval. Jo Harris, the designer who later worked with him on Circus Circus, attributes the casino's success to it's being laid out as a spoked wheel with the gambling area as the hub, so whichever direction you walk, it is in view.

The 5-acre (2-hectare) **Garden of the Gods**, named after the Baths of Caracalla frequented by ancient Rome's elite, has three swimming pools and two whirlpool spas, the whole complex landscaped with sweeping lawns, graceful fountains, and classically inspired statuary. Even the lifeguard stands are designed to resemble imperial thrones. A sign at the entrance reads, "European-style topless bathing is permitted at Caesars' pools. We prefer that this is restricted to the Venus pool area." As with most hotel casinos, the pool is for the hotel guests only, and admission is strictly patrolled, access granted only upon the production of a room key.

Caesars' 4,000-seat **Colosseum** is designed to recall the ancient Roman one, and was built specifically to showcase the talents of Canadian singer Celine Dion. The singer agreed a $45 million contract to give five shows a week for three years.

Dion said that what convinced her to sign on the dotted line was seeing the spectacular Cirque du Soleil show, *O*, performed on their permanent, custom-built stage at Bellagio. "I knew that I wanted to have a show like this and have, like, 60 performers on stage with me, making every song a visual appearance," she says. "It's kind of impossible to travel with a show like this; the effects and the decor and the whole thing make it technically impossible without a base. We found that in Las Vegas."

Artists off the road

This may be the forseeable future for pop singers and other performers. "Artists are looking to get off the road and do something that's more interesting, both for the audience and themselves," says Tom

Gallagher, CEO of Caesars' owners. Gary Bongiovanni, who edits a trade magazine devoted to the concert business, said, "It may be the best of all worlds for the artist. In a way Celine Dion may be pioneering that in the pop world and what better place for it than Las Vegas?"

True to her wishes, the 22,000 square-foot (2,000 square-meter) stage built for Dion's performance is designed by Franco Dragone, who was also responsible for the Cirque du Soleil productions.

Elton John has also been signed to play 75 concerts at the Colosseum when Ms Dion is resting. Unlike the Canadian, however, John's concerts do not run consecutively, but are spaced throughout the three-year period. These shows are also tailor-made for the venue and provide a unique spectacular unlike any other concerts perfomed by the British pop legend.

The most desirable hotel rooms at Caesars Palace are those in the towers, and, quick to spot the trend, Caesars received permission in 2004 to begin construction on yet another tower. The 29-story **Palace Tower** has more than 1,100 deluxe guest rooms and suites, all with huge whirlpool bathtubs and great views. The 24-story **Forum Tower** is made up of two-story, four-bedroom apartments known as Fantasy Suites, themed in Roman or Egyptian style and designed for special guests who travel with families or retinues.

Fantasy Suites are available only to the resort's invited guests, with one exception; honeymoon couples who have their wedding at the hotel may rent them for around $3,000 per night.

Caesar salads

Food in Las Vegas always comes in colossal amounts: 21 tons (19,000 kg) of smoked salmon and 2,700 ounces (76 kg) of caviar are consumed in the hotel's various restaurants *(see page 145)* every year, as well as 336,000 of the aptly chosen Caesar salads. The salad, incidentally, is thought to hail from the 1924 recipe of an Italian immigrant to the US chef, Caesar Cardini.

Map on page 108

BELOW:
palatial pools.

Sports gods

Caesars also has a long association with sporting events, having been the first hotel in Las Vegas with satellite equipment to relay events. They employed former world heavyweight champion Joe Louis as their greeter up to his death in 1981. Frank Sinatra and the Reverend Jesse Jackson delivered eulogies at his memorial service, and the former champ is remembered with a 7-foot (2-meter) marble statue standing at the entrance to the Race & Sports Book, inside which are 90 video screens, hundreds of electronic panels and reader boards, and larger-than-life murals of famous performers.

More than 160 major boxing contests, starting with the bout with Larry Holmes which ended Muhammad Ali's ring career in 1980, and other championship events have been staged in the hotel's spacious grounds.

Among the events which drew heavy betting were Wayne Gretzy playing for the Los Angeles Kings against the New York Rangers in a National Hockey League game on an unseasonably hot day in 1991 (300 tons of refrigeration equipment was installed to make the ice); tennis champions Jimmy Connors and Martina Navratilova battling on the Palace courts in 1992; and soccer star Pelé in a World Cup game the following year. Oscar de la Hoya, Julio Cesar Chavez, Evander Holyfield, Riddick Bowe, Marvin Hagler, and Sugar Ray Leonard have all fought championship contests on the premises.

Forum Shops

The classy arcade known as the **Forum Shops** features Dior, Versace, Gucci, Bulgari, Ferragamo, and others, and is always crowded. Revenue per square foot is said to be the highest in North America. Stores range from a clock shop called Roman Times to "Warnerius Fraternius Studius Storius" (Warner Bros Studio Store). Customers are welcomed to Magnet Maximus by a perpetually flying pig. A domed ceiling emulates a changing sky over the arches, columns, fountains,

BELOW: this man in the Forum Shops is really a movie star; see him play a scene with Sharon Stone in the film *Casino*.

and central piazza, where Wolfgang Puck's Spago restaurant *(see page 145)* adjoins a replica of the Trevi Fountain. One of the liveliest places late at night is the fun, floating cocktail lounge known as **Cleopatra's Barge** with furled sails, ostrich-feather fans and waitresses dodging between the dancers, bringing drinks across the gangplank to spectators in the tiered seats.

At one end of the arcade, beneath a pale blue ceiling with puffy white clouds, is an enormous statue of Minerva. Bacchus presides over another piazza, on an elevated throne. Now and again the throne revolves, the god raises a beaker to his lips and speaks, as laser-driven planets, stars, and constellations race through the sky above.

Plutus, god of wealth, controls the music and dancing waters, and Apollo strums a modern fiber-optic lyre. A major attraction just off the magnificent **Great Hall** is the world's first IMAX 3-D simulator adventure rider. *Race for Atlantis* is a convincingly scary ride which is amazing even without the 3-D glasses.

Approaching the entrance from the **rotunda** with circular aquarium, the arcade is filled with Aqua Massage tanks, while Japanese slot machines allow you to box and dance with partners on screen, and a photo booth will place you in front of scenes from around the world, or show you what your future child might look like.

Exiting the Forum Shops at the Cyber Station end of Caesars, you can see the bright blue-and-violet windows of the **Casino Royale** ⑰ just across the Strip. You have to take the moving walkway all the way back through the casino to exit, though. Inside the Casino Royale, which has a 25¢ roulette table, for a fee you can don a Victorian costume and be photographed against an appropriate background at Madame Bloomer's Old Time Photo.

Harrah's

William Harrah was building casinos in the town of Reno and at Lake Tahoe as early as the 1930s, but **Harrah's** ⑱ (3475 Las Vegas Boulevard South, tel: 369-5000 or

Map on page 108

If times are tight, Casino Royale has a 25¢ roulette wheel.

BELOW: Celine Dion shows off her new home at Caesars.

What Price Power?

In 2004, one of the biggest resorts on the Strip had to close for a night, leaving thousands of guests to check in elsewhere. Bellagio was hit hard after a main power line failed, and although by the next day normal relations were restored, the incident was yet another example of Sin City's almost crippling dependency on power. And power means big bucks. "I guess I'll have to go to another casino to lose money," quipped one displaced guest – not the sort of comment any gaming establishment wants to hear.

Energy problems in the desert are now a constant worry. Three years prior to this incident, Vegas's natural gas prices rose and many casinos began to impose small "per room per day" energy surcharges. Since the turn of the millennium, electricity charges to businesses have risen by 65 percent; more for residential customers. A hotel-casino on the Strip can use up as much energy as 10,000 private homes, and rising electricity bills have come as a shock to the neon-happy resorts.

At the MGM Grand and other hotels, the 750 watts of light in many rooms has been reduced to 500. Motion sensors turn off the lights in empty offices. The current generation of slot machines are designed to consume 25 percent less electricity than their predecessors. Intelligent thermostats are reducing the air conditioning in empty convention rooms.

Seeing power bills rise so steeply, Bally's, Paris Las Vegas and Caesars Palace adopted more energy-efficient lighting, and Fitzgerald's casino shut off exterior spotlights at 2am. The Las Vegas Hilton also cut back its hours of floodlighting. At Caesars Palace – whose monthly electricity bill is more than $3.7 million – "smart thermostat" systems have been installed.

The city's convention center was luckily between shows, when Nevada Power asked customers to "shed load." Lights in the building are now being steadily replaced with low-wattage fluorescent bulbs. To take advantage of off-peak rates, the Cashman Center delayed the start of its home baseball games, so that they now begin (at cheaper rates) at 7:15pm.

Nevada Power is one of the state's oldest comp anies, and at the same time has made itself one of the most unpopular. The state's Public Utilities Commission rejected almost half the $922 million the company sought in increased charges. Local politicians blame much of the utility's troubles on bad public relations.

As of the last decade, there were 15,000 miles (24,000 km) of neon on the Strip. The Rio's 125-foot (38-meter) high marquee, voted the city's best neon sign, uses 12,930 feet (4,000 meters) of neon tubing and over 5,000 lightbulbs; the Stardust's 18-foot (6-meter) sign, with 40,000 bulbs, uses enough electricity to light a town of 30,000 people.

Nevertheless, the glare and glitter of the fantasy city in the desert is sacred to the casinos. John Marz of the Mandalay Group said, "Las Vegas has an image and a certain cachet that it has to live up to, and that includes the exterior lighting, the neon and the marquee. It's what people come here to see, and reducing those would be the last thing we do." ❑

LEFT: midnight cowboy.

800-427-7247) on the Las Vegas Strip dates back only to 1992, having opened 20 years earlier as the Holiday Casino. Its famous riverboat facade was replaced – and lamented by some regulars – by a glitzy exterior with gold-trimmed harlequins, and celebrated its $200 million new look with a high-wire walk 100 feet (30 meters) above the Strip by Tino Wallenda.

Major player

Harrah's is a major player in gaming circles, having at one time or another owned or managed at least 18 other casinos in the United States, including properties in New Orleans and Mississippi. The company was also instrumental in partnering with Californian Native American tribes, particularly in the Escondito region.

In Vegas itself, Harrah's owns the Rio casino west of the Strip, and a free shuttle bus runs between the two. In 2004, Harrah's stepped in virtually overnight to manage the venerable Binion's Horseshoe casino *(see page 181)* amid rumors

that in subsequent years, the early rounds of the World Series of Poker will move from Binion's Downtown to Harrah's on the Strip.

Harrah's **La Playa Lounge**, with multicolored palm trees, illuminated rocks, and three-dimensional mural, evokes "a day at the beach," the fantasy enhanced by tropical drinks in exotic glasses. There's an outdoor swimming pool and an entertainment plaza, **Carnaval Court**, with added blackjack tables and stage performers.

There is also a bar where bartenders are selected for their skills in singing, dancing, juggling glassware, and breathing fire. Other entertainment includes Budd Friedman's **Improv Comedy Club** in a 350-seat showroom. Among the shops are the Jackpot store selling magazines, newspapers, and books as well as fresh flowers and Harrah's logo merchandise, and the Old Fashioned Chocolate Shop and Soda Fountain from San Francisco's Ghirardelli Chocolate Co.

The casino's happily named Fresh Market Square Buffet offers a

Map on page 108

BELOW:
streetlife in Sin City.

lavish champagne brunch from 10am to 4pm on weekends.

Harrah's is an exuberant place, where the nickel video-poker machines are just inside the door. The Bally Pro Slot machines at Harrah's are advertised as having a noisy stainless-steel tray, to make the pay offs even more exciting. The trays are even designed to prevent coin cups being placed in them, in an attempt to modestly deaden the sound.

Phil Sartre, CEO of Promus, Harrah's Memphis-based holding company, says that Bill Harrah was the first casino operator to emphasize slot machines over table games. He began the chain with a bingo parlor in Reno in 1937. The popularity of slot machines has almost doubled since the 1970s, and they now typically account for 62 percent of a casino's winnings. The stakes are much higher, too.

"Most casinos are getting on the slot band wagon," says Sartre. "They recognize that it's the most stable customer base. They are not trying to win real big, it's people who are there for fun. They'll be back if they have fun."

Imperial Palace

The **Imperial Palace** (3535 Las Vegas Boulevard South, tel: 731-3311 or 800-634-6441) opened in 1979 with an Oriental theme, the roof covered in blue tiles from Japan. Inside are carved dragons, giant wind-chime chandeliers, and bars called Geisha and Ginza.

Until his death in 2003, owner Ralph Engelstad was the only sole proprietor of a major Las Vegas casino, earning himself an untold fortune; currently the premises are being operated by representatives of the Engelstad family trust. Engelstad was acclaimed for his friendly policies toward disabled people, who form 13 percent of the 2,600 employees here.

John Stuart's *Legends in Concert* show, which has been running for 13 years, features impersonations (of varying verisimilitude) of luminaries like Liberace, Michael Jackson, Madonna and, of course, Elvis Presley. Stuart rotates a cast of about

BELOW: "Tina Turner" belts it out at the Imperial's *Legends in Concert* show.

100 celebrity lookalikes, most of whom obsessively study videos of their models. "I loved everything about the way he wore his clothes, his hair, the way he sang. I would study myself doing his smile in a mirror," said Graham Patrick, who plays Elvis, his upper lip curling.

Imperial impersonators

Impersonators in Vegas are almost as common as high rollers. Another "Elvis," Jim LeBoeuf at the Riviera, owns a dozen costumes, worth up to $4,000 each. He buys teddy bears which he tosses into the audience. "Everybody understands a free teddy bear. (It's) a portion of Elvis' generosity that everybody remembers him for."

Doug Sparks, who portrayed Sammy Davis Jr in the Sahara's show *The Rat Pack is Back*, recalls the night when Davis's widow watched the show. "It was a weird feeling (but) she said she enjoyed it, that I had the mannerisms down" but told him that Sammy wouldn't have worn "that suit." Sparks was quick to accommodate.

"That suit has not been back on stage," he says.

Imitating Madonna, Coty Alexander explains: "Right before I go on stage I feel like Madonna. When you're impersonating, you're acting. Sometimes you're really into it and the character overcomes you. When you impersonate somebody every night, your facial expressions actually change."

The Oriental-style, 2,700-room hotel has all the usual amenities including an Olympic-sized swimming pool, 24-hour wedding chapel for those impulsive proposals, and an independent on-site medical center.

Gamblers should be on the alert for the sometimes short-lived promotions like the Imperial Palace's "New Member Mania." Under this plan, enrollees could qualify for a variety of freebies ranging from room vouchers to car-rental days, concert tickets, spa passes, free meals, and even airline credit vouchers. The only drawback is that there seems to be a requirement for around six hours of straight gambling to qualify.

Map on page 108

In the 1950s, great motels on the Strip were commonplace, but now most of the originals have been pulled down.

BELOW: mobster Bugsy Siegel slept here. He really didn't like being called "Bugsy."

The Imperial's owner, Ralph Engelstad, was renowned for his antique cars, which are now on show as the **Imperial Palace Auto Collection**. An animated figure of John Wayne stands beside the Duke's silver 1931 Bentley, welcoming guests to the impressive 200-car collection. Priceless motors include a $50 million array of 1930s Duesenbergs; Liberace's 1981 Zimmer with a candelabra hood ornament; Howard Hughes' baby-blue Chrysler; a 1929 Isotta Fraschini of the type seen in *Sunset Boulevard*; and a replica of Karl Benz's 1886 three-wheeler said to have reached speeds of up to 8 mph (13 kph).

Also on show are cars formerly owned by Hitler, Kruschev, and many US presidents. The blue-and-white 1976 Cadillac for which Elvis Presley paid $14,409 – including extras like brass hubcaps – and Marilyn Monroe's 1955 Lincoln Capri convertible, in which the screen goddess clocked up only 26,000 miles (42,000 km), are cars that have motor-mad fans eating their room vouchers with envy.

The Flamingo

The **Flamingo** ⑳ (3555 Las Vegas Boulevard South, tel: 733-3111 or 800-732-2111) of today is a far cry from the "carpet joint" of Bugsy Siegel's day. Almost the last traces of the mobster disappeared in 1995 when his bullet-proof casino office with its elaborate escape routes was bulldozed.

This was all part of a master plan which included razing the outmoded, motel-style buildings at the rear of the property and constructing a $104 million tower addition. The hoodlum might well have been forgotten by now but for the success of Warren Beatty's 1991 movie *Bugsy*, with himself in the title role. Though the movie was more fantasy than fact, it did kindle enough popular interest for the hotel to open the **Bugsy Celebrity Theater**.

Historians like to recount that, tough as he was, Benjamin Siegel did not faze everybody. Since paying tax was not one of his top priorities, he was once challenged by Robbins Cahill from the Nevada Tax Commission, who sent an

LEFT AND RIGHT: the Barbary Coast has what it claims is the world's largest "Tiffany-style" stained-glass mural.

Map on page 108

employee to collect $5,000 owed in gaming taxes. "What'll you do if I don't pay?" the mobster asked. He was told that his license would be revoked, and replied, "You wouldn't dare." The employee reported back to Cahill who told the hoodlum, "Maybe you'd better try us." Siegel backed out of the challenge and wrote a check.

Six months later, in June of 1946, Siegel was murdered by a shotgun blast at the Beverly Hills mansion of his girlfriend, Virginia "Flamingo" Hill. A plaque near the Flamingo's garden buffet pavilion wryly commemorates the mobster's demise, announcing that his "preoccupation with safety proved to be geographically misplaced." The late Las Vegas historian Frank Wright mused that, "In a sense, Siegel's death was a great advertisement for the city of Las Vegas. It certainly brought attention, and created a sort of sense of illicit excitement."

The 15-acre (6-hectare) garden, with more plastic flamingos and real penguins, is quite charming at night, which, even though only steps away from the bright-heat roar of the Strip, is filled with the sound of crickets. There are pools, waterfalls, a lagoon, and a turtle observation bridge, plus an entire wildlife habitat, with koi, swans, ducks, and – of course – Chilean flamingos. The garden is open to the public most days, to hotel guests only at night.

Barbary Coast

Down the block, the **Barbary Coast** ㉑ (3595 Las Vegas Boulevard South, tel: 737-7111 or 888-227-2279) stresses "Victorian charm and elegance," more or less sustained by chandeliers with big white globes, Art-Deco glass signs, and waitresses who wear red garters over black-net stockings. Along with its decorative windows in the Victorian Room is what it claims is the world's largest "Tiffany style" stained-glass mural. Some tables are set aside for *pai gow*, a form of poker adapted from an Asian domino game, and there is a poker machine played with gold coins which pays $250,000 for a royal flush, or a mere free drink for two pairs. ❑

RESTAURANTS

Hyakumi Japanese and Sushi Bar
Caesars Palace
Tel: 702-731-7731
Open: D daily; noodle and sushi bar 11am–4pm.
$$–$$$$
Every type of sushi is available here.

The Palm
Caesars Palace
Tel: 702-732-7256
Open: L & D daily. **$$$$**
Gourmet steak and seafood, veal or, for anyone interested in lighter dishes, pasta.

Terrazza
Caesars Palace
Tel: 702-731-7731
Open: D Tues.–Sat. **$$$**
Beautiful restaurant featuring excellent Italian dining, with jazz nightly in the lounge.

Chinois and Spago
The Forum Shops at Caesars Palace
Tel: 702-737-9700
Open: L & D daily; sushi bar 3–11pm. **$$$**
Wolfgang Puck offers Chinese with a Gallic attitude. Specialties

include Shanghai lobster with coconut curry sauce, stir-fried string beans, catfish, duck, and much more. A few steps away is a branch of Puck's California-inspired **Spago**. **$–$$**

Asia
Harrah's
Tel: 702-369-5000
Open: D Fri.–Tues. **$$$**
An elegant mix of Chinese, Japanese, and Asian cuisine presented in a lovely atmosphere.

Drai's
Barbary Coast
Tel: 702-731-7111
Open: D daily. **$$$**

Ex-Hollywood producer Victor Drai brings an upscale ambiance to this beautiful room. Dishes include seared jumbo scallops with citrus ginger sauce.

Michael's
Barbary Coast
Tel: 702-731-7111
Open: D daily. **$$$$**
Victorian-style gourmet room featuring classic Continental cuisine like chateaubriand.

● ● ● ● ● ● ● ● ● ● ● ●
Price includes dinner and a glass of wine, excluding tip.
$$$$ $40 and up, **$$$** under $40, **$$** under $30, **$** under $20

MIRAGE TO THE STARDUST

Pirate battles, erupting volcanos, white tigers, leaping dolphins, one-armed bandits, and the hotel where Elvis played his first Vegas gig. Need we say more?

Map on page 148

In 1989, when he was about to open the **Mirage** ❶ (3400 Las Vegas Boulevard South, tel: 791-7111 or 800-627-6667), entrepreneur Steve Wynn said that there had been "a terrible sameness" to earlier Vegas casinos. "I wanted to take it to a new level. We presented this place as an alternative for people. I always knew others would follow, as they have, but it happened much faster than even I expected."

The Mirage certainly was different. From the erupting volcano just off the sidewalk to the tigers' glass-enclosed habitat in the arcade of smart shops underground, it drew huge crowds of curious spectators right from the beginning. Within three years, the casino was the biggest money-maker on the Strip. Even though the hotel needed to take more than a million dollars a day to break even, it never seemed to be a problem.

The spectacular appeal of the Royal white tigers and their magician owners, Siegfried & Roy, was enough to fill the 1,500-seat show room 480 times a year. Despite tickets costing $100 or more, the shows were usually sold out weeks – if not months – in advance. But Siegfried & Roy have not performed since October 4, 2003, when Roy was attacked and dragged off stage by one of his tigers. Roy is never expected to fully recover, and the show is now permanently closed.

Rare species

Nevertheless, Siegfried & Roy's white tigers are safe and well in the **White Tiger Habitat**, and the **Secret Garden** (admission fee) displays even more wild animals, this time set in semi-tropical splendor. Past azure-blue pools where dolphins swim are 40 rare or endangered species, including the Royal

LEFT:
the Strip, looking north.
BELOW:
pirate battle at T.I. (Treasure Island).

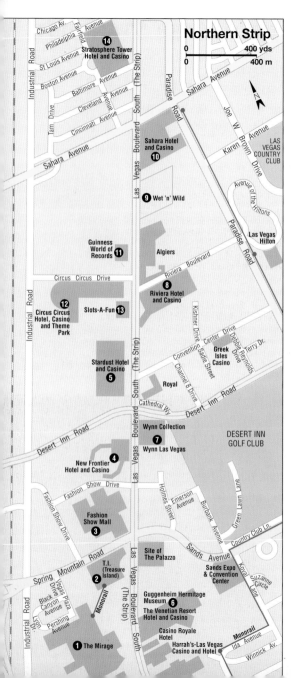

Northern Strip

0   400 yds
0   400 m

white tigers and white lions. "Recording sticks" offer an anodyne narration.

Sharks and exotic sea life swim in a 20,000-gallon (75,700-liter) tank behind the Mirage's registration desk, inside a glass-enclosed atrium 90 feet (27 meters) high filled with lush gardens, palm trees, and tropical foliage. The **Dolphin Habitat**, which houses 10 Atlantic bottle-nose dolphins in 2.5-million gallon (9.5-million liter) saltwater tanks, has been visited by half-a-million schoolchildren since it opened in 1990. As for **the Volcano**, it erupts 128,000 recirculated gallons (480,000 liters) of water a minute down its sides, a phenomenon powered by a natural-gas pipeline; the sulfuric odor of the burning gas is masked by a piña colada scent released into the air.

The Mirage promoted itself aggressively across the USA in the Wynn era, with a traveling show which clearly helped to make it one of the state's biggest tourist attractions. The hotel's elegant rooms are nearly always filled, and the guests spend more than $700,000 a day on non-gambling pursuits. Revenue from the casino is what makes the extravagances possible. Less than 5 percent of the Mirage's 4 million square feet (372,000 square meters) are devoted to gaming, but that's still where the big bucks are made.

T.I.

At least as interesting is **Treasure Island**, which shares the 100-acre (40-hectare) site with the Mirage and is connected by a free monorail. Treasure Island is month-by-month shedding its family image and rebranding itself as **T.I. ❷** (3300 Las Vegas Boulevard South, tel: 894-7111 or 800-944-7444). T.I.'s showroom hosts Cirque du Soleil's *Mystère*, where over 70 singers, dancers, jugglers, and acrobats deliver an athletic and metaphorical journey through life. Be sure to book ahead, as tickets are popular.

Outside, a vast lagoon is the spectacular scene of the *Sirens of T.I.* – a stand-off between a group of tempting sirens and a band of renegade pirates. The crowd is different from those that gathered to watch the now-defunct pirate battle. That audience was kids; this audience is hip and ready to spend money, the most commonly held theory as to why the resort is rebranding itself.

After 10 years, the casino was ready for a change. Out have gone the kids' costumes. In have come scantily clad girls and T-shirts saying "TI girl." This is all a process back to adult entertainment that has taken place since the millennium, a throwback to the naughty Vegas of the 1950s and 60s. A long pedestrian bridge crosses the Strip to connect T.I. with the Venetian resort, which is useful when traffic is heavy.

Although the overwhelming majority of the city's 36 million visitors each year do some gambling while they're here, most of them claim that it's not their main reason for visiting. More than half of them, however, do some shopping, spending an average of $183 each ($252 for foreign tourists), according to a recent survey. "Given the quality and depth of the luxury and consumer goods available," says retail analyst George Connor, "we now have one of the heaviest concentrations of retail in the world."

Shop till you drop

One of the major beneficiaries of this heavy spending is the well located **Fashion Show Mall** ❸ (tel: 369-0704), whose recent $350-million expansion, which doubled its size, has added Nordstrom's to its seven flagship retail giants such as Neiman Marcus, Saks Fifth Avenue, and Macy's – making more than 250 stores altogether.

The eye-catching complex has a movable stage with retractable runways, state-of-the-art video, and lighting and sound equipment to enhance runway fashion shows. A canopy area known as **The Cloud**, onto which images are projected

Map on page 148

BELOW:
The Cloud at the Fashion Show Mall.

after dark, stretchs along a major part of its Strip frontage. The mall houses several bistros and sidewalk cafes. Open weekdays from 10am to 9pm (till 7pm Saturday, noon–6pm Sunday), the mall is easily accessed via a (free) underground garage.

The New Frontier

The **New Frontier** ❹ (3120 Las Vegas Boulevard South, tel: 794-8200 or 800-634-6966) attracts a younger crowd, partly perhaps because of its lower prices. The atrium is an indoor garden with fountains, pools, and waterfalls. It is also the longest-established hotel on the Strip, and has a venerable history. Not only was it the place where Kirk Kerkorian – the city's richest man – began his Las Vegas career with junkets on his fledgling airline, but it was also the venue where Liberace and later, Elvis Presley, first played in Vegas.

Kerkorian had made a fortune selling surplus military aircraft, and began gambling in Las Vegas in the 1940s and 1950s, sometimes losing $50,000 a night. In 1962 he bought

BELOW: an Atlantic dolphin, one of the stars at the Mirage.

80 acres (32 hectares) across the Strip from the Flamingo for less than $1 million, and acquired the narrow piece of land that separated it from the Strip. He then made a deal with Jay Sarno, who was building Caesars Palace, and sold him the property for $5 million. Later, the Frontier narrowly escaped closure by an employee strike that ran from September 1991 to February 1998.

Old-fashioned one-armed bandit slot machines with pistol-arms you can pull stand as a greeting in the doorway, and Micky Gilly's clone of his now-defunct Texas nightclub, scaled-down but with a bucking mechanical bull, packs in the punters every evening. Thursday is always Ladies' Night, offering cheap drinks and free bull rides. The huge site on which the New Frontier stands is due for development as the site for Phil Ruffin's projected City by the Bay.

A San Francisco-themed resort is planned with attractions based on Coit Tower, Lombard Street and an Alcatraz restaurant, as well as a 1,500-room hotel-casino where the former Silver Slipper once stood. Ruffin and New Yorker Donald Trump also have plans for Trump Tower, a luxurious condominium project similar to the one the developer and Atlantic City casino mogul currently owns in Manhattan.

The Stardust

The **Stardust** ❺ (3000 Las Vegas Boulevard South, tel: 732-6111 or 800-634-6757) has 2,300 rooms, a highly rated Track and Sports Book, a much-loved low-stake poker room, the Wayne Newton Theater, and a very Las Vegas history. The casino was begun in 1955 by Tony Cornero, in his time a bootlegger, hijacker, rum-runner, and operator of offshore gambling boats before he started work on the Stardust. It was nearly three-quarters finished

Map on page 148

when he died of a heart attack after gambling at the Desert Inn.

The Stardust has an exterior bathed in lines of purple light with colored fountains beside the entrance. It was also owned for 10 years by former bootlegger and racketeer Moe Dalitz *(see pages 32–33)*, who had operated small gambling parlors in Cleveland and other parts of the eastern United States before moving out West. Dalitz met future Teamsters boss Jimmy Hoffa through his laundry business and was able to use Teamster funds to finance the purchase of the Stardust, and possibly the Desert Inn, in which he had a 13.2-percent stake when it opened in 1950.

Stardust memories

Although Moe Dalitz once said "How was I to know those gambling joints were illegal? There were so many judges and politicians in them I figured they had to be all right." In his later years, through charitable donations and the friendship of Nevada senator Pat McCarran, the mobster was able to achieve a measure of respectability bordering on popularity.

He was honored as a humanitarian by the American Cancer Research Center and given an award by B'nai B'rith. Stardust executive Herb Tobman said that Dalitz never neglected a chance to contribute to charity, both national and local, and was legendary for it around town, "There has never been a greater influence on this city," he said. Ovid Dermaris and Ed Reid, authors of *The Green Felt Jungle*, took a more crisp view: "He was a sanctimonious little mobster from Cleveland," they concluded.

Wayne Newton was once listed in the Guinness Book of Records as the world's highest-paid entertainer with earnings of around $325,000 a week. The singer is now fulfilling a lifetime engagement at the Stardust's **Wayne Newton Theater**, where his show, with lots of handshaking from stage to audience, is perennially popular. He is also one of the growing number of celebrities who has chosen to live permanently in Las Vegas. ❑

Wayne Newton has played here more times than anyone can count.

RESTAURANTS

Mikado
The Mirage
Tel: 702-791-7223
Open: D daily. **$$$$**
Teppan tables and a sushi bar. Choose from tempura, hibachi lobster, steak, chicken, or fresh shrimp.

Moongate
The Mirage
Tel: 702-791-7223
Open: D daily. **$$$**
Fine Chinese food graced by a classical Chinese courtyard. Soothing and tasty.

Onda
The Mirage
Tel: 702-791-7223
Open: D daily. **$$**
Regional and classic Italian dishes with North American innovations, featuring homemade pastas, breads, fresh seafood, and meats.

Buccaneer Bay Club
T.I. (Treasure Island)
Tel: 702-894-7223
Open: D daily. **$$$**
Dine from a US-Continental menu as a pyrotechnic sea battle

on the Strip takes place before your very eyes.

Island Paradise Café
The Stardust
Tel: 702-732-6111
Open: 24 hours daily. **$–$$**
The Stardust's 24-hour restaurant is good value, if a little light on frills. For fans of steak-and-lobster dinners, this is *the* place: tasty, quick, and so inexpensive there'll be change left over to hit the gaming tables again.

Sushi King
The Stardust
Tel: 702-732-6111
Open: D daily. **$$**

Fresh sashimi and sushi, as well as yaki shitake and tempura. Over 140 different items on the menu, with much of the seafood flown in every day.

Tony Roma's
The Stardust
Tel: 702-732-6111
Open: D daily. **$$**
Tony Roma's is known for ribs, and this branch is no exception. Smother in barbeque sauce.

● ● ● ● ● ● ● ● ● ● ● ●
Price includes dinner and a glass of wine, excluding tip.
***$$$$** $40 and up, **$$$** under $40, **$$** under $30, **$** under $20*

VENETIAN TO THE STRATOSPHERE TOWER

Glide in a gondola past great shops, enjoy world-class
art, scare yourself silly on top of the tallest tower in
the West, and see the tattooed stripper from Seattle

The lovely **Venetian** ⑥ (3355
Las Vegas Boulevard South,
tel: 414-1000 or 888-283-
6423) was conceived by maverick
Sheldon Adelson, ebullient founder
of the annual computer convention
Comdex. Adelson, the son of a
Boston cabbie, financed the Venetian partly from the $900 million
proceeds of the sale of Comdex.
After their marriage, Adelson and
his wife Miriam, an Israeli doctor,
spent their honeymoon in Venice
and subsequently set a pair of historians to work compiling a photographic catalog of original Venetian
artwork and architectural details.

Built to be beautiful

Built at a cost of $1.5 billion on the
site of the former 44-year-old Sands
Hotel, the Venetian was designed to
be the world's largest hotel and convention complex under one roof.
The rooms are almost twice as large
as the average, and the bathrooms
have data ports. The restaurants are
served by chefs on the critics' Top-
10 lists, the luxurious 65,000-
square-foot (6,000-square-meter)
spa and fitness club is operated by
the renowned **Canyon Ranch**, and
the complex has enough marble-
and-stone flooring to cover a dozen
football fields. It adjoins a pool deck
modeled after a Venetian garden.

"We anticipate seeing a new
brand of tourist," says Robert Gold-
stein, the Venetian's president. He's
betting a great deal on this assessment with the hotel's acquisition of
a museum that easily fits into the
world-class category. The Guggenheim Hermitage is a partnership
with Russia's renowned Hermitage
Museum in St Petersburg, and for
the Las Vegas property, 63,700
square feet (5,850 square meters) of
exhibition space was built and fine-
tuned. This could be the start of

Map
on page
148

LEFT AND BELOW:
the Venetian.

something big. Jim Mann, curator of the Las Vegas Art Museum on West Sahara, predicts that other museums will follow the Guggenheim and Venetian partnership because of the huge potential audience.

Campanile Bell Tower

Viewed from the Strip, the lavish Venetian really does look like Venice, from the **Campanile Bell Tower** roaring 300 feet (98 meters) above the **Grand Canal** to the *gondolieri* in striped shirts. Like their Italian counterparts, they serenade their sometimes embarrassed passengers, but at least the gondola rides are cheaper than the originals. Adding to the realism, thousands of pigeons have been trained to fly out and swirl around at least twice a day.

Along with the **Doges Palace** and **Rialto Bridge**, the resort sports a scaled-down **Piazza San Marco** in which jugglers, singers, and dancers seem to be continually performing. The square is the culmination of the **Grand Canal Shoppes** which begins with a colorful, awe-inspiring frescoed ceiling and segues into

the bluest skies ever seen. Dozens of contemporary celebrities are portrayed at **Madame Tussaud's** in wax near the hotel's entrance, and the tiny but fascinating **Houdini Museum** (open 9am–11pm) exhibits memorabilia from the famous magician.

In 2003, a 22-story tower opened, including 12 stories of rooms and 10 stories of parking, bringing the resort's total to 4, 049 rooms. This will be augmented considerably when the Venetian's new resort and tower (which is thought will not have an Italian theme) is built on the corner of Twain Avenue and the Strip. Demolition on the existing site began in early 2004, when one of the most poignant casualties was the destruction of the family-owned Tam O'Shanter motel, in business since 1959.

The motel's distinctive Irish neon sign has been donated to Vegas's Nevada sign museum. As the family considers its future, they will no doubt garner solace from the price of selling their site, which is said to have been in the region of "several million dollars."

BELOW: guarding just one of the treasures at the Guggenheim Hermitage.

Guggenheim Hermitage

Even the most casual art lover will recognize these names: Camille Pisarro (1830–1903), Vincent Van Gogh (1853–90), Paul Gauguin (1848–1903), Henri Rousseau (1844–1910), Paul Cézanne (1839–1906), Pierre Auguste Renoir (1841–1919), and Pierre Bonnard (1867–1947).

Works of these 19th- and 20th-century artists are exhibited in just the *first* room of the highly regarded **Guggenheim Hermitage** museum (daily 9am–11pm, tel: 414-2440). In subsequent rooms of the museum are famous works by other familiar names: the *Green Violinist* by Marc Chagall (1847–1985), the *Nymph and Satyr* by Henri Matisse (1869–1954), *Woman in Armchair* by Pablo Picasso (1881–1973), *Woman Holding Vase* by Fernand Léger (1881–1955).

There are also pieces by Robert Delauney (1885–1941), Amedeo Modigliani (1884–1920), and Vasily Kandinsky (1866–1944). It's a first-rate collection which has drawn a crowd since opening in 2001.

The state-of-the-art gallery space was designed by architect Rem Koolhaas. Its exterior and interior walls are covered with panels of Cor-Ten steel, never used before as the structure of a museum gallery. The streamlined, textured metal is meant to evoke the velvet walls of the St Petersburg Hermitage while providing a contrast with the over-the-top architecture of the Venetian.

In an even larger gallery at the Venetian was the Guggenheim Las Vegas museum. Its premiere exhibition, "The Art of the Motorcycle," brought from the Guggenheim in New York City, captivated casual visitors and aficionados alike with its comprehensive history of the motorbike, but at the end of a long run, the Guggenheim Las Vegas closed after this first and only show.

Wynn's Las Vegas

On the 200-acre (80-hectare) site of the old Desert Inn, north of the Venetian, Steve Wynn's $1.6 billion **Wynn Las Vegas** ❼ is rising, and due to open in 2005.

The resort, accessible via a new

> Map on page 148

Most Las Vegans believe "if it's worth doing it's worth overdoing."

– JOHN SMITH

BELOW: glide in a gondola past gorgeous garments at the Grand Canal Shoppes.

walkway crossing above the Strip, will have a glassed-in 48-story tower with 2,611 rooms, a 120,000-square-foot (11,000-square-meter) casino and two showrooms, a huge pool, and a 3-acre (1 hectare) lake. Water has always played a key role in Wynn's creations.

For a while he even contemplated flooding two Downtown streets and turning Fremont Street into a canal to create a Venice-like environment. It remains a fantasy unfulfilled. Although man-made lakes are prohibited in Clark County, he alone probably had the political muscle to pull it off.

Wynn may well be the best known person in Las Vegas, and there has been endless speculation about his new project, just as there was preceding his Mirage and Bellagio ventures. He is incurably drawn to the spectacular, and to showmanship. After he appeared with Frank Sinatra in jokey commercials on US TV a few years ago, his face became familiar to millions of Americans outside of Las Vegas.

The impressive new casino will be a suitably stylish venue for the tycoon's impressive collection of art, called of course, the Wynn Collection. The hangings include paintings by Picasso, Modigliani, Matisse, Cézanne, Monet, and Van Gogh. Wynn and the Venetian's Sheldon Adelson have recently been granted licenses to open casinos in Macau in eastern Asia, and each is expected to invest around $500 million in the new venture.

The Riviera

Breaking new ground in the 1980s, the **Riviera** ❽ (2901 Las Vegas Boulevard South, tel: 734-5110 or 800-634-6753) shifted from headliners to more broad-based stage shows. The first one was *Splash,* which features performers and specialty acts centered around a huge aquarium. Nine drag artistes perform, led by Frank Marino impersonating Joan Rivers.

Following this was *An Evening at La Cage,* and the latest version is a rather tawdry skin show called *Crazy Girls,* which begins with the audience being mooned by eight

BELOW: *rasul* is an exotic treatment available at the Venetian spa.

pairs of bare buttocks. Seven bronze Crazy Girls, their rears shiny from being caressed by thousands of eager hands, flank the casino's sidewalk entrance.

The fast-food court just off the sidewalk is a convenient and inexpensive place to eat with a choice of hot dogs, yoghurt, burgers, Chinese dishes, sushi, pizza, espresso and pastries. There are half-a-dozen other restaurants including a hot-dog counter in **Nickel Town**.

Among the stores is one selling pearls right from the oyster; a magic shop; and one representing Pahrump Valley Vineyards, the state's only commercial winery. The hotel, with its Olympic-size swimming pool, exercise rooms, spa, tennis courts, and a video arcade, was the setting for Martin Scorsese's 1995 film *Casino*. Its casino is slightly bigger than that of Circus Circus, although with fewer slot machines. When the Riviera opened in 1955, it had only 116 of them.

Liberace was a Las Vegas veteran with 10 years of performances behind him when he opened the Riviera in April 1955. He was backed by his 23-piece orchestra, and Joan Crawford acted as official hostess. Wearing a white tuxedo by avant garde designer Christian Dior, the camp pianist was drawing $50,000 a week, an astonishing fee at a time when a house could be bought for less than a fifth of that figure. The first high-rise hotel in Vegas had been planned to make an impact, and it quickly became entertainment central.

Vegas veterans

The Clover Room was headlined by 1950s' stars Marlene Dietrich, Milton Berle, Harry Belafonte, Orson Welles, Dinah Shore, Red Skelton, Ginger Rogers, Mickey Rooney, and Zsa Zsa Gabor. For the next three decades the hotel built more towers – up to the present five – and the stars kept coming. Carol Channing, Louis Armstrong, Cyd Charisse, George Burns, Eddie Fisher, Tony Bennett, and Dean Martin all played in the Riviera's **Versailles Theater**.

How are you going to cool off when the temperature hits 110

Map on page 148

The Riviera's bronze "Crazy Girls" have rear ends shined to perfection by an eager public.

BELOW: the Riviera has a very Vegas history.

degrees, which it often does in this desert oasis? Well, one way is to take the 76-foot (23-meter) plunge or just catch the waves at **Wet 'n' Wild** ❾ (2601 Las Vegas Boulevard South, tel: 871-7811, daily till dark, fee) which packs rides, slides, chutes, shoots, and floats into its watery 15 acres (6 hectares).

The Sahara

When the **Sahara** ❿ (2535 Las Vegas Boulevard South, tel: 737-2111) opened in 1952, it featured real camels and a North African theme. Marlene Dietrich and Tony Bennett made their Las Vegas debuts in the Congo Room, where Mae West and later George Burns appeared. Don Rickles debuted in the Casbar Lounge in 1959. In 1963, Elvis Presley and Ann-Margret filmed segments of *Viva Las Vegas* in the hotel.

The venerable hotel-casino was originally built by the Del Webb Corp. which also later owned The Mint, the Thunderbird, and the Lucky Club, and when owner Milton Prell wanted to extend the Sahara, he received the first Bank of Las Vegas casino loan.

The Sahara is entered via a dramatic, neon-lit rotunda with a motif of neon camels and a **NASCAR Café** that features racing on giant projection screens with surround sound. A score of authentic stock cars are displayed, including the world's largest, Carzilla, a Pontiac Grand-Prix that weighs three tons. It has a **NASCAR Cyber Speedway** at the rear where visitors can choose a type of car and course to take on a virtual-reality adventure, sitting in the life-size racing cars which shake and sway up and down and side to side as a fast-moving racetrack is projected onto a nearby and enveloping screen.

"Speed-The-Ride" lasts only 45 seconds, but riders are propelled from zero to 35 mph (56 kph) in two seconds, in what a local writer described as "an adrenaline junkie's crack pipe;" a loop skywards and then back down. The Sahara was one of the first casinos to display the video poker machines on which a pair of phantom hands on screen

BELOW: try virtual-reality NASCAR racing at the Sahara's Cyber Speedway.

"deal" the cards, and there are new gimmicks all the time. Recent machines have featured Elvis Presley singing when you hit the right combination, plus Sinatra and two talk-show hosts from US television, Regis Philbin and Alan Trebek. Today's slot machines are controlled by microchips which constantly generate a series of random numbers whether the machine is being played or not. The precise fraction of a second at which you pull the handle or press the button determines which numbers (represented on the reels by symbols) show up.

"The Rat Pack is Back," a sign proclaims, promoting a show which captured some of the ambiance of the old days when Sinatra, Dean Martin, and Sammy Davis Jr hung out here. In the main showroom, magician Steve Wyrick is on an eight-year contract.

World records

For unfathomable reasons, a local man, Brad Rodgers, has collected more than 8,400 shot glasses and hundreds of them are displayed in the **Guinness World of Records ⓫** (2780 Las Vegas Boulevard, tel: 792-3766, daily 9am–5pm). Then there's Nick Vermeulen who, even more mysteriously, has gathered more than 2,000 air-sickness bags from 470 airlines. "Somebody has to do it," he explains, though he doesn't say why.

Most of the other exhibits are equally bizarre; a stripper from Seattle, every inch of whose body is covered with tattoos, a wax figure of the late Shigechiyo Izumi who claimed to be 120 years old when he died in 1986 (allegedly he was born in 1866, the year Abraham Lincoln was assassinated).

Then there's a picture of Ken Edwards, a British man who ate 36 medium-size cockroaches in one minute; videotape of other champion eaters include a guzzler downing 250 oysters in three minutes. The museum includes dozens of astounding facts and figures: did you know that the loudest measured snore clocked in at 90 decibels while a pneumatic drill tops in at only 70 to 80 decibels?

Map on page 148

LEFT: the tattooed stripper at the Guinness World of Records.
RIGHT: the Stratosphere Tower rises above the Strip.

Jugglers, trapeze artists, and clowns perform here above the gaming hall from 11am until midnight.

BELOW: this family-oriented resort packs in the punters.

Circus Circus

Before **Circus Circus** ⑫ (2880 Las Vegas Boulevard South, tel: 734-0410 or 800-444-2472), Jay Sarno had the vision for Caesars Palace, and everything since has progressed from there. The title of "Mr Las Vegas" has been casually awarded to many people in the town's history and several seem like worthy candidates, but most would agree that the kind of spectacle that Las Vegas displays today owes more to Sarno than to any other individual.

How proud he would be if he were able to see how his vision for palaces of fantasy, crafted around single themes, have grown. "Sarno was ahead of his time," said Bob Stoldal, a local TV writer. "People said, 'Circus Circus just doesn't work. It's not Las Vegas.' Clearly that wasn't true."

With free circus acts and a midway lined by carnival concessions, ample opportunities for inexpensive food, a vast family amusement park, bargain deals for hotel rooms, and 5,100 parking spaces, some making up an RV park called **Circusland** with its own pool, laundromat, and general store, Circus Circus always seems crowded.

"On the Strip," wrote Aaron Betsky, curator of architecture and design at San Francisco's Museum of Modern Art, "you are part of the most elaborate urban theater ever assembled. After four decades of trying, Las Vegas has finally managed to turn Hollywood into reality, and what we can learn from today's Vegas is that streets can also be theaters, buildings can become their own signs."

Preoccupied with the gaming, Circus Circus gamblers rarely look up to where another world above is populated by crowds jamming the midway attractions as acrobats, jugglers, aerialists, trapeze artists, and clowns perform in the world's largest permanent circus from 11am till midnight. Miniature camels race along plastic tracks, children's faces are painted by a clown, and an endless line of hopefuls try to win prizes by bringing a big rubber mallet down heavily enough to propel a rubber chicken into a cooking pot.

Gambling fever

Every day for over 20 years it has packed in the crowds, but this kind of success eluded Sarno himself. An inveterate gambler – he once won $10,000 betting that he could sink a long shot on a basketball toss – his instincts failed with Circus Circus, which took a long time to recover from opening with no hotel rooms. It was only after William G. Bennett and his partner Bill Pennington took over and concentrated on the then-untapped family market that it became a money machine.

One explanation for the turn-around comes from Mel Larson, a one-time VP of the casino. "I found out that half the people coming to town did not have reservations and more than half were driving," he recalled. "So we just hammered on the radio on the stations that reached people on the freeway. We captured all this walk-in business, which was unheard of at the time. Everybody else was after the upper-income people but we just wanted a lot of folks." Sound strategy.

Now this aggressively successful downmarket, family-oriented resort is owned by the Mandalay Resorts Group, which also operates the Luxor, Monte Carlo, Excalibur, and the Mandalay Bay, and now controlling more hotels in the city than any of its competitors.

Next door, **Slots-A-Fun** ⑬ (2800 Las Vegas Boulevard South, tel: 734-0410) offers free beer to all players and has penny slot machines, but as they only take dollar bills you get to play 100 pennies at a time. There's a glass case near the door exhibiting Polaroid photos of earlier winners and usually somebody handing out free ticket booklets and offering a free pull. In some casinos you can find machines that take $500 tokens, but not in Slots-A-Fun, which is distinctly downmarket.

Making money

Satellite casinos like this one are heavy on slot machines, which have become by far the biggest money-making sector in the gaming industry. The old one-armed bandits, now historical relics, have been replaced by electronic machines

Map on page 148

BELOW: outdoors at night on the northern stretch of the Strip.

with TV screens instead of reels. Collectively clearing $17 million in daily profits, the casinos use any gimmick they can think of to keep the money rolling in. One of the most successful is the slot club, where members are given key cards which both operate the machines and keep a tally of their wins and losses.

Players are also rewarded with a variety of items from key rings to free meal tickets – all part of the $2 million the casinos spend every day in comps ("complimentaries," which are freebies given to gamblers as rewards or inducements) of one kind or another, with high rollers, of course, more likely to receive free rooms, limos, or seats in the showroom.

Almost all machines now operate on multiple coins, often feeding into a master jackpot which any machine in the group can win. These jackpots grow into an astronomical amount. The groupings can be a number of machines in one casino, or can be tied to all of the same machines in the entire state. Progressive machines can be identified by flashing electronic pay-off signs displayed either on top of the machine or above a grouping of them.

Stratospheric

The **Stratosphere Tower** ⓮ (2000 Las Vegas Boulevard South, tel: 380-7777 or 800-998-6937) is the tallest building west of the Mississippi River and the tallest free-standing observation tower in the country. It is owned by wheeler-dealer Carl Icahn, one of the world's richest men.

Speedy elevators whisk visitors to a height of 1,149 feet (345 meters) in an ear-popping 30 seconds, where on a clear day California and Arizona are visible. The deck is also a favorite nightspot for visitors, who relish the finest view of the world's best display of neon. The casino offers some of the Strip's more competitive odds.

The 1,500-room resort is topped by a revolving restaurant and offers rides hundreds of feet above ground on the **High Roller Roller Coaster**. The thrilling **Big Shot** is a kind of

Anyone who completes a ride on the Stratosphere Tower's Big Shot and manages to stay alive becomes a member of the "Scream Team," to whom discounts are offered.

BELOW: thrill-ride with a view.

Map on page 148

reversed bungee jump that shoots riders high into the air. A recent rider said, "I didn't want to do it, my kids made me. It was the most terrifying thing I ever did. I couldn't wait to do it again." The Stratosphere also features the extreme **X Scream**, which thrusts riders out over the top and edge of the casino, then rocks them slowly back to safety.

The resort has a showroom, a pool and spa, and a choice of restaurants including the **Around the World** buffet, the **Top of the World** revolving restaurant with the best view on – and of – the Strip, and a 1950s diner. Romantically inclined visitors can get married near the top of the tower.

The best-known denizens of the Stratosphere Tower are the team of Steve Lieberman and Officer Dex, who garnered press around the country and appeared on NBC TV's *Nightly News*. Officer Dex – a two-year-old German shepherd trained to sniff out explosives – is greeted with big smiles as he cuts through the crowd. Together with his partner he underwent a training course as a K9 security unit in Indiana, and they have been patroling the casino together ever since. "They have been great publicity for us," says PR manager Michael Gilmartin.

Dream weaver

Bob Stupak, the man who originally dreamed up the idea for the tower, was described by local newspaper columnist John L. Smith as "perhaps the greatest huckster in Las Vegas history," something of an accolade given the competition. Stupak ran illegal card games right after leaving school, almost killed himself racing motorcycles, and had a brief career as a singer.

In 1974 he acquired what Smith called "the worst piece of real estate on Las Vegas Boulevard," a former used-car lot, and built Bob Stupak's World Famous Historic Gambling Museum, a grandiose name that Stupak says "was about one foot longer than the casino." After it burned down, he followed up with the 20-story Vegas World, where the cash flow helped to pay for the $550 million Stratosphere Tower. ❏

The Big Shot ride on top of the Strat Tower is truly terrifying.

RESTAURANTS

Delmonico Steakhouse
The Venetian
Tel: 702-414-3737
Open: L & D daily. **$$$**
Emeril Lagasse dishes up delicious Creole flavors in his personal steakhouse.

Lutece
The Venetian
Tel: 702-414-2220
Open: D daily. **$$$$**
Classic, family-style and *nouvelle* French cuisine are all on offer in this elegantly modern restaurant.

Postrio
Grand Canal Shoppes at The Venetian
Tel: 702-796-1110
Open: L & D daily. **$–$$$$**
Wolfgang Puck's San Francisco-style eatery serves modern American cuisine with Mediterranean accents. Try the signature dish: baked loup de mer en croute.

House of Lords Steakhouse
The Sahara
Tel: 702-737-2111
Open: D daily. **$$**

Beautiful waterfalls and plush seating highlight the cozy ambiance, while the menu features prime beef and seafood.

NASCAR Café
The Sahara
Tel: 702-737-2111
Open: L & D daily. **$**
Two-level restaurant features NASCAR stock cars, sports screens, and auto merchandise. north American food.

The Steak House
Circus Circus
Tel: 702-794-3767
Open: D daily; champagne brunch Sun 9.30 and 11.30am, also at 1.30pm. **$$**

Steaks, seafood, and chicken cooked over an open grill. A display case shows customers the variety of beef available.

Top of the World
Stratosphere Tower
Tel: 702-380-7711
Open: L & D daily. **$$$**
Revolving restaurant with the best view of the Strip in town. This can overshadow the main-stream menu, but the sunset is fabulous.

● ● ● ● ● ● ● ● ● ● ● ● ●
Price includes dinner and a glass of wine, excluding tip.
$$$$ $40 and up, **$$$** under $40, **$$** under $30, **$** under $20

BEYOND THE STRIP

Elvis and Liberace, bountiful buffets, and a spa that
offers "fruity body slushes" in piña colada for the skin.
Who says it all happens on the Strip?

Map
on page
166

Located about three blocks east of the Strip, the **Hard Rock Hotel ❶** (4455 Paradise Road, tel: 693-5000 or 800-693-7625) is a magnet to rock fans with its lively vibes, guitar-shaped chandeliers, and glass cases filled with the ephemera of rock aristocracy, including a large Rolling Stones display with a couple of "Keef's" guitars and one of Mick's leopard-skin jackets. It has 657 rooms, luxury suites, a spa, and a huge Beach Club. Restaurants include the Pink Taco, a version of the Japanese restaurant Nobu, and a steak house said to be reminiscent of 1950s' Las Vegas. But a sad piece of rock history was made here; the day before a US tour was to commence, John Entwhistle, bass player of The Who, died on June 27, 2002.

If the casino business resembles what marketeers define as the ideal television audience, then the swinging style of the Hard Rock is probably delighted with its clientele who, unsurprisingly, tend to be the right age demographic, young adults in their 20s and 30s. Competition is fierce between casinos and it's probably no surprise to learn that the Hard Rock and other places use the services of men to entice "whales" (Vegas term for big spenders). One of them is Steve Cyr, who applies what a recent magazine profile called "a mixture of genial charm and rocket-fueled salesmanship." Cyr says he takes care of people who don't think twice about gambling $100,000. "My goal," he says, "is that a guy loses a hundred grand, shakes my hand and says, 'Steve, I had a great time and I'll see you again next month.'"

Topless magicians

The smaller **Hotel San Remo**, 115 East Tropicana Avenue (tel: 739-9000 or 800-522-7366) is less frenetic

LEFT:
Elvis-A-Rama.
BELOW:
a magnet to
music fans.

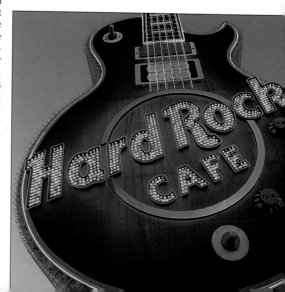

than some of the Strip casinos. It has around 700 rooms, many overlooking a pleasant garden pool. The San Remo's showroom features a popular presentation called *Showgirls of Magic,* whose late-night show is performed topless.

The **Las Vegas Hilton** ❷ (3000 Paradise Road, tel: 732-5111 or 800-687-6667), is a hotel familiar to high rollers who enjoy its opulent, marble-floored penthouse apartments with chandeliers, fireplaces, gold-plated bathroom fixtures, individual pools, 24-hour butler and room service, and workout facilities. Even a "media center," is turned over free to players who spend in excess of $2 million.

The 3,174-room hotel introduced a million-dollar blackjack tournament, where the $1,000 entry fee includes a three-night stay at the hotel. There are 13 restaurants, a pool, a spa, a spacious casino, and *Star Trek: The Experience* in which

visitors can assume the identity of a Starfleet or alien crew member and participate in virtual-reality and video adventures. The Hilton also has a showroom where Elvis Presley famously performed 800 times.

Elvis really was here

The late singer, just about the biggest star to hit this town, was living in one of the Hilton's rooftop suites when Barbra Streisand came calling in August 1974. She had starred in the hotel's showroom when it opened as the International five years previously.

She was currently hot from her famous Oscar-winning appearance in *Funny Girl* and her rapturously received concert in Manhattan's Central Park. The singer tried to interest Elvis in her remake of *A Star is Born.* Why it didn't work out is still disputed, but the role was taken by Kris Kristofferson.

Since his disastrous debut at the

BELOW: Elvis and Liberace swap instruments – and jackets, 1956.

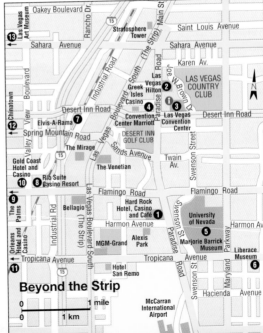

Beyond the Strip

Frontier in 1956, Presley had spent a lot of time in Las Vegas but, until 1969, as a visitor more than a performer. Then Frank Sinatra hosted a "Welcome Home" TV special for Elvis when he left the army in 1960, and they sang each other's songs. "We're working the same way only in different areas," Sinatra told the enraptured audience.

On July 31, 1969 Presley made his comeback performance on the Hilton's stage. He had studied by sneaking into the Flamingo showroom after the lights went down, to watch singer Tom Jones, described by Nick Naff as "among the horniest men I ever knew." Elvis couldn't project that sex image, says Naff, an executive at the International, "but he could suggest to females that he was the nicest guy in the world. That's the very reason they love him today. He played on his own projected qualities – the nice guy, the shy guy."

Opening night was packed with celebrities, high-rollers, and the press, and any Presley fan who could spring for the price of a hotel room and a ticket for an event of this magnitude. "His audience were now ready," said Bill Willard, who was there. "The kids had grown up and had the nostalgia thing going." His gigs at the hotel were a major draw for years and very important to an off-Strip hotel whose showroom was its major draw. Hundreds were turned away for almost every show, and there were two each night, at 8pm and midnight.

"The Colonel had him on a brutal schedule," recalled one observer, Lamar Fike. "If somebody did it now they'd die on-stage. I think Vegas contributed as much to his demise as anything else. He literally worked himself to death."

By the mid-1970s, interest was beginning to wane, probably exacerbated by the singer's fading appearance. Not only the grueling work schedule but his drug-enhanced lifestyle and unhealthy diet were taking a toll. "The last two years he still filled the house but it was the diehards at that point," recalls *Las Vegas Sun* columnist Stan Delaney. Elvis Presley played

Map on page 166

Vegas works hard to claim the largest, the tallest, and the best of everything.

BELOW: the World Gaming Convention at the Las Vegas Convention Center.

his final Las Vegas engagements from December 2 to 12, 1976. He died eight months later.

Convention central

Las Vegas is the convention capital of the US, hosting at least 27 corporate jamborees each year. (Chicago is way back in second place with 11.) The **Las Vegas Convention Center ❸** (3150 Paradise Road, tel: 892-0711) was financed in the 1950s with a hotel and motel room tax which, in 2001, provided $135 million of the $184-million budget. Four million trade-show participants generated $4.8 billion for the city in non-gaming revenue that year.

With new expansion, the convention center now has 3.2 million square feet (300,000 square meters) of space. Las Vegas now has three of the country's seven largest convention centers.

Adjoining the Las Vegas center is a **tourist information office** (tel: 892-7573) which supplies maps, brochures, and leaflets. The 278-suite **Convention Center Marriott ❹** (3225 Paradise Road, tel: 796-

9300) has meeting rooms of various sizes, a grand ballroom, business services, a whirlpool, a health club, an outdoor pool, and a restaurant. Set in attractively landscaped grounds, the 496-room **Alexis Park** (375 East Harmon Avenue, tel: 796-3300) is a tranquil, all-suite hideaway with no gambling.

The **Greek Isles Casino** (305 Convention Center Drive, tel: 952-8000 or 800-633-1777), has the blue-and-white decor of a typical Greek village and Cyrillic-style signs for the bar and restaurant. The Greek Isles was formerly owned by the financially troubled Debbie Reynolds casino, then briefly owned by the WWF (World Wrestling Foundation).

The showbusiness display has been replaced with an empty lounge, although the showroom itself remains. Check out the electronic roulette machine and admire the long mural running along the outside wall depicting a prototypical fishing village.

Located on the campus of the University of Nevada, the informa-

BELOW: Liberace first performed in Vegas in the 1940s.

Liberace

In 1944, after Walter Liberace debuted at the Frontier casino, he got an offer he didn't know how to refuse. Mobster Bugsy Siegel offered to double his $2,000 weekly salary if the piano player would move to the Flamingo. But Bugsy died, so Liberace stayed at the Frontier, using in his show the signature candelabra copied from the one he'd seen on Frederic Chopin's piano in the biopic *A Song to Remember*. Liberace's flamboyant manners and costumes went on to make him a Vegas legend and a tremendous draw with the ladies, despite his obvious gay mannerisms.

When he visited England, *Daily Mirror* columnist William Connor called him a " deadly, winking, sniggling, snuggling, chromium-plated, scent-impregnated, luminous, quivering, giggling, fruit-flavored, mincing, ice-covered heap of mother love." Liberace sued, and won $22,400 in damages. In the early 1960s his young companion, Scot Thorsen, sued for palimony (but lost) after being ejected from Liberace's home. In 1972, the "ice-covered heap of mother love" opened at the Las Vegas Hilton for $300,000, playing his final show at Caesars Palace in August, 1986.

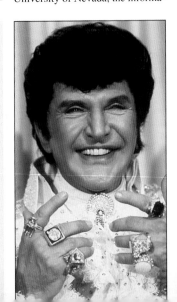

tive **Marjorie Barrick Museum** ❺ (4505 South Maryland Parkway, tel: 895-3381, weekdays 8am–4:45pm, Sat 10am– 2pm) is best approached from Paradise Road on the east side. Live lizards, Gila monsters, a tortoise, and a thin, red snake greet visitors from inside glass cases in the lobby, and in the museum are sandy dioramas of Mojave desert life. Stuffed birds from sandpipers to pelicans decorate an oasis filled with cholla cactus, desiccated wood, and a tiny kit fox. In another room are three large bears: black, polar, and grizzly.

There are also exhibits on the Southern Paiute Native Americans, including turquoise belts, rugs and baskets, Navaho pottery, and an explanation of the weaving process with samples of the natural dyes brazilwood and cochineal. Alongside are Mexican masks, colorful Guatemalan *huipiles* (embroidered blouses), and Mayan ceramics whose jars resemble contemporary pottery. Pierced ears were common, one exhibit explains, because it was believed that without them passage to the "other world" would be

impossible. There's an explanation of the pictures in a reproduction of the *Codex Barbonicus*, an ancient pictorial manuscript which stretches for several feet, and a display of prewar Vegas slot machines and Hoover Dam exhibits.

Behind the museum is the delightful **Xeric Garden** (from the Greek word *xeros*, meaning dry), with cacti, desert plants, and a bird-watching verandah. Ask for the pretty free brochure which identifies and describes all the plants, an activity miles away in spirit from the jangling slots of the Strip.

Diamond pianos

The brochure for the **Liberace Museum** ❻ (1775 East Tropicana Avenue, tel: 798-5595, Mon–Sat 10am–5pm, Sun 1–4pm) says that "though the Strip may sparkle and the neon may shine, nowhere in Las Vegas can be found a more dazzling spectacle than the museum." Even today, the idea of somebody wearing a five-tiered violet cape of ostrich feathers with lavender sequins – as Liberace did for a 1985

Map on page 166

BELOW:
eat, drink and be dumbfounded at the Liberace Museum.

television show – is an extravagance that's hard to beat. But here it's just one of a roomful of outrageous items on show.

A black-diamond mink is lined with 40,000 Austrian rhinestones and a separate display exhibits the world's biggest rhinestone, measuring in at 115,000 carats and weighing 50 lb (23 kg). The entertainer was fond of jewelry – like the piano-shaped watch and a piano-shaped 260-diamond ring – antiques, including an inlaid, ormolu desk that belonged to Czar Nicholas II of Russia, as well as cars and musical instruments. A hybrid Rolls Royce Volkswagen (license plate RRVW) is one of the 19 cars on display (he owned more than 30 including a Rolls decorated in brilliant red, white, and blue).

There are dozens of pianos, pride of place given to a 1920 Chickering grand on which George Gershwin composed, plus a hand-painted model which Chopin once played, and Schuman's Bosendorfer. Even rarer is a piano built in 1786 by John Broadwood, credited along with Bartolommeo Christofori as one of the instrument's inventors. Many of the musical artifacts on show – an old English hand-held street organ, for example – appeared in Liberace's television shows, on which there were always candelabras. He even had a candelabra-shaped ring.

Sagamore of the Wabash

Liberace had a Spanish-style home in Palm Springs, the bedroom of which is recreated here, but during his Vegas career, he bought two adjoining homes on East Tropicana Avenue and had Michelangelo's painting from the Sistine Chapel reproduced over his bed.

The houses were turned into a museum after his death on February 4, 1987, but this museum – topped with an enormous symbolic piano – in which visitors now admire his opulent collection is a recent one; it opened in 2002. On a wall near restroom doors painted violet is a certificate from the state of Indiana granting him the title Sagamore of the Wabash, the highest honor the governor can bestow.

BELOW: eat Filipino, Vietnamese, or Chinese food in Chinatown.

West of the Strip

Even those people who aren't card-carrying fans of "the King" will most likely get a big kick out of **Elvis-A-Rama** ❼ (3401 South Industrial Road, tel: 309-7200, open daily 10am–7pm) where a colorful embroidered sampler offers his post-mortem message: *Life is fragile; handle it with care.*

Elvis imitators pop up everywhere in Vegas – in wedding chapels, accompanying showgirls, dropping in by parachute, or just dispensing handbills, but in this museum is the genuine article, or at least some genuine artifacts. Some exhibits, like a 16-foot (5-meter) boat, a piano, and the 1955 Cadillac bought with the $5,000 check he received on signing with RCA, are important enough to stand alone, but many of the museum's displays are categorized in glass cases.

One display devoted to the singer's army career shows his uniform and a collection of letters between him and his fiercely manipulative manager, "Colonel" Tom Parker. Others show a red-trimmed karate robe, rhinestone-speckled jumpsuits worn for performances, and a pair of blue-suede shoes which were insured for one million dollars. A soundtrack of the familiar, mellifluous voice accompanies the visitor's passage down halls and past walls plastered with movie posters and record album covers, while videos play all day. An impersonator performs on the hour from 11am. Access to the museum from the Strip is west via Spring Mountain Road or Desert Inn Road onto Industrial Road, which bisects both of them. Alternatively, call for a ride on the free shuttle.

West of the freeway is the ostentatiously lit **Rio** ❽ (3700 West Flamingo Road, tel: 252-7777), an all-suite hotel, the smallest of which are 600 square feet (56 square meters) and the largest, almost three times that size, featuring wrap-around windows and great views. The hotel promotes a Latin American aura with its Samba Theater, Copacabana Showroom, VooDoo Lounge, and Ipanema Bar. Try to catch the panoramic view from the

Map on page 166

The Rio sign is said to use almost 13,000 feet (4,000 meters) of neon tubing.

BELOW: sunglass city.

TIP

Be sure to book Vegas shows months in advance. When in town, call the box-office directly, as there may be one or two seats left on the night that ticket-bookers do not know about. Many theaters are dark on Mondays.

Rio's 52nd floor where the specialty of the VooDoo Lounge is a bubbling, smoking concoction of five rums and three liqueurs which goes by the name of Witch Doctor. The tropical lagoon, complete with waterfalls, has four pools, five whirlpool spas, and a sandy beach.

Life is a masquerade

The spectacular 12-minute show *Masquerade in the Sky*, which takes place four times every afternoon and evening except Tuesday and Wednesday, is performed above spectators' heads as a procession of gaily decorated floats moves steadily around a 950-foot (290-meter) track. Exotically dressed performers sing and wave from a balloon, and from vehicles decked out as gondolas or riverboats.

For a fee, casino guests can join the parade – especially enticing to children – and leave with a photograph. All of this takes place in the lively **Masquerade Village**, complete with eating, shopping, and gaming facilities.

The Rio is one of the properties owned by Harrah's, and a free shuttle runs between the two casinos every 15 minutes until midnight (until 1am on weekends). Guests can also use the **Rio Secco Golf Club**, which is located 15 miles (24 km) from the resort.

Oversized beds

Just west of the Strip on Flamingo Road, the opening of **The Palms** ❾ (4321 West Flamingo Road, tel: 942-7777) late in 2001 was eagerly awaited because it was the first new hotel for 15 months, a lifetime in this town of non-stop construction. From the beginning it was promoted as the hip place to be, and fielded an unprecedented 120,000 applications for the 2,500 available jobs.

Its owner, George Maloof, owner of the National Basketball Association's Sacramento Kings, planned to cross-promote the two enterprises via the hotel's huge hot-air balloon emblazoned with a 36-foot (11-meter) logo of the Palms. Two dozen of the hotel's 455 rooms are equipped with massively oversized beds. "Our players complain that

BELOW: the pool at the Palms is the color of "sapphires and amethysts."

they stay at hotels and the beds are too small," Maloof said. "We looked into it and there is actually such a thing as an NBA bed." It is 16 inches (40 cm) longer than usual.

Designed by the celebrated architect Jon Jerde with an understated Polynesian theme, the 42-story hotel is decorated in soft color schemes of beige and taupe and has exterior lighting that can be seen from miles away but which, according to a recent guest, pours too much glare indoors at bedtime.

The five bars include the stylish 55th-floor **Ghost Bar**, accessed by high-speed elevators, with extensive views of the city's skyline and an open-air deck in whose floor is inset a plexiglass window. Apparently guests find it exciting to jump up and down on this despite the fact that there is nothing below it but 54 stories of space, then the asphalt of the parking lot.

Fiber optic-lit drink rails rim the bar both here and in the steak house, **Nine**, where it encircles the champagne and caviar bar. The nightclub, called **Rain in the Desert**, has a color-changing wall of water and an elaborate electronic system that produces fog, haze, fireballs, and dancing fountains. Near the swimming pool, which is "the color of sapphires and amethysts," is a spa offering "fruity body slushes" in a yummy choice of amaretto sour, margarita, or piña colada.

Mardi Gras and Dixieland

One of the earliest hotels to open west of the Strip, the **Gold Coast** ❿ (4000 West Flamingo, tel: 367-7111) has been renovated with a fitness center overlooking the pool area. Dixieland jazz has long been a mainstay in the lounge, and there's a bowling center with its own snackbar nearby. Thursday night is seafood night at the Ports of Call buffet, while anyone wishing to learn the intricacies of that liveliest of table games – craps – should roll out of bed and into the casino on a Friday, Saturday or Sunday at 11:30 am for a free lesson.

A free shuttle runs over to the company's sister hotels, the Barbary Coast and the **Orleans** ⓫ (4500

Map on page 166

Gambling is a way of buying hope on credit.

– ALAN WYKES

BELOW: don't try to sneak past security.

Map on page 166

West Tropicana Avenue, tel: 365-7111), whose New Orleans-type attractions include the French Quarter, Garden District, and Mardi Gras. Cajun and Mexican cuisines are available. The buffet is good value, especially at crowded Tuesday lunch times when surplus seafood from the previous night's buffet is carried over for a meal at half price – terrific if you're short of funds.

Showroom tickets at the Orleans are inexpensive compared with Strip hotels, a bargain to see acts like Frankie Valli; Frankie Avalon; Bobby Rydell; Peter, Paul and Mary; and Neil Sedaka. Other veterans who still pack out Las Vegas lounges include Paul Anka, Chuck Berry, Chubby Checker, Little Richard, and the British rock group the Moody Blues.

Chinatown and Chagall

Chinatown ⑫ (4235 Spring Mountain Road, tel: 221-8448) is easily spotted just west of the Strip by a long row of red pagoda-style roofs. They shelter shops and restaurants with cuisines including Filipino and Vietnamese (some of which have fresh seafood flown in daily). Chinatown culminates in a plaza with a gold-colored statue and an enclosed mall in which is a central restaurant surrounded by shops bearing Chinese signs. This small area is a great place for souvenirs. There's a good shop for gifts, and, for more esoteric friends and family, try Great Wall Books for the Chinese edition of *Time* magazine.

The **Las Vegas Art Museum** ⑬ (9600 West Sahara Avenue, tel: 360-8000, Tues–Sat 10am–5pm, Sun 1–5pm; admission charge), about 10 miles (16 km) west of the Strip in the Sahara West Library building, is an affiliate of the Smithsonian Institute. It was founded as the Las Vegas Art League in 1950 by a group of volunteers who believed in the need for a local arts venue. It has since gone on to present a series of major exhibitions, including Marc Chagall, Salvador Dali, Dale Chiluly, and Auguste Rodin. With a changing series of programs, it aspires to be one of the country's leading visual arts institutions. ❏

RIGHT: showgirls, showing off.

RESTAURANTS

Carnival World Buffet
Rio All-Suite Hotel
Tel: 702-247-7923
Open: B, L & D daily. **$–$$**
Acknowledged by many as the best buffet in town, you can have a dozen international meals for one price. Around 70 types of pastries are on offer.

Alizé
The Palms
Tel: 702-951-7000
Open: D daily. **$$$$**
Celebrity chef André Rochat ascends to the top (literally) of the Palms Hotel to present his award-winning French cuisine and excellent wine list. Good views.

Big Al's Oyster Bar
The Orleans
Tel: 702-365-7111
Open: L & D daily. **$$$**
Creole-cajun-style shucked oysters and clams, voodoo mussels, shrimp scampi, bouillabaisse, and pasta.

Nobu
Hard Rock Hotel
Tel: 702-693-5090
Open: D daily. **$$–$$$**
A Nobu Matsuhisa restaurant. The sashimi has South American flair, and the menu features inventive Japanese fare like Kobe beef carpaccio and tiradito with chili paste and cilantro.

Battista's Hole in the Wall
4041 Audrie Street
Tel: 702-732-1424
Open: D daily. **$$**
This casual Italian has 30 years' worth of celebrity photos and mementoes. The menu features one-price meals of pasta, seafood, or veal, which includes all the wine you can drink. The wandering accordion player is a local legend.

Ruth's Chris Steak House
3900 Paradise Road
Tel: 702-791-7011
Open: L & D daily. **$$$**
Ruth Fertel opened her first restaurant in New Orleans in 1965; now these reliable, good-value steak houses can be found all over the US.

• • • • • • • • • • • •
Price includes dinner and a glass of wine, excluding tip.
$$$$ $40 and up, **$$$** under $40, **$$** under $30, **$** under $20

DOWNTOWN

Downtown is where gaming began and where myths were made. Gambling odds are good, as is the Fremont Street Experience, but all is not well on the Street of Dreams

The area between the Stratosphere Tower and Downtown is often overlooked by visitors as they speed down the Strip going from one part of town to another. In fact, its anonymity contributes to the charm, for this part of the Strip retains a pleasantly funky feel more reminiscent of 1950s Vegas than any faux re-creation. Popular chapels like the **Little White Chapel**, and inexpensive motels, like **Viva Las Vegas** with its themed rooms, are a respite from the hurly-burly that swarms around the rest of the city.

Anything that glitters

The ultimate destination, of course, is **Downtown**, where gambling started in Las Vegas; the birthplace of the gaming paradise which has migrated to the twinkling glitz of the Strip. Downtown, the neon beats brightly in a dense concentration of billboards and marquees with the very signs that made Las Vegas famous, like "Vegas Vickie," the cowgirl fronting **Glitter Gulch**, and her equally photogenic sweetheart, "Vegas Vic."

But nowadays, Downtown is fighting for a slice of the action that its younger brother up the Strip has grabbed for itself. A new shopping mall, **Las Vegas Premium Outlets** at Grand Central Parkway, has 120 stores and will hopefully help. The **Neonopolis ❶** complex, at the junction of Fremont Street and Las Vegas Boulevard, is another attempt at a revival. The three-level mall has shops, a food court, a 14-screen movie theater, and underground parking for 600 cars, but so far Neonopolis remains mostly empty. To ease the pain of being away from the Strip, most casinos have parking garages, some charging a small fee which is refunded in the casino itself.

Map on page 178

LEFT:
Vegas Vickie.
BELOW: heading toward Downtown from the Strip.

The **Neon Museum** (tel: 229-5366) is not actually a building, but a collective title for the old neon signs that have been hung all around Downtown. Some of the more colorful exhibits hang on an 85-foot (26-meter) tower in Neonopolis's interior plaza. These recall the 1920s era of Thomas Young's Electric Sign Company (YESCo) where clients included those of the now-defunct Thunderbird and Hacienda hotels as well as the Tropicana, the Aladdin, and the Sands. "It was a town known for its neon," reminisces Mark Laymon, foreman of

what is today the country's largest sign company, still deriving one-third of its income from casinos. Today, however, many of the neon signs are indoors, beckoning gamblers to the slot machines.

Young, who leased his neon signs to smaller businesses to make them affordable, was obliged to deal with mobsters who were behind many of the original casinos. "People would say, 'You're really in a hotbed down there,' but I can honestly say that was never apparent in our dealings. We had something they needed and we were the only ones who could

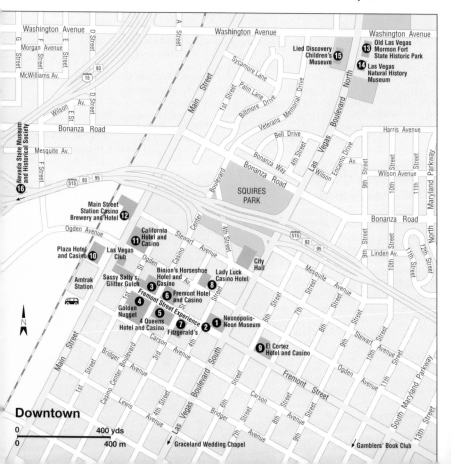

Downtown

0 ___ 400 yds
0 ___ 400 m

produce it. And they paid their bills. They were people of honor so far as we knew."

Many of the historic neon signs here have been "curated" from other cities; Hunick's Lounge was an Orange biker bar back in the 1950s, the Hunt's Red Car motel sign came from Compton, California.

Experience the street

Fremont Street throws off enough neon to read by, but it's all switched off before each performance of the **Fremont Street Experience** (after dark every hour, on the hour), an eye-popping computer-generated light spectacular that spans five city blocks in a frame nearly 100 feet (30 meters) overhead.

Two million lights and 208 speakers blast a ten-minute moving picture show across the latticework ceiling, projecting streams of jet fighters, thundering herds of buffalo, a tropical jungle with exotic birds and flora, morphing into a space odyssey, a cartoon orchestra, thunder and lightning, and rows of dancing girls kicking to a samba

beat. If you happen to be playing a slot machine regularly, working for a pay off, keep your eye on it as you walk outside to watch the show because there are those who wait for just such a chance to jump on your chair. The balcony at Fitzgerald's (10 seats) or Starbuck's sidewalk cafe (eight tables) are the only places to sit, but you have to get there early. It costs about $6 million a year to operate the show, but it has disappointed its backers; the show is not doing enough to reverse the decline in Downtown players. What may well help is the Downtown extension of the monorail, but there is no firm completion date.

In addition to the mall and the casinos, Fremont Street has plenty of liquor stores, strip joints, and junk-filled souvenir shops with every kind of useless object from chopped-up dollars-in-a-bottle to T-shirts with the slogan "if I can't win, I don't want to play."

The eastern end of the street, one of the most dangerous areas in all of Downtown, crawls with "feral losers in a city built on the idea that

Map on page 178

Examples from the Neon Museum can be found on many Downtown streets.

BELOW: take a limo to the Fremont Street Experience.

BELOW: Downtown is suffering an identity crisis, and no one can agree how to solve it.

anybody can be a winner," according to the *Los Angeles Times*.

Urban downtown areas are in trouble all over the USA, and Vegas is no exception. "When I came here in 1964," says Oscar Goodman, the city's effervescent mayor, "we had a place called Vegas Village, a marketplace where everyone came and did their shopping. The politicians were there, the gangsters, the actors. That's the kind of feel I want to reinvent for Downtown."

While there is consensus on the need for a revival, there is little agreement over how to bring it about. Some think that the big buildings and glitz that pull tourists to the Strip will do the trick. Others see a solution in developing Downtown on a small scale from what's already there, creating, "a neon, desert version of New Orleans, naughty but eminently livable," as *Las Vegas Life* puts it.

The magazine suggested that the light show has maybe been more of a distraction than an attraction, and that the street that was once one of the country's most famous now has,

"the emotional drag of an e-mail greeting card. We have taken our (historic) past, wrung it out, sterilized it and put it in a mall."

Urban problems

The city has acquired the 61-acre (25-hectare) site of a former railway switching yard, sandwiched between current Downtown and the two major freeways. Mayor Goodman describes it, with typical Vegas verve, as "the greatest piece of urban real estate in the country. A blank slate on which to create a whole new environment." Proposals include a 2,200-foot (670-meter) Millennium Tower, a minor league baseball stadium, a golf resort, TV and film production studios, and an "extreme" sports park with snow skiing and hot springs.

City planners pin their hopes for a revival not only on flashy buildings but adventurous urban pioneers willing to resettle in refurbished lofts in the currently near-deserted area between Charleston Boulevard and Bonneville Avenue, which a group of younger architects hope to

revitalize by redeveloping existing buildings. "In many ways architecture reflects a community's cultural standards and sense of identity," says Goodman. "We deserve to be surrounded by beautiful buildings. We are not content to settle for mediocrity."

Fremont Street ❷, now 100 years old, was where Las Vegas gambling began, the site of the first city traffic signal, the city's first paved street, and the city's first telephone. The first gaming license was issued to the long-defunct Northern Club at 13 East Fremont. Tony Cornero's Meadows Club was the place to be when gambling was legalized in 1931, with its rooms providing hot water and electricity, along with the residency requirement for divorce being reduced to six weeks, but it didn't last for long.

The next year the Apache Hotel on Fremont Street was the first Las Vegas resort with an elevator, and the Horseshoe was the first to fit carpets, leading to the quaint term "carpet joint," slang for an up-market gambling establishment.

A local legend

Benny Binion arrived in the 1940s, a colorful Texas gambler with a trademark buffalo-hide overcoat and a big, white cowboy hat. He took over the Eldorado Club, renamed it **Binion's Horseshoe ❸** (128 Fremont Street, tel: 382-1600 or 800-237-6537) and began a 40-year career which endeared him to his customers. He was almost always accessible, sitting at a corner table wearing a cowboy shirt with gold coins for buttons and no tie. His son Jack remembered, "He just liked people more than other people liked people. He worked hard to make them like him."

Binion died in 1989 and his statue on horseback sits at Ogden Avenue and Casino Center Boulevard. "He was a guy you could shake hands with and feel you had met a real American character," says Howard Schwartz, of the Gamblers Book Club. From the very beginning, Binion welcomed big bets. He established a craps limit of $500, 10 times what other casinos were allowing, and barely blinked on the

Map on page 178

BELOW: girls, girls, girls.

Pawn Shops

More than one Las Vegas taxi driver has talked of driving some unfortunate gambler to McCarran International Airport only to be told that his fare has no money – and been obliged to accept a watch or a wedding ring as payment. But for some big losers there is one stop before that taxi ride: the pawn shop. There are seven pages of pawn shops listed in the Las Vegas Yellow Pages, some with half a dozen branches or more, and many emphasizing that they are open 24 hours a day: just what a down-on-his-luck gambler might most want to hear.

Pawnbroker ads invariably include a long list of what they'll loan money on, ranging from rifles and shotguns to tools, camcorders, and paintings. A few specialize in automobiles, with one firm promising that you can drive your car away – just so long as you leave them the title.

But jewelry tops the charts at most shops. "Watches, rings, necklaces, you name it," said one dealer. "We had one gent in here along with his girlfriend. Made her take off her earrings and then even an ankle bracelet. It was gold. Truth is, I wasn't feeling happy about serving him, but well, you know, that's the way it is in business."

Surprisingly, between 80 and 90 percent of pawnshop customers subsequently return to redeem their items. By law, shops must keep items for 120 days before disposing of them, allowing redemption by the customer within that grace period. The standard *vigorish*, or interest, is 10 percent, although some places charge more – as much as they can in a few establishments.

As a general rule, pawn shops worldwide have a negative reputation but one local dealer said that he was merely performing a service for his needy clients, making money on somebody else's money "the same way a bank makes interest on a loan."

In most places in the US, pawn shops are to be found in poor neighborhoods because that's where the customers are, but in Las Vegas not only is there at least one pawn shop a mere stone's throw from the Strip, but customers cut across all income levels and social classes. Habitual gamblers are more likely to face ups and downs than ordinary people, hence their need for this 24-hour service industry.

Pawnbroking is a profession so old that it is mentioned in the Bible, which warns Christians against usury, and forbids the taking of the necessities of life as security or any pledge whose loss would severely injure the borrower. "If you take a neighbor's cloak in pawn, you shall return it to him by sunset," admonishes the text in *Exodus* (xxii, 25–26), "because... it is the cloak in which he wraps his body; in what else can he sleep?"

No local pawnbroker admits to taking his neighbor's cloak, but fur coats have occasionally turned up (in the desert) as well as hand-tooled leather boots, ivory-topped walking sticks and bicycles.

The world's oldest pawnbroker is undoubtedly Vienna's Dorotheum, founded by Emperor Joseph I in 1707 to provide the poor with easy credit. This venerable institution is still in operation, which only goes to show that where there's a need, someone will always be around to fill it. ❑

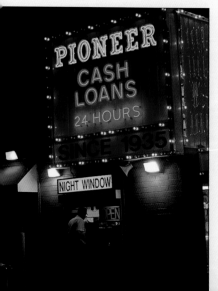

LEFT: serving 24/7. Pawnbroking is a profession so old it's mentioned in the Bible.

day in 1980 when a gambler named William Lee Bergstrom asked if he could bet a million. Given the okay, Bergstrom arrived later with a suitcase filled with $770,000, placed his bet on the "Don't Pass" line, won, and was escorted out to his car with two filled suitcases by Ted Binion. He subsequently bet other large sums, always winning, and four years later finally brought in one million dollars. Which he bet and lost on one toss of the dice.

Benny once said that the toughest decision to make in a casino was when to extend credit, but he wasn't so attentive filing tax returns. He served more than three years of a five-year stretch at Leavenworth prison for evasion. He lost his license as a casino operator but the family took over, and he was paid as a consultant. The year before he died he told an interviewer, "I suppose if I had to do it over again I would almost certainly be a gambler because there's nothing else an ignorant man can do."

From 1964, and for more than 20 years, Binion's casino kept a glass-fronted display case showing a million dollars in 100 sequentially numbered $10,000 bills, which were eventually sold to an anonymous collector. Five million visitors came to have their pictures taken in front of the display, spending time, and money in the casino while the pictures were developed, which was, of course, the whole point.

The Horseshoe, which made $28 million in one year, had originally cost the Binions $3 million, and even 30 years ago was worth almost three times that.

World Series of Poker

Benny had lost hundreds of thousands of dollars at the poker table in his early Las Vegas days, but nevertheless in 1970 he took over the running of the popular **World Series of Poker**. The game began in Reno, and now fills the 80-room Horseshoe every April through May with 4,000 stony-faced players. For a $10,000 stake anybody can join in, and the match has so far spawned around 25 millionaires. The World Series of Poker soon outgrew the

Map
on page
178

And if you discover that you're not, get outta town reel fast.

BELOW: Binion's Horseshoe, site of the World Series of Poker.

TIP

Veteran Vegas writer
Deke Castleman rec-
ommends visiting slot
machines around
seven in the morning
when the crew emp-
ties the change buck-
ets; the ones with the
least quarters *might*
be the loosest.

casino (although it later moved back to the Horseshoe), so the Binions bought another corner of the famous Downtown intersection, a 296-room casino called the Mint, with a small rooftop swimming pool and a huge illuminated clock face, still the only clock that can be seen Downtown.

Gradually the tournament has broadened so that now some competitions cost less than a dime to enter. Would-be world champions beware, though, the value of money is always minimized by gamblers: a "dime" means a thousand dollars, a "nickel" refers to a $5 chip and a "quarter" equals $25. "A dollar straight" is a hundred-dollar bill.

Game of many skills

A frequent tournament player, British writer Al Alvarez says, "Poker is a game of many skills. You need card sense, psychological insight, a good memory, controlled aggression, enough mathematical know-how to work out the odds as each hand develops, and what poker players call a leather ass – patience! Above all, you need the arcane skill called money management, the ability to control your bankroll and understand the long-term implications of each bet so that you don't go broke during a session." Sounds simple enough, doesn't it?

The Horseshoe, whose carpets are patterned with the crossed-T brand used on the family's cattle ranch in Montana, offers late-night gamblers a New York Steak Dinner for around $3 (10pm–5:45am), which the *Las Vegas Advisor* called "the greatest Las Vegas meal deal of all time." Downtown's older casinos have always had a battle to woo the punters from the Strip, so they give free food to almost three quarters of them. In contrast, the Strip casinos give nearly half their customers free drinks, which is a slightly better ratio than Downtown.

"Everybody comped big players, but Benny Binion was the first I ever knew who comped little ones," said Leo Lewis, a former Horseshoe executive. Referring to Binion's policy of offering free drinks to slot players, he quoted Binion's dictum that "If you wanna get rich, make

BELOW: the 4 Queens
is popular with slots
players.

little people feel like big people."

The Wine Spectator included Binion's in its top-ten list of casinos, right between Bellagio, number one, and Caesars Palace, in third place. "No celebrity chef. No gold leaf. No marble. The denizens of this Downtown institution are resolutely unconcerned with Renaissance art, crystal chandeliers and soothing pastel color schemes," the magazine said. "Binion's Horseshoe is famous for one thing: gambling." Almost everywhere on the planet, casinos charge a 5 percent commission on winning baccarat bank bets, but the Horseshoe charges 4 percent. Also, while the norm is eight-deck blackjack games dealt from a plastic shoe, at the Horseshoe it's mostly a handheld single deck which gives much better odds to the players.

In early 2004, the Becky Binion-run Horseshoe closed overnight. It re-opened in a deal partnered by Harrah's. The World Series of Poker is still staged at Binion's (the casino name may change to just "the Horseshoe,") but in future years early rounds might be held at Harrah's.

Generating heat

There are four glittering, pulsating casinos at the main intersection of Fremont Street and Casino Center Boulevard, but the **Golden Nugget** ❹ (129 Fremont Street, tel: 385-7111 or 800-634-3454) stands out against the neon crassness of its neighbors, with its classy white exterior trimmed with soft gold lights. The Golden Nugget has retained the Victorian style that it displayed when it first opened as a saloon more than 50 years ago, an era when horses could still be seen on the streets. Crystal chandeliers reflect off polished brass and marble in the lobby.

Brass and granite squares shine from the surrounding sidewalk. Its buffet always has long lines, especially for champagne brunch on Sundays. An outdoor pool sits in landscaped gardens with tall palm trees, the terrace is lined with white alabaster swans and bronze sculptures of fish. In the Spa Suite Tower, the Grand Court is modeled on a room in the Frick Museum of New York. On display in the casino is the

> **Map on page 178**

BELOW: Downtown neon nirvana.

See the world's biggest gold nugget, the Hand of Faith, at the Golden Nugget.

world's biggest gold nugget, weighing a staggering 59.84 lb (27.2 kg), and called the Hand of Faith. It was discovered in Australia. One of the casino shows features country and western lookalikes.

Recreation business

In 1972, Steve Wynn more or less began his career at the Golden Nugget, becoming the youngest corporate chairman in Las Vegas history at the age of 31. He added hotel rooms and suites of which there are now almost 2,000. *Time* magazine once said that Wynn was on a mission to gentrify gambling, cleaning it of its associations with high life and low life while delivering it to a suburb near yours as the innocuous extension of the middle-class weekend. "I am in the recreation business," Wynn claims. "What I do for a living and what keeps me young and happy is creating places where people go 'Wow!' and have fun. It's not that I'm insatiable, it's just that I love the exercise."

BELOW: the Boneyard, where old signs fade away.

The **4 Queens ⑤** (202 Fremont Street, tel: 385-4011) casino claims that some of its slots have a 97.4 percent payback, which is better than the Downtown average of 95.6 percent. Downtown slots, according to *Casino Player*'s Jim Hildebrand, pay almost 2 percent more than the 25¢ machines on the Strip. Those differences don't look huge from the 95–97 percent end of the telescope, but the 1.8 percent shift (from 95.6 to 97.4) means that the house "take" is reduced by 23 percent.

Largest blackjack table

The biggest gambling bargain in the downtown casinos, like El Cortez or the Golden Gate, are the 25¢ craps tables, and often the drinks are free. Don't forget to tip the waitress. Whether or not it's justified, the 4 Queens describes itself as "the jackpot capital of the world."

The Queens promotes both, "the world's largest blackjack table" and "the world's largest slot machine," which can be played by six people at a time. Magnolia's Veranda offers views of the casino as you eat, and Hugo's Cellar has had good reviews from food critics. The Queens is one

Map
on page
178

of the few casinos that invites visitors to take photographs, although not of people, and no video is allowed.

Completing the neon quadrant of hotels is the **Fremont Hotel & Casino** ❻ (200 East Fremont Street, tel: 385-3237 or 800-634-6460) which claims that with 450 seats in its garden buffet, would-be diners don't get stuck in the usual long line-ups. The hotel has three other restaurants, including a Tony Roma's and the 24-hour Lanai Café. If you hit $100 on the slots, there's a free T-shirt.

Nickel zone

Next door to the 4 Queens is **Fitzgerald's** ❼ (301 Fremont Street, tel: 388-2400 or 800-274-5825), which has 200 slot machines in its Nickel Zone. It claims that it has paid out over a billion nickels. Fitzgerald's will give you a free O'Lucky Bucks card to improve your gambling chances and offers trinkets like key chains, beanie animals, autographed sports memorabilia, and free meals. Displaying shamrocks everywhere, Fitzgerald's

is so Irish in theme that it has instituted a "Halfway to St Patrick's Day" celebration in mid-September with green beer and Irish stew.

Just two blocks away is **Lady Luck** ❽ (206 North 3rd Street, tel: 477-3000 or 800-523-9582), which began as a small newsstand with slot machines, but has grown to become a casino hotel with 792 rooms, an outdoor pool, and three restaurants. (It was recently bought for $14.5 million by Isle of Capri Casinos, which may change its name to Isle of Capri after spending $35 million.)

The casino's Mad Money Slot Players can receive complimentary rooms, limo transfers, and arena seats in the casino's private box for rodeos, concerts, and sports events. The casino's coveted free "fun-book" includes a one-night stay and a free long-distance phone call.

One of the ways that casinos increase loyalty is to offer free club membership. Members get a card to use in a slot machine which allows them to play for credit. It also tracks how much and how often members gamble. Even small-time players

LEFT: play as you go.
RIGHT: sassy
salsa chicks.

This Neon Museum exhibit positively glows with health.

can earn rewards like $10-a-night motel rooms or 1–2 percent of their gambling money returned in gifts. Near the buffet is a red British telephone booth, equipped with a modern phone. A free limousine service runs hourly from McCarran airport.

Beyond Neonopolis is Jackie Gaughan's 308-room **El Cortez Hotel & Casino** ❾ (600 East Fremont Street tel: 385-5200 or 800-634-6703), one of the last places with penny slots. A man once won $76,000 playing them. They are undoubtedly a reflection of Gaughan's attention to the less affluent corner of the market. He is an expert on slot machines, especially where to place them to maximize yield. About his penny slots he says, "You use them to make a place look alive because people stay there longer playing them. They collect the pennies people have in their pockets and want to get rid of, and they make a little money."

Old-time gambler

Bill Boyd called Jackie Gaughan "one of the few old-time gamblers left in Las Vegas. He grew up in the business and his word is his bond." Gaughan was running a book and illegal games while he was in the Army Air Corps at Tonopah north of Vegas, after getting his start as a bookie in the Midwest. In 1946, he arrived in Vegas and bought 3 percent of the downtown Boulder Club then, a few years later, 3 percent of the Flamingo.

School for dealers

Jackie's son Michael trained at El Cortez, ran a school for dealers, and then opened the Gold Coast Casino on West Flamingo, popular with Las Vegas locals, where he has space for a bowling alley, a dance hall, and a movie theater. Beginning with El Cortez in 1963, where he lived in a five-room penthouse, Gaughan acquired the Union Plaza, the Gold Spike, the Las Vegas Club, Nevada Club, and the Western Hotel & Bingo Parlor. In 2003, all Gaughan casinos merged with Boyd Gaming, cementing the liaison.

Back up toward the glittering intersection of Fremont and Casino

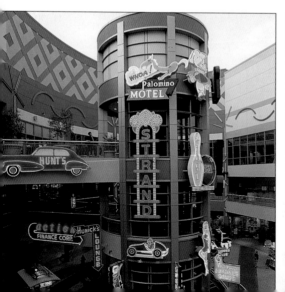

Center Boulevard are more old-style casinos. Next to Binion's Horseshoe and pitching itself as the city's only sports-themed casino is the **Las Vegas Club** (18 East Fremont Street, tel: 385-1664 or 800-634-6532), decorated with framed pictures of sports heroes, medals, and trophies. Old posters abound near the Sports Book, and even the gift shop is called the Short Stop.

Towering at the top end of Fremont Street, the neon-lit, 1,000-room **Plaza ❿** (1 Main Street, tel: 386-2110 or 634-6575) has become the first downtown casino to install cashless slot machines. There are eight daily sessions of bingo upstairs, and free music in the Omaha Lounge. Behind the Plaza are the railroad tracks, currently used only by freight trains, although it is constantly rumored that passenger service to Los Angeles will eventually resume.

One block from the Las Vegas Club is Sam Boyd's **California ⓫** (Ogden and 1st Street, tel: 385-1222 or 800-634-3484), promoting what it calls, "an aloha spirit," derived

from Boyd's five years working in Hawaiian bingo parlors making contacts with travel agents who helped fill the place with visitors from across the Pacific. "Dad worked the Hawaiian market like you couldn't believe," Bill said. "He became something of a god to the people in Hawaii."

Urban cowboy

The hotel's arcade shops sell foods, souvenirs, clothes, and other items from the 49th state. Boyd, described by author and screenwriter Jack Sheehan as "an urban cowboy with the ever-present Stetson hat and string tie," was a non-stop worker who, even as a multi-millionaire, would still clear tables, deal craps, or work in the casino cage. He had begun working in an amusement park as a carny and pitchman for games of chance.

Sam Boyd emigrated from Oklahoma in the Depression years and learned his trade while working on gambling boats off the coast of California. He got his start in Las Vegas in 1941, working at the Jackpot

Map on page 178

LEFT: right on the money.
RIGHT: cool dude in the hot city.

Club where Binion's Horseshoe now sits. He also worked at El Cortez, at El Rancho Vegas, and at the Flamingo as shift boss after Bugsy Siegel was killed. For a time he was pit boss at the mob-infiltrated Thunderbird, which was topped by a neon sign in the shape of the mythical Navaho Native American bird.

Sam Boyd died in 1995, and many of the multi-million dollar Boyd Gaming Corporation's employees are stockholders.

Main Street

An overhead bridge crosses the street beside the Aloha Cafe to the **Main Street Station** ⑫ (200 North Main Street, tel: 387-1896 or 800-713-8923), which boasts of its "turn-of-the-century opulence." Some of the stained-glass windows (surprisingly underlit) were originally given to Lillian Russell by "Diamond" Jim Brady and, along with beveled glass panels, came from the actress's Pittsburgh mansion. There are Belgian street lamps from 1870, century-old chandeliers from the opera houses of Paris and

San Francisco, and bronze doors from a Kuwaiti bank.

Along the sidewalk, passers-by can peer into a beautifully preserved and antique-filled Pullman railroad car in which "Buffalo" Bill Cody lived as he toured the country a century ago with its guest quarters occupied, separately, by Teddy Roosevelt and Annie Oakley.

Here also is the downtown area's only micro brewery, which produces a range of beers from light German-style ale to dark malty Porter. In the bar, television screens show sports and music videos, and the pub serves food from lunch through to late-night suppers.

Two other well-known Downtown landmarks are George L. Sturman's **Fine Arts Gallery** (Main Street and East Charleston, tel: 384-2615) where the main collection focuses on the 1930s to 1980s and includes Dali, Warhol, and Calder. Also on view are glass sculptor Dale Chiluly's paint-spattered sneakers, and a watercolor by Robert DeNiro Sr, father to the more famous son. Luv-it Frozen Custard, at the corner

RIGHT: a recreated living room in the Old Mormon Fort, Nevada's oldest building.

Gamblers' Book Shop

There's hardly any aspect of gambling that the Gamblers' Book Shop (630 South 11th Street, tel: 382-7555) doesn't have something about on its shelves, and when Brooklyn-born manager Howard Schwartz can't find anything on a subject he usually commissions somebody to write it. "I have a lot of respect for people who buy books so they can understand the games," he says.

Many of the titles were written by John Luckman, who in 1964 with his wife Edna founded the store. It now stocks more than a thousand titles, plus all the manila folders on everything from card tricks to slot-machine crooks that have been amassed over the years. About half of the store's sales derive from its extensive mailing list of 25,000 customers, whose demands are increasingly for computer games and videotapes. But whatever the subject, Schwartz can't emphasize enough the advantage of doing necessary homework. "This generation has a short attention span," he muses, "but knowing what you're doing allows you to slow down your losses." Fledgling gamblers who don't bother to educate themselves, he jokes, "might as well mail in their wallets."

of Las Vegas Boulevard and Oakey since 1974, is a local, much-luvved favorite.

Beyond Downtown

At the corner of Las Vegas Boulevard and Washington Avenue is one of the state of Nevada's most venerable buildings, the **Old Mormon Fort**, in what is technically the **Old Las Vegas Mormon Fort State Historic Park ⑬** (500 East Washington Avenue, tel: 486-3511, daily 8:30am–4:30pm). The fort was built by Brigham Young's pioneers in 1855 to protect missionaries and settlers en route to California. Inside the high adobe walls, a reconstructed tower looks over a plaza deserted except for a broken-down wagon and the iron pegs for throwing horseshoes.

The only surviving part of the original structure is the building nearest to the little creek which, rising from underground aquifers a few miles west, supplied a water source running through the fort, nourishing the poor soil in which the hopeful missionaries planted potatoes, tomatoes, squash, grapes, peaches, barley, and wheat. Some of these same plants are grown today on the museum premises in a demonstration garden.

After the Mormons left, a miner named Octavius D. Gass acquired the site along with other land to assemble a sizable ranch, subsequently bought by Archibald Stewart whose widow Helen ran the ranch after her husband was killed in 1884 and later sold the property to the railroad. The site on which the Stewart home stood is scheduled for excavation to unearth any secrets that may be underneath.

A walk through time

Sharing a wall is the **Las Vegas Natural History Museum ⑭** (900 Las Vegas Boulevard North, tel: 384-3466, daily 9am–4pm) whose hallway proclaims it to be "a walk through time in which each foot represents a million years." The animated dinosaur reproductions move convincingly and a huge Tyrannosaurus Rex growls impressively when a button is pressed.

Map on page 178

BELOW: efforts are being made to pretty up Downtown.

Interactive exhibits include an African Rainforest feature ("To Africa" says the sign on the elevator) where avid spectators can create a thunderstorm against a backdrop of Mount Kilimanjaro and bring to life in Vegas a savannah packed with zebra, gazelle, rhino, hippo, baboon, and cheetah, all cohabiting peacefully at the neutral zone of the waterhole.

Striped baby sharks

A large room is filled with lions, bison, leopard, antelope, musk ox, ibex, peacock, ostrich, geese, vultures, and flamingos. The shimmering blue walls of the next room are like a rippling ocean in which striped baby sharks swim in an open tank. Other fish swim in a separate aquarium, all compatible and "of the same size so no fish considers another a possible dinner." The sharks are fed at 2pm on Monday, Wednesday, and Saturday.

Two huge sleepy pythons named Bonnie and Clyde sprawl behind glass. They are from Burma and are said to have "highly developed heat sensors for detecting warm-blooded animals." Pythons naturally grow to a length of 24 feet (7 meters) and can devour animals as big as leopards. With a digestion like that, it's not surprising that one good meal might last these canny reptiles several months.

Leaflets are offered to parents with questions and suggestions to stimulate interest among younger visitors. In the **Young Scientists Center** there are exhibits challenging children to identify familiar aromas and teaching them about different tastes.

Something for the kids

There's plenty to engage the attention of adults as well as kids in the nearby **Lied Discovery Children's Museum** ⓯ (833 Las Vegas Boulevard North, tel: 382-3445, Mon–Sat 10am–5pm, Sun 1–5pm), which shares the ground floor of the city's library. (Note a common mistake: the name of the museum is pronounced "leed," not "lied.")

If you ever wondered what a million pennies ($10,000) looks

In the 1990s, Vegas attempted to lure families to Sin City by building "kid-friendly" resorts. Although these are successful, the trend since the millennium has been back to the adult market.

BELOW: mammoth kidding around in the Nevada State Museum.

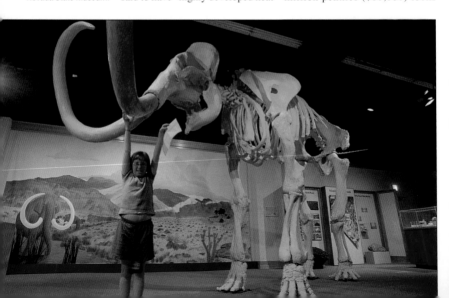

like, here's an exhibit that will show you. Also in the make-believe post office, young, would-be customers can sort, weigh, and mail packages.

Irresistible to all ages is the Discovery Grocery Store, which makes shopping a game and a musical pathway with which you can play a tune by jumping on different panels. There's a tube stretching up several floors, which you can put your head in and talk to hear the echo; an overhead ropeway with moving buckets that can be filled and emptied; sand in which to move rubber cacti around; a place to pump bubbles up viscosity tubes or to draw a picture of yourself on grid sheets while looking in a mirror.

Planet walking

Heavy boots can be donned for Planet Walking, which demonstrate the difference in gravity. What weighs 80 lb (36 kg) on earth would weigh 95 lb (43 kg) on Saturn, Uranus, and Neptune, 188 lb (85 kg) on Jupiter, and 2,232 lb (1,012 kg) on the Sun. And maybe now they've

got that Language Map in operation. It lights up, speaks, and shows the location where a particular language is spoken.

Worth a visit

"Work your claim until you have all the gold from it and do not gamble away the money," and "Do not make gold the most important thing in life," were among the nuggets of advice offered to miners in an 1853 letter in the **Nevada State Museum and Historical Society** ⑯ (Lorenzi Park, Valley View, and Bonanza, tel: 486-5205, open daily 9am–4:30pm, library weekdays only) which explores the history of arid but interesting southern Nevada.

Even though it's off the beaten track and has nothing whatsoever to do with farming, the museum is well worth a visit, if only for its mining exhibit and the relics from the days when Las Vegas was still a dusty frontier town. The boots of Rex Bell, the local rancher turned movie star who became governor and married movie star Clara Bow, accompany his picture. ❑

Map on page 178

RESTAURANTS

André's French Restaurant
401 South Sixth Street
Tel: 702-385-5016
Open: D daily. $$$$
This Downtown version of André's is rustic and friendly, with small rooms for intimate dining. André Rochat serves classics such as sole meunière, rack of lamb, and outstanding soufflés surrounded by country charm. In an area not known for fine dining, this branch consistently wins "best Vegas food" awards.

Bay City Diner
Golden Gate Hotel
1 Fremont Street
Tel: 702-385-1906
Open: 24 hours daily. $$
Located in the oldest hotel in town, this diner has long been famous for a deal that's hard to beat: shrimp cocktails for 99¢.

The Burgundy Room
Lady Luck Casino
206 North Third Street
Tel: 702-477-3000
Open: D daily. $$$$
This lovely room has

Continental fare at reasonable prices. Dishes include beef Wellington, fettucine Alfredo, veal Oscar, and perfectly cooked rack of lamb.

Stefano's
Golden Nugget
129 Fremont Street
Tel: 702-385-7111
Open: D daily. $$$
Good wines, singing waiters, and classic dishes lashed with garlic and sauces make this pleasant eatery unmistakably Italian. The osso buco is a favorite; the lobster-tail Milanese is outstanding.

Triple 7 Brewpub
Main Street Station
200 North Main Street
Tel: 702-385-7111
Open: B, L, & D daily; stays open until 7am. $–$$$
Among copper-clad brewing pots, choose between five kinds of burger, gourmet pizzas, barbecue ribs, or pale-ale battered shrimp. There's also a sushi bar, but the real attraction is the beer.

● ● ● ● ● ● ● ● ● ● ●
Price includes dinner and a glass of wine, excluding tip.
$$$$ $40 and up, **$$$** under $40, **$$** under $30, **$** under $20

RED ROCK CANYON LOOP

How to leave Sin City, visit an old Western town,
hike in a geological phenomenon, and be back
in town in time to hit the Strip that night

A 40-mile (63-km) loop from the Las Vegas Strip will take in most of the sites immediately to the south and west of the city. Begin with a drive south down Las Vegas Boulevard, past the Mandalay Bay casino. This will bring you to the first destination, the **Las Vegas Outlet Center** (7400 Las Vegas Boulevard, tel: 896-5599), formerly known as Belz) where aisles are lined by familiar names like Liz Claiborne, Nike, Reebok, and Waterford Wedgwood among the 130 stores. Savings are promised with the "no middlemen, no mark-up" outlet ethos. There is ample parking space and a central food court. A fleet of taxis line up outside, waiting to take passengers and their purchases back to the Strip.

Wild West

Only a few hundred yards beyond the outlet, opposite the site of a new casino, SR 160 heads west to the community of **Blue Diamond**, a company town for a gypsum producer, where SR 159 curves right through Red Rock Canyon. But first comes **Bonnie Springs Old Nevada** ❶ (tel: 875-4191), a faux Olde Western town where the motel (tel: 875-4400) has themed rooms with decor ranging from Covered Wagon to Chinese. Everything, except for

an apparently never-used chapel, is covered with dust and sports an old and probably intentionally decrepit appearance.

There was a ranch here in 1843, used as a stopover to refresh passengers on wagon routes bound for California via the old Spanish Trail. Today's visitors throng to the subterranean wax museum, too dimly lit to read the captions below crude figures representing a mountain man, a missionary, a prospector, and a native Paiute. Abraham Lincoln's lips move

Map
on page
198

PRECEDING PAGES:
leaving Las Vegas.
LEFT:
Summerlin and the
Strat Tower.
BELOW:
take a bike to
Bonnie Springs.

almost in synch with a recorded speech. Brigham Young, the explorer Jedediah Smith, and President James Buchanan complete the motley group. Lining the main street are a disused opera house and the dingy shacks of a sheriff's office, a shaving parlor ("teeth pulled here") and a store doubling as a museum. Exhibits include an 1897 washing mangle and medicine bottles.

Where the street ends in a central square, a crowd gathers three times a day to watch a "melodrama" which closes with the mock hanging of two wisecracking bank robbers. Although there are a couple of cafe-saloons, the best place to eat is a restaurant beside the entrance overlooking a murky pond.

Spring Mountain Ranch ❷ (Blue Diamond Drive, tel: 875-4141) was the home of wealthy Vera Krupp, who raised cattle on thousands of adjoining acres. The ranch dates back a century to when moun-

tain man Bill Williams, one of explorer John Fremont's guides, camped here. The original sandstone cabin and blacksmith's shop were built in 1864 and can still be visited. Along with the Old Mormon Fort in downtown Las Vegas, they are the oldest buildings in the valley.

Today's visitors begin their tour at the attractive modern ranch house (daily 10am–4pm) built by Chester Lauck who played Lum in the famous early radio show, "Lum and Abner." He built the 3-acre (1-hectare) reservoir still used for irrigation, naming it Lake Harriet after his wife, and bred racehorses on the ranch with his partner, screen actor Don Ameche.

The Krupp diamond

Additions to the property, including the swimming pool, were added by Mrs Krupp, wife of the notorious German "cannon king" Alfred Krupp. In 1959, Vera was robbed at gun-

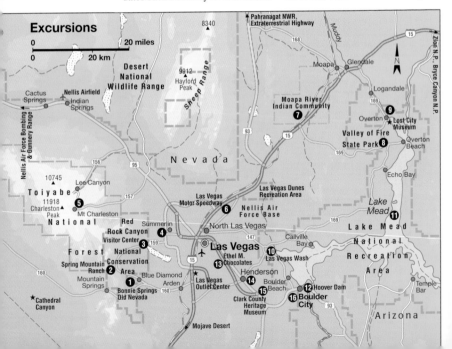

Map on page 198

point in her living room, and a ring set with a 33.6-carat diamond was taken. The ring was recovered a few weeks later, and, after her death, bought by Richard Burton for $305,000 for Elizabeth Taylor. The living room in question now serves as the **visitor center**.

In 1967, Howard Hughes bought the ranch as part of his Las Vegas spree, but probably never visited, although his deputy, Robert Maheu, occasionally entertained guests here. After one more owner, Spring Mountain Ranch was bought for $3.25 million by the Nevada State Parks Department, and is now used for summer concerts and other activities. There are guided tours, beginning at noon, and the picnic grounds are open until dusk.

More than a million visitors a year travel SR 159 to explore 197,000-acre (80,000-hectare) **Red Rock Canyon National Conservation Area ❸**, managed by the Bureau of Land Management. The informative **Red Rock Visitor Center** (daily until 4:30pm, tel: 363-1921) is at the end of the 13-mile (21-km) loop if

you come from Bonnie Springs, or at the beginning if you enter from West Charleston Boulevard. There are day excursions from Las Vegas; if you opt to travel with ATV Action Tours (tel: 566-7400 or 888-288-5200), you can explore some of the hidden dirt tracks in an off-road vehicle. Despite its desert appearance, the canyon is often a few degrees cooler that the streets of Las Vegas, and offers a tiny breeze, which is very welcome in summer.

Sculpted vistas

Red Rock Canyon really ought to be called "red-rock and green-tree canyon," because the far side of the loop is green and fertile compared to the arid beauty of the near side. Along the way are sculpted vistas, hidden waterfalls, and desert vegetation, as well as bighorn sheep, coyotes, antelope, wild horses, and donkeys. (Please remember not to feed the animals.)

There are trails, both long and short, for hikers and cyclists; picnic areas; a campground (for permits, call 647-5050); and a rock-climbing

BELOW: Summerlin and other green suburbs are in easy reach of the Strip.

Map on page 198

center (tel: 363-4533) which offers instructional classes.

Traces of the Paiute tribe have been found at Willow Spring, where a well-preserved panel of five red-painted pictographs and petroglyphs survive. Some archeologists say that the paintings, "reflect the belief that the rock face was a permeable boundary between the natural and supernatural worlds… the door the shaman entered to visit the spirits."

The magnificent colors of the ochre and gray morning landscape come from ferrous minerals in the rocks, and change color as the day progresses. When the evening shadows grow long, the canyon turns a deep terracotta red. After heavy winter rains, wildflowers are abundant and in late spring the air is filled with the aroma of blossoming cliffrose, a tall, attractive shrub covered with tiny, cream-colored flowers.

An endangered species

Mojave Desert flora and fauna are displayed both inside and outside the visitor center – the only place in the park where water is sold, so be sure

to buy a bottle. Behind the visitor's center are endangered desert tortoises. This soil-colored desert reptile co-habits in an area of less than a square mile for its life span of 50 to 100 years. As the shells of young tortoises do not harden, they are most vulnerable in their youth. It is illegal to take a desert tortoise from the wild but adoption can be arranged via the Tortoise Group (tel: 739-8043), which redistributes legally acquired former pets.

Dominant shrubs like the creosote bush sprout yellow flowers whose nectar and pollen sustain millions of bees, as does the rabbit brush which blooms from August to October. The roundish, woody saltbush shrub is a common desert plant that sustains wildlife, and the weedy, yellow sunflower known as groundsel has value in traditional medicine for Native Americans.

Heading back toward Vegas on SR 159 offers, just north of the road, a chance to drive through plush **Summerlin ❹**. An expensive, self-contained suburb for around 60,000 residents – and growing – , it has rich, tropical landscaping and offers several well-appointed golf courses among the resorts.

The **JW Marriott Hotel Resort** (Rampart Boulevard and Summerlin Parkway, tel: 869-7777 or 800-695-8284) has two lavish pools with lagoons, a spa, a casino, and restaurants. Nearby are half a dozen golf courses. Marriott has taken over the Resort at Summerlin (221 North Rampart Boulevard, tel: 869-7777, fax: 869-7771), comprised of two hotels: the Regent Grand Spa, decorated in Spanish-Revival style with a giant spa; and the more formal Regent Grand Palms with its gourmet restaurant.

Stopping at one of these resorts is perfect for a tranquil late lunch or early dinner before hitting the frenetic gaming tables of the Strip. ❑

BELOW: a desert bighorn ewe.
RIGHT: blowing his own horn at Red Rock Canyon.

NORTH OF LAS VEGAS

Northwest of Las Vegas there are
snow-covered mountains and blazing desert;
northeast, a lost civilization and sandstone cliffs.
But hey – is that a UFO hovering overhead?

To reach the refreshing slopes of a desert mountain, head north on US 95 and then west on SR 157. Rising to a peak of around 12,000 feet (4,000 meters), rugged, craggy Charleston Peak at **Mount Charleston ❺** is high enough to support both summer and winter activities – skiing and sleigh rides in winter, horse-back riding, wagon rides, and hiking in the summer, when the temperature is typically in the 70s°F (21°C).

This is one of the reasons Mount Charleston is such a popular summer day trip from the sweltering streets of Sin City, where temperatures are likely to be considerably higher. At other times of the year, people flock to the **Las Vegas Ski & Snowboard Resort**, (tel: 593-9500) with 10 ski trails spread over 40 acres (16 hectares) in **Lee Canyon**. The season lasts from late November until the early spring.

Mount Charleston captures enough westerly precipitation to support varied vegetation. Sagebrush, crimson blooming cactus, yellow wildflowers, and bristle cone pines are among 30 species of plants endemic to the region. Named after two brothers who operated a sawmill more than a century ago, **Kyle Canyon** has a campground and RV site; there are other camping sites (for reservations, tel: 877-444-6777) and a few picnic areas. Not far away is the **Mount Charleston Lodge** (tel: 872-5408), with log cabins available at reasonable rates.

Pioneer territory

A golf resort is emerging near the pleasantly rural **Mount Charleston Hotel** (tel: 872-5500) where a roaring fireplace dominates the huge lobby. The hotel has no casino but a good dance floor, and makes an ideal spot for a quick honeymoon if

Map
on page
198

LEFT:
slots in the
supermarket.
BELOW:
cabins in Mount
Charleston.

Take to the slopes at the Las Vegas Ski & Snowboard Resort.

you happened to have gotten hitched in one of Las Vegas' chapels earlier in the day.

The glass-enclosed Cliffhanger Lounge and vast dining room offer grand mountain views, as does the relaxing sauna. There is an adjoining nine-hole golf course. The hotel has a free pamphlet listing hiking trails ranging from less than a mile to a grueling 11-mile (18-km) loop to the mountain peak.

There are scenic drives, hiking trails, and horses for rent for those who seek to explore the **Toiyabe National Forest**, a unique example of forested mountains hemmed in by desert. Thousands of years ago, as the water that once covered the valley dried up, plant and animal life retreated to the higher ground which today still supports deer, elk, wild turkey, wild horses and donkeys, bighorn sheep, and even the occasional mountain lion.

Continuing north on US 95, the road skirts the western border of the 3.5 million-acre/1.5 million-hectare **Nellis Air Force Bombing and Gunnery Range**, in an area known

RIGHT: diamonds are forever, or until the next losing streak.

as Pioneer Territory. Originally built to train B-29 gunners during World War II, it eventually became the training ground for the nation's ace fighter pilots. Many key military personnel assigned to Nellis during World War II later returned as civilians to take up permanent residency in Las Vegas. Today, thousands of active duty personnel, civilian employees, military dependents, and military retirees are connected to Nellis. The base is only open to the public on one "open house" day each fall.

Almost 60 years ago, the first atomic bombs were tested at Yucca Flat, and the Federal government's occupation of this area finally led to **Yucca Mountain** being selected as a repository for 77,000 tons of radioactive waste. The waste will be stored in supposedly "safe" canisters in concrete-lined chambers. Nobody knows just how safe this will actually be, particularly since the discovery that the mountain's interior is not as waterproof as had previously been thought.

The plan was vetoed by Nevada's

Reno

Reno (446 miles/718 km northwest of Las Vegas) trumpets itself as "The Biggest Little Town in the World," with an arch of neon Downtown. It does, in fact, offer a broad range of entertainment and recreation, with excellent opportunities for hiking, biking, climbing, golf, water sports, skiing, and snowboarding.

The green-baize tables and shiny slots still have huge pulling power, and just as Las Vegas is the gambling mecca for Angelenos, Reno is the gaming resort of choice for San Franciscans. But as well as the fun of gambling, shows, and super-swift divorce, Reno offers a pretty full cultural life. There is an opera society, and at least two groups of players mount outdoor summer Shakespeare festivals. Many of the old-school Las Vegas casino hotels are represented by sibling establishments here. There is a Circus Circus, a Harrah's, and a Flamingo Hilton. The Eldorado is a favorite with many visitors for its atmosphere, service, and value.

The Downtown arch is in fact the Little Town's second; the original arch from 1926 is on show at the National Automobile Museum (tel: 775-333-9300).

governor but his veto was overridden by a vote in the Senate. Nuclear waste has been stored at more than 130 separate above-ground power plants and research labs; some of the opposition to the Yucca Mountain site has come from people worried about the hazards of transporting the waste across the country to Nevada.

Northeast of Las Vegas

The fastest route from Las Vegas northeast is via Interstate 15, which soon passes the **Las Vegas Motor Speedway** ❻ (tel: 644-4444). The Speedway features celebrity races, NASCAR events, MotoX, and even hosts events like the George Strait Chevy Truck Country Music Festival. Track tours are available from Mondays to Fridays 9am–4pm.

If the idea of all that speed starts a thrill in your veins, the track occasionally offers "test and time" events. Show up with a street-legal car that passes a technical inspection and you can try it on the track and get an official report. It's advisable to arrive with an alternate ride home – your car may not be quite so tech-

nically excellent after you've thrashed it up the track. If you're even more serious, the Speedway offers a range of training courses, from three-hour sessions to some lasting three days.

Flanking both sides of I-15 are the grounds of **Nellis Air Force Base**, where fighter pilots have been trained since World War II. A left turn north off I-15 leads to US 93, which runs along the eastern border of the Nellis Air Force Bombing and Gunnery Range. Beyond the **Pahranagat National Wildlife Refuge**, US 93 bumps into what some consider the strangest feature of this alien landscape, SR 375. Also known as the **Extraterrestrial Highway**, SR 375 has been the site of more than the usual number of UFO sightings, and has its coterie of devoted fans.

The little community of **Rachel**, little more than some trailers and a bar called the Little A'e'Inn, is a rallying point for UFOlogists from around the world. Their credibility is strengthened by rumors that the Air Force studies alien visitations at

Map on page 198

ATVs (all terrain vehicles) are a great way to explore.

BELOW: Highway 375 is the site of many UFO sightings.

Map
on page
198

Overton's Lost City Museum traces the history of the indigenous Anasazi.

BELOW: Valley of Fire State Park.
RIGHT:
flying the flag.

nearby **Groom Lake**. The very existence of any such facility is officially denied. Needless to say the base – where top-secret aircraft are tested – is heavily guarded and intruders are detained if not arrested.

Back down on I-15 and still heading northeast, the road slices through the **Moapa River Indian Community ❼**, or technically, a corner of it. The reservation is not open to the public, but Native Americans man a truck stop where souvenirs, liquor, cheap cigarettes, and gas can be purchased.

A right-hand turn off the highway along SR 169 loops through the fine **Valley of Fire State Park ❽**, the name derived from the jagged sandstone cliffs which appear to be ablaze in sunlight. A leaflet is available from the toll booth at the entrance and also from the wonderfully sited **Visitor Center** (daily 8:30am–4:30pm, tel: 397-2088) about midway through the route. Take plenty to drink as even the center is sometimes without water and has no soft-drinks machines. **Mouse Tank**, a trek of almost half a mile

from the road, is where the indigenous Paiute used to drink from rainwater collected in the stone basin. Carvings and petroglyphs can be seen, mostly around **Atlatl Rock**, depicting a prehistoric hunting tool, forerunner of the bow and arrow. Several movie companies have taken advantage of the scenery.

Lost City

Where SR 169 leaves the Valley of Fire State Park is **Overton ❾**, a small town in which the **Lost City Museum** (daily 8:30am–4:30pm, tel: 397-2193) documents the history of the long-lost Native American Anasazi. Living in the area for centuries, they left as long as 800 years ago, probably because of a prolonged drought. Ironically, the area that was home to the Anasazi is now deep beneath the waters of Lake Mead.

The museum exhibits some of the beads, polished shells, pottery, baskets and, intriguingly, bone gambling counters, salvaged by archeologists before the lake and Hoover Dam were built. In Overton on North Moapa Valley Boulevard are the funky Overton Motel (tel: 397-2463) and a Best Western (tel: 397-6000).

In the northern arm of Lake Mead are two waterfront resorts about 10 miles (16 km) apart. For those with time, the meandering **Northshore Scenic Drive** offers attractive scenery and occasional sightings of bighorn sheep. Following it south curves around the lake and eventually ends up near Lake Mead marina and the chance to catch a boat to Hoover Dam *(see page 212.)*

On the way, you can take smaller roads to **Overton Beach** (tel: 394-4040), **Echo Bay Resort & Marina** (tel: 394-4000), or to **Callville Bay**, originally established by Anson Call in 1864 as a freight outlet for Colorado River steamboats. ❑

LAKE MEAD AND HOOVER DAM

This giant lake in the desert offers unlimited
recreational opportunities all year round.
It was only made possible by a masterpiece
of 1930s engineering

The most popular day trip from Las Vegas is to Lake Mead and Hoover Dam, about 35 miles (56 km) to the southeast. Sightseeing excursions can be arranged from Las Vegas by light airplane, by helicopter, or by bus if you don't have a car. If you're traveling by road, stops can be made at Henderson and Boulder City *(see pages 216 and 218)*, best appreciated for their museums after a trip to the dam.

Also on the way is the opulent **Lake Las Vegas** Resort (tel: 565-0211), a $7-billion development. The entrance is off SR 147, locally known as Lake Mead Drive. At the Discovery Center (tel: 564-1600) near the entrance a free video is shown continuously, depicting the development of this European-style waterfront village. When the project is completed in 2010, it will have 5,500 homes arranged in five neighborhoods.

Already in operation is the 496-room **Hyatt Regency** (tel: 800-554-9288). Decorated in hues of aqua, cayenne, and gold with two-story arched windows, and with upper galleries overlooking the courtyard in a Mediterranean style, it offers a spa, a fitness center, two swimming pools with cabanas, and a water slide, a sandy beach, a casino, and five restaurants including a 24-hour

coffee shop. Julia Roberts and Billy Crystal's movie *America's Sweethearts* was filmed here shortly after the hotel opened in 2001.

Private casbahs

Montelago Village, at the west end of the lake, opened in late 2002, centered around the **Ritz Carlton** hotel. Around 75 of the rooms are on a bridge, styled after the Ponte Vecchio in Florence, with an arcade of classy shops. There are 47 suites with lake or mountain views and

Map
on page
198

LEFT:
a Nevada Wildlife boat
on Lake Mead.
BELOW:
angling is encouraged.

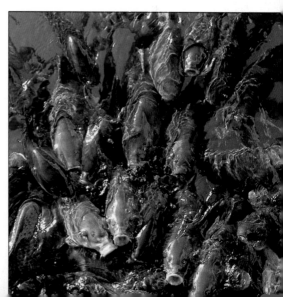

There are ample opportunities for boating on the lake.

BELOW: burning brown and ochre hills hide Lake Mead from view.

four larger "casbahs," with private entrances. The beach area, with a lawn and picnic areas, was constructed with 350 tons of imported white sand. Overlooking it all is the hill-top Monte Catini, an exclusive development with only 19 residences in the $3 million range, all named after Renaissance families.

The complex, with a lakefront walkway, cobbled streets, shops, and the **Reflection Bay Golf Club** designed by Jack Nicklaus, is likely to become a tourist attraction in its own right. It has already proved an attractive lure for successful corporate people, including a former pro auto racer, a football Hall-of-Famer, and Celine Dion, who established a home here during her residency at Caesars Palace.

The **Las Vegas Wash** ❿, wetlands between Lake Las Vegas and Lake Mead, is a prime spot for nature-viewing, providing for birds and other creatures an oasis refuge from the desert. At the eastern end of Tropicana Avenue, a parking area affords access to the Duck Creek Trail, part of a 165-acre (66-hectare)

preserve dotted with "sitting shelters" in which to wait for waterfowl to appear.

Four miles (6 km) before coming to Lake Mead, a casino-hotel called the **Hacienda** (Highway 93, Boulder City, tel: 293-5000 or 800-245-6380) has replaced the Gold Strike, which burned down. It has proven popular with locals, especially those from nearby Boulder City, where gambling is not allowed.

Lake Mead

Lake Mead ⓫, with a jagged shoreline of 550 miles (885 km), contains enough water to cover the entire state of New York to a depth of about 1 foot (0.5 meters). The lake is 500 feet (152 meters) at its deepest point in late fall and early spring, but averages about 200 feet (61 meters) deep for its 100-mile (160 km) length. The water has an average daytime temperature of 86°F (30°C) in summer, so visitors hanging their beer and soda over the side of a boat to cool find the drinks come up warmer than when they went in. The recreational areas on

and around the lake attract 9 million visitors a year. Unfortunately, as of 2004, the lake was in the fifth year of an on-going drought. It is 80 feet (24-meters) lower than previously, and is expected to go much lower before the drought ends.

The first glimpse of the lake, when arriving from Las Vegas, is refreshing. Turning off just before Boulder City, the hot, desert landscape becomes more gentle. A sudden curve, a hill and from the top, the lake – ice-blue against brown rolling hills. The drive to the marina is through the fragrant national park, with more coyotes and mountain goats than people.

At the marina, **Lake Mead Cruises** (tel: 293-6180) offer a variety of excursions (most available with hotel pick-up in Las Vegas). The *Desert Princess* is a triple-decked paddle wheeler and the largest boat on the lake. Throughout the year she hosts 90-minute cruises, plus weekend dance cruises and dinner cruises. The two-hour dinner cruise is particularly pleasant, with appetizing entrées and a well-stocked bar. After a turn-around at Hoover Dam, the return is timed for the setting of the sun behind the ochre-and chocolate-colored hills.

Fast-moving cat

More adventurous is the *Velocity*, a fast-moving catamaran that gives close-up views of canyon walls and glimpses of wildlife. The catamaran has open windows but no air-conditioning. Normally, the breeze off the lake is cool enough for comfort, but in the fiery summer months, some might prefer the climate-controlled *Desert Princess*.

Nevada Highway 169, which is also called the **Northshore Scenic Drive**, runs for miles along the shore, then heads north toward Overton Beach and the Valley of Fire State Park *(see page 206)*. There are no roads on the south side.

Angling on the lake goes on year round but a license is required. The lake has many camping spots and there are several places that offer boat rentals and provisions for overnight camping. Houseboats can also be rented.

Map on page 198

BELOW: there are a variety of cruises to be taken aboard the *Desert Princess*.

*Hoover Dam took
less than five years
to complete.*

BELOW: you can stand
on the Hoover Dam
with one foot in
Arizona and the other
in Nevada.
RIGHT: the dam
became a symbol of
man's ability to
harness nature.

Map
on page
198

Hoover Dam

Straddling the Arizona–Nevada border, **Hoover Dam** ⓬ is anchored to the rugged volcanic walls of the Black Canyon and towers 726 feet (221 meters) above the Colorado River. It was for years, and occasionally still is, known as Boulder Dam. The reason for both names was due to the unpopularity of the 31st president, Herbert Hoover, who had largely been responsible for the successful outcome of a series of delicate negotiations to push the project forward.

Dedicated by President Franklin D. Roosevelt in 1935, the Hoover Dam was built primarily as a flood-control measure, but with 17 generators, it was able to produce enough energy to supply a million residences for 20 years. The lake that resulted from filling the deep canyons behind it supplies nearly 25 million people with water, including Las Vegans.

After the snow melts in the Rocky Mountains, the run off pours into the 1,400-mile (2,250-km) long Colorado River, roaring through the Grand Canyon before beginning its 100-mile (160-km) journey into Lake Mead. This is where the Hoover Dam halts its flow. The river heads south, providing the state border with Arizona all the way into Lake Mohave, which is blocked at the southern end by the **Davis Dam**.

A visit to the dam is more rewarding than it might first seem. A masterpiece of engineering, it has striking sculptures by Oskar J.W. Hansen which might well be the largest monumental bronzes ever cast in the US. On a two-hour tour, visitors – there are a million each year – are treated to a talk inside the circular, state-of-the-art **Visitor Center** (last tour 3:30 pm, tel: 294-3523). After a 25-minute movie including vintage film of the dam's construction, an elevator takes visitors to a scenic overlook.

Before the river could be managed, its waters had to be divided equally among the six states it serves, an apportionment that was made by the creation of the Colorado River Compact in 1922; Mexico was later allocated a share in a treaty made in 1944. More than one and a half million acres (607,000 hectares) of land are irrigated in the United States and Mexico by management of the water.

Construction of the Hoover Dam cost $60 million, a massive figure at the time, and workers were busy for four years, enduring exacting conditions under the veteran dam builder, Frank T. Crowe.

The dam, 660-feet (200-meters) thick at its base, and 45-feet (14-meters) thick at the top, required 4.5 million cubic yards (3.5 million cubic meters) of concrete. Because of the heat generated by concrete as it settles, the concrete was first poured into a series of interlocked columns inset with miles and miles of tubes through which cooling water flowed. ❑

HENDERSON AND BOULDER CITY

Two different towns lie only a short distance from Vegas. Henderson is fast-growing and fast-moving, while Boulder City feels like a sleepy community in the Midwest

Henderson and Boulder City could hardly be more different – from each other or from Las Vegas. Henderson, one of the USA's fastest growing cities, is now primarily a service suburb for Vegas. The landscape turns from desert scrubland to small communities so fast that maps are updated every year, and taxi drivers are perpetually lost. Many hotel and other service staff make the 13-mile (21-km) commute to the Strip or Downtown at least once a day. Boulder City is older and distinctly more genteel. Growth is restricted to 120 inhabitants per year by city ordinance.

On the way to Henderson (about 9 miles/14 km southwest on Interstate 515), the 50-room **Sam's Town** (5211 Boulder Highway, tel: 456-7777) has something for everybody. The rooms are decorated in a "19th-century southwestern theme," and two huge RV parks have swimming pools, spa, laundry, pet runs, and clubhouse.

A complimentary shuttle runs (8:30am–11pm) to downtown Las Vegas casinos. The hotel's A Place for Kids (tel: 450-8350, daily noon–midnight, till 10pm Sundays) offers computer and art centers, group games, and a quiet area. For a fee, children (3–12) will be supervised at play.

Yummy factory

Northwest of Henderson is **Ethel M. Chocolates** (1 Cactus Garden Drive, tel: 888-627-0990. Around 60 different varieties of the yummy candy are made in this factory, including a "chocolate postcard" bearing your own personal photograph. Visitors can watch some of the chocolate production on a self-guided tour between 8:30am and 7pm every day. A ton and half of chocolates are typically enrobed in the course of a shift and the com-

Map on page 198

LEFT:
casino cowboy.
BELOW:
Bob will be happy
to serve you.

pany's 70 stores throughout the West have at least $150 million annual sales. Employees, of whom there are 200, are given sensory training that includes learning which flavors are tasted on which parts of the tongue. The company was founded by "Mr Mars Bar," Forrest Mars, whose worldwide business grew from his parents' candy store in Tacoma, Washington.

Mars was described by author Joel Glenn Brenner as "the Howard Hughes of candy." In his book, *The Emperors of Chocolate: Inside the Secret World of Hershey and Mars*, Brenner says that Forrest, who lived until the age of 95, dying in 1999, resided mostly in Miami but for about two months of the year stayed in a penthouse above the Las Vegas factory – watching the employees through one-way mirrors. He established the business in Nevada "because it is one of the few states that allowed the sale of liqueur-filled cordials."

The adjoining cactus garden has many varieties of prickly plants – it's a good place to learn to identify them – and receives about 700,000 visitors a year.

Henderson

North of Henderson, the hilltop **Green Valley Ranch** (2300 Paseo Verde Parkway, tel: 614-5283), has a 10-screen cinema, an Irish-style pub, and a pancake house. Claiming inspiration from a typical Argentine *estancia* (cattle ranch), it is aimed squarely at a local, middlebrow audience.

The city of **Henderson** ⓮ began as a satellite of Las Vegas when the latter's population was a mere 8,500. Henderson's infrastructure cannot keep up with its current rapid-fire expansion, and doctors and teachers are welcomed with open arms.

Henderson's earlier development was spawned by the US Defense Department's partnership with Cleveland entrepreneur Howard Eells for the production of magnesium. At first, many of the 13,000 workers lived in shacks, trailers, and tents along the Boulder Highway, but the company town of Henderson soon came into being with a bill

BELOW: Ethel M. Chocolates' employees receive sensory training. And candy, too.

pushed through the Senate allowing residents to buy their homes. A **Farmer's Market** is held on Water Street from 4pm on Thursdays, and several Henderson hotels have collaborated to offer golf packages at half-a-dozen local links. Call 800-481-7890 for information.

Thousands of panes of stained glass are subtly lit to denote the passing day in the ceiling of **Sunset Station Hotel Casino** (1301 West Sunset Road, Henderson, tel: 547-7777). Iron balconies, windows, and weathered brick give the sense of a stroll in a Spanish village. The Mediterranean-style architecture is enhanced by a bar in the style of Modernist architect Antoni Gaudí. The 457-room hotel has a microbrewery, a 13-screen movie theater, and an outdoor amphitheater.

Between Henderson and Boulder City is southern Nevada's first museum, set up in 1949 by Anna Parks who, with her husband Gene, had opened a mortuary in Boulder City in 1932 for the remains of those killed during the construction of the Boulder Dam.

Pioneer life

The museum was the forerunner of the now-expanded **Clark County Heritage Museum** ⓯ (1830 South Boulder Highway, just before Lake Mead Drive, tel: 455-7955, daily 9am–4:30pm), which can be reached by taking the Boulder Highway route into Henderson. In the lobby are shelves of interesting books about Native Americans and the geology of the region.

The history of southern Nevada is shown in exhibits which begin with a diorama of the desert as it was 12,000 years ago, with petrified logs on sandy wastes, turtles, cacti, and a tall extinct beast described as a camelope. A Pauite camp is displayed with rabbit pelts woven into a blanket, baskets, and other finely detailed craftwork.

The pioneer life of trappers, farmers, and ranchers is represented by a woman sitting in her kitchen beside a big spinning wheel along with a baby in a rocker. Other exhibits are diverse: there's Fanny Soss's 1930 dress store, the first local shop with window mannequins, as well as a

Map on page 198

Native American goods make great souvenirs to take back home.

BELOW: Henderson is one of the fastest-growing areas in the US.

depiction of the notorious Block 16, the downtown Las Vegas area where low-class saloons and gambling dives abutted on the Arizona Club with a second-floor brothel. Singer Ella Fitzgerald donated two of her dresses to the collection, which includes items from the Tropicana, the Hacienda, and the Thunderbird.

Boulder City

Established mainly because the government wanted to keep men building the nearby Hoover Dam away from hard liquor, gambling, and prostitution, pretty **Boulder City**  (pop: 15,500) still has no gaming, no neon, and a strictly controlled growth policy.

When the town was created, the Secretary of the Interior appointed Tennessee-born Sims Ely, a former newspaper editor, to be city manager of Boulder City and he proved to be a strict guardian of the city's morals. Cars were searched at the entrance to town and impounded if liquor was found. Alcoholic beverages were not legalized until 1969

and prostitution is banned to this day. Off-duty workers went to Las Vegas for entertainment – although a (still-existing) casino called the **Railroad Pass** was quickly erected in 1931 west of town, making it one of the state's oldest gaming houses. Sims, who died in 1954, had totally dictatorial powers – a "little Hitler" – one disgruntled worker called him, giving orders to the police and granting or refusing all commercial or residential leases.

Today, this pretty city is proud of its history and strives to preserve its small-town atmosphere. It is the only major city in Nevada that does not allow gaming. Upon entering, the speed limit announces the countdown – from 65 miles an hour on the main road down to 15 miles in town – all advertised in ever-decreasing increments.

Local tale

One local tale is that, for a while at night time, a police car was stationed just outside the city limits to enforce the speed countdown. The shadowy figure inside the car was-

BELOW: do not take wooden nickels from this man.

Hiking, biking, and birdwatching

A recent survey established that about 8 million of Las Vegas's annual visitors – 22 percent – visit public lands and recreational areas around the Las Vegas Valley. What might sound like an unlikely stop is Henderson's 147-acre (60-hectare) Water Reclamation Facility (Moser Drive, near where Sunset intersects the Boulder Highway, tel: 566-2940, daily 6am–3pm), which has been designated as a Bird Viewing Preserve where a local branch of the Audubon Society has documented 200 different species. Early morning is the most rewarding time to visit.

The hills north of Boulder City are a mecca for mountain bikers. Well-established trails now have approval from the city, which maintains a road to the top of what locals call Radar Mountain. At its base are a shower and washroom. The International Mountain Biking Association has certified Bootleg Canyon as a rare "epic" ride. Hikers can explore the Historic Railroad Trail from the visitor center at US 93 and Lakeshore Drive, just east of Boulder City. Part of the trail runs through tunnels built to ferry construction materials to Hoover Dam.

n't a real cop but a realistic dummy, and kids loved to "decapitate" him for kicks.

The town's charm is best discovered in the historic district. Centered around the Boulder City Theater on Arizona Street, the attractive little houses with red-tiled roofs and stuccoed walls on nearby Cherry and Birch streets were built to house employees of the dam's power companies.

The houses were eventually auctioned off for about $75,000 each, but the area looks much the same, with its trees, sidewalks, a diner, and a pizza parlor – a complete contrast to Sin City only 23 miles (36 km) away. By 9pm all is quiet – even the McDonalds on the strip mall outside town shuts early.

A life-size climber conquers a canyon wall in the **Boulder City Hoover Dam Museum** (1305 Arizona Street, tel: 294-1988, daily 10am–5pm, Sun noon–5pm), offering an imaginative demonstration of the day-to-day tasks of building the dam. It's a pleasant little museum where you can play your part in an old debate by casting your vote for the name "Hoover Dam" or "Boulder Dam."

An ancient switchboard allows visitors to plug in and listen to residents reminisce about the old days. A film shows how hard the men worked – "muckers" shoveled out after each blast with short-handled spades called banjos for just $4 a day. The cafe serves buffalo burgers and a cowboy breakfast named after Will Rogers, who played in the town's theater in 1935.

Famous hotel

The museum, and a gallery showing the work of local artists, are situated inside the refurbished, 22-room **Boulder Dam Hotel** (tel: 293-3510). Here the friendly atmosphere of a bed-and-breakfast inn has welcomed guests including John Wayne, Doris Day, Shirley Temple, Bette Davis, and Dean Martin. It's a good base for tours of the dam, or excursions on the lake. Lake Mead Air (tel: 293-1848) operates flights to the Grand Canyon from Boulder City's airport. ❑

TIP

Unless otherwise stated, all phone numbers in this book are preceded by the telephone code 702.

LEFT AND RIGHT:
Boulder City.

TRANSPORTATION

GETTING THERE AND GETTING AROUND

GETTING THERE

By Air

McCarran International Airport, 5757 Wayne Newton Boulevard, tel: 702-261-5211, is the hub for air travel into and out of southern Nevada. It becomes particularly busy on weekends.

By Train

There are no trains, but there are rumors that eventually high-speed services will be resumed to and from Los Angeles.

By Bus

The national bus line, Greyhound (tel: 800-231-2222), operates daily services to Las Vegas from most parts of the country. The Downtown depot of Greyhound is at 200 South Main Street (tel: 384-9561). There are several inexpensive hotels and motels within walking distance.

By Car

Around 26 percent of Las Vegas visitors are from Southern California. Those who come by car usually follow Interstate 10 from LA (or I-215 from San Diego) to join I-15 north of Riverside. At Barstow, I-15 is intersected by US 58 which takes travelers from the northwest. Traffic on I-15 is fast moving, mainly through desert, and there are many accidents. From the north, the most direct route is US 95.

GETTING AROUND

Orientation

Although casinos, hotels, attractions, and activities are spread virtually everywhere throughout the Las Vegas Valley, there are essentially two main areas where visitors will find the highest concentration of places to stay, sights to see, and things to do, all of which are designed to entertain and make any stay enjoyable. These two are the Las Vegas Strip and downtown Las Vegas. To reach the Strip, tourists need only travel south on Las Vegas Boulevard, which becomes the Strip at Sahara Avenue. Travelers coming from the west arrive at the Strip first.

Downtown starts at Jackie Gaughan's Plaza Hotel Casino and runs east on Fremont Street. Five blocks from the Plaza, Fremont Street intersects with Las Vegas Boulevard.

From the Airport

McCarran Airport is about 1 mile from the Strip and about 5 miles (8 km) from downtown Las Vegas. A taxi ride from McCarran to the Strip costs about $10; the fare to Downtown can run up to $20. A shuttle bus service runs continually from the airport and costs much less.

Some airborne sightseeing excursions to the Grand Canyon and elsewhere take off from the North Las Vegas Airport, 2730 Airport Drive, tel: 261-3800. Public transportation is limited and the North Las Vegas Airport is best reached by cab.

Taxis

All taxi service in Las Vegas is heavily regulated by the Nevada Taxicab Authority (tel: 486-6532). There are a limited number of companies and the service is metered. Unlike in most cities, Las Vegas cabs are prohibited by law from picking up hailing customers on the street. Not that it doesn't occasionally happen, but visitors shouldn't feel snubbed if they hail an empty cab but it doesn't stop to pick them up

However, there are nearly always lines of taxis at the airport, or by major hotels on the Strip and Downtown; also at some restaurants. Taxis can also be ordered by telephone 24 hours a day. Services include:

A Cab. Tel: 369-5686.
A-North Las Vegas Cab. Tel: 643-1041.
ABC Union Cab. Tel: 736-8444.
Ace Cab. Tel: 736-8383.
Checker Cab. Tel: 873-2000.
Deluxe Taxicab Service.
Tel: 568-7700.
Desert Cab. Tel: 386-9102.
Designated Drivers. Tel: 531-6959.
Henderson Taxi. Tel: 384-2322.
Lucky Cab Company of Nevada.
Tel: 477-7555.
Nevada Yellow Cab Corporation.
Tel: 933-2141.
Star Cab Co. Tel: 873-8012.
Western Cab Company. Tel: 736-8000.
Whittlesea Blue Cab. Tel: 384-6111.

Trolleys & Buses

A trolley on wheels mainly for the convenience of tourists connects many of the Strip resorts with each other but this is not well publicized; look for a sign or a bench at the side or even the back of a particular casino. The trolley operates from 9:30–1:30am on a 2-hour loop

system and a trolley (supposedly) arrives every 15 minutes, but it is a slow way to get around. Be sure to have the exact fare when you board.

Public transportation is provided by Citizen's Area Transit (CAT) buses, which can be found in the Las Vegas Valley including the towns of Boulder City, Mesquite, and Laughlin. A guide detailing routes, scheduling, and service is available by calling CAT-RIDE (tel: 228-7433). There are customer-service representatives at that telephone number who can help plan a trip.

CAT operates 5:30am–1:30am daily on residential routes. Some routes run 24 hours a day, and some only during peak service hours Monday to Friday, except major US public holidays.

Helpful CAT phone numbers are 228-7433 (CAT-RIDE) for transit information; 676-1500 for RTC administrative offices; and 228-7433 for lost and found. Websites include www.rtc.co.clark.nv.us for general RTC information, and www.catride.com for specific CAT information.

All buses have electronic fareboxes that accept dollar bills and coins, but do not give change. If you plan to transfer to another bus to complete your one-way trip, ask the driver for a transfer.

Monorail

The RTC's much-anticipated monorail system is now under construction. The first phase, completed in early 2004, extends from Tropicana Avenue to Sahara Avenue. The second, which will run from Sahara Avenue to Downtown will (perhaps) be completed in 2007. The project will connect with many CAT bus routes. There is a charge to ride the monorail, and day passes are also available.

On the other side of the Strip, there is a free private monorail system that connects

the Excalibur, the Luxor, and the Mandalay Bay casinos, all three of which are owned and managed by the same development company.

Sightseeing

Limousines

Cruising the Las Vegas Strip in a limousine is an exciting way to see the sights and provides the ultimate in traveling luxury. As with taxis, the limousine service in Las Vegas is strictly regulated. However, unlike taxis, limousines are not metered. The cost is agreed upon at the time of rental.

A Luxury Limo Referral Service.
Tel: 737-8899.
Ambassador Limousine. Tel: 888-519-5466.
Bell Transportation. Tel: 383-7060.
Fox Limousine Inc. Tel: 597-0400.
Larson's Van Service. Tel: 456-4791.
Las Vegas Limousines. Tel: 888-696-4400.
Lucky 7 Limousines. Tel: 739-6177.
On Demand Sedan and Limousine Service. Tel: 386-2715.
Presidential Limousine. Tel: 800-423-1420.
Rancho Limousine Service.
Tel: 645-7634.
Rent-A-Limo. Tel: 597-9696.
Vegas Now (Door-to-Door Travel).
Tel: 765-6552.

Charters and Tours

Adventure Charters and Tours, 1305 North Main Street. Tel: 385-0500 or 800-255-5482.
ATV Action Tours, 175 Cassia Way, Henderson Tel: 566-7400 or 888-288-5200.
Off-road vehicle tours to Red Rock Canyon, Death Valley, and others.
Bell Trans/Limousines and Buses, PO Box 15333. Tel: 382-7060 or 800-274-7433.
www.bell-trans.com.

Coach USA, 4020 East Lone Mountain Road. Tel: 644-2233 or 800-559-522. www.Paulina.salen @coachusa.com

Gold Carriage Charter and Tour, 1305 North Main Street. Tel: 383-8160.

Greyhound Charter Service, 200 South Main Street. Tel: 800-454-2487.

Lake Mead Cruises, 480 Lakeshore Road, Boulder City Tel: 493-9765.

Travelways, 1455 East Tropicana Avenue. Tel: 739-7714.

Vegas Now, 1350 East Flamingo Road. Tel: 765-6552 or 877-669-6900. www.vegasnow.com

World Bus Tours, 3500 West Naples Drive. Tel: 597-5545 or 888-931-2432.

Air Tours

A Tour 4U, 8981 Fort Crestwood Drive. Tel: 233-1627, 888-609-5665. www.atour4u.com

Air Vegas Airlines, 1400 Executive Airport Drive Suite A, Henderson. Tel: 736-3599 or 800-255-7474. www.airvegas.com

Grand Canyon Discount, 2990 East Oquendo Road. Tel: 433-7770 or 888-600-8281. www.gcflight.com

Heli USA Flights, 275 East Tropicana Avenue, Suite 200. Tel: 736-8787 or 800-359-8727. www.heliusa.com, Tours over the

Strip, to the Grand Canyon, and other destinations.

Maverick Helicopters, 6075 Las Vegas Blvd S. Tel: 261-0007. www.maverickhelicopter.com

Papillon Grand Canyon Helicopters, 245 East Tropicana Avenue. Tel: 736-4359 or 888-635-7272. www.papillon.com

Scenic Airlines, 2705 Airport Drive, North Las Vegas. Tel: 638-3291 or 800-634-6801. www.scenic.com

Sundance Helicopters, 5596 Haven. Tel: 736-0606 or 800-653-881. www.helicoptour.com

Car Rental

Many rental car companies have outlets at McCarran International Airport on the aptly named Rent A Car Road. Some companies also have offices inside hotels, casinos or resorts.

There is little difference between Nevada driving regulations and other places in the United States. All speed limits are posted, seat belts are required and their use is strictly enforced, and drivers can turn right on a red light.

One major difference about Nevada roads is the center lane, which is not used for travel but for left-hand turns only. Nearly every major hotel has free valet

parking with an attendant who, although optional, is usually rewarded with a tip of $1 or $2 per car every time you park.

A Lloyd's Rent-a-Car, 3735 Las Vegas Blvd South. Tel: 795-4008 or 800-795-2277. www.xpressrac.com

AA Prestige Auto Center, 1719 Industrial Road. Tel: 388-7580.

Alamo Rent-A-Car, 6855 Bermuda Road. Tel: 263-8411 or 800-462-5266. www.goalamo.com

Avis, 5164 Rent A Car Rd. Tel: 261-4038 or 800-822-3131.

Budget Car and Truck Rental, 5188 Paradise Road. Tel: 736-1212 or 800-922-2899. www.budgetvegas.com

Dollar Rent-A-Car, 5301 Rent A Car Road. Tel: 739-8408 or 800-826-9911. www.dollarcar.com

Enterprise Rent-A-Car, 5032 Palo Verde Road. Tel: 795-8842 or 800-736-7222.

Express Rent A Car, 3735 Las Vegas Boulevard South. Tel: 795-4008.

Hertz Rent A Car, 5300 Rent A Car Road. Tel: 736-4900 or 800-654-3131. www.hertz.com

National Car Rental, 5233 Rent A Car Road. Tel: 261-5391 or 800-227-7368. www.nationalcar.com

Rent A Limo, 4990 South Paradise Road. Tel: 791-5466.

Rent A Wreck, 2310 Las Vegas Boulevard South. Tel: 474-0037 or 800-227-0292.

Thrifty Car Rental, 376 East Warm Springs Rd. Tel: 896-7600 or 800-8847-4389.

Motorcycles

Eagle Rider-Las Vegas Motorcycle Rentals, 5182 South Arville St. Tel: 888-916-7433. www.eaglerider.com

Las Vegas Harley-Davidson, 2605 South Eastern Avenue, tel: 431-8500. www.lvhd.com

Street Eagle Las Vegas, 6330 South Pecos Road. Tel: 346-8490. www.streeteagle.com

ACCOMMODATIONS

SOME THINGS TO CONSIDER BEFORE YOU BOOK A ROOM

What to Know

Las Vegas hotel rates vary enormously but one constant is that hotel rooms cost more on weekends. Rates also tend to go up and down depending on demand with few bargains available, for example, when a big convention or sports event is being held.

At other times there are some- times astonishing deals but it may be necessary to consult the travel pages of a US newspaper – the Sunday edition of the *Los Angeles Times* is good – to find them. That is where you will also find ads listing free 800 telephone numbers and such websites as **Vegas.com** and **hotels.com** which sometimes offer a choice of as many as 100 hotels from $30 per night. As a rule, downtown Las Vegas is cheaper than the Strip but there are often comparable bargains to be found on the latter, too.

Booking a Room

Most large hotels have smoking and non-smoking floors. Be sure to ask when reserving a room.

ACCOMMODATIONS LISTINGS

THE STRIP

RESORT HOTELS

As room rates vary, the dollar signs here are an approximate guide only; sometimes it's possible to bargain on the spot before check-in.

Aladdin Resort and Casino
www.aladdincasino.com
3667 Las Vegas Boulevard South.
Tel: 785-5555 or
877-333-WISH.
Fax: 736-7107. **$$$**

Algiers
www.algiershotel.com
2845 Las Vegas Boulevard South.
Tel: 735-3311 or
800-732-3361.
Fax: 792-2112.
A quiet haven with pool and patio café but minimal slot machines, located across from Circus Circus. **$$**

Bally's Las Vegas
www.ballyslv.com
3645 Las Vegas Boulevard South.
Tel: 739-4111 or
800-634-3434.
Fax: 967-4405. **$$$**

Barbary Coast
www.barbarycoastcasino.com
3595 Las Vegas Boulevard South.
Tel: 737-7111 or
888-227-2279.
Fax: 894-9954. **$$$**

Bellagio
www.bellagioresort.com
3600 Las Vegas Boulevard South.
Tel: 693-7111 or
888-987-6667.
Fax: 792-7646. **$$$$**

Boardwalk Casino-Holiday Inn
www.hiboaradwalk.com
3750 Las Vegas Boulevard S.
Tel: 735-2400 or

800-635-4581.
Fax: 739-8152. **$$**

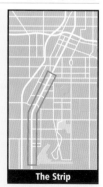

The Strip

Caesars Palace
www.caesars.com
3570 Las Vegas Boulevard
South.
Tel: 731-7110 or
800-634-6661.
Fax: 731-7172. **$$$**

Circus Circus
www.circuscircus.com
2880 Las Vegas Boulevard
South.
Tel: 734-0410 or
800-444-2472.
Fax: 734-5897. **$$**

Excalibur
www.excaliburcasino.com
3850 Las Vegas Boulevard
South.
Tel: 597-7777 or
800-937-7777.
Fax: 597-7009. **$$**

Flamingo Las Vegas
www.flamingolv.com
3555 Las Vegas Boulevard
South.
Tel: 733-3111 or
800-732-2111.
Fax: 733-3353. **$$$**

Four Seasons
www.fourseasons.com
3960 Las Vegas Boulevard
South.
Tel: 632-5000 or
877-632-5000.
Fax: 632-5195.
$$$$

Hard Rock
www.hardrockhotel.com
4455 Paradise Road.
Tel: 693-5000 or
800-693-7625.
Fax: 693-5010. **$$**

Harrah's
3475 Las Vegas Boulevard
South.
Tel: 369-5000 or
800-HARRAHS.
Fax:369-5008. **$$**

Imperial Palace
www.imperialpalace.com
3535 Las Vegas Boulevard
South.
Tel: 731-3311 or
800-634-6441.
Fax: 735-8578. **$$**

Las Vegas Hilton
www.lv-hilton.com
3000 Paradise Road.
Tel: 732-5111 or

800-732-7117
Fax: 794-3611. **$$$**

Luxor
www.luxor.com
3900 Las Vegas Boulevard
South.
Tel: 262-4000 or
800-288-1000
Fax: 262-4404. **$$**

Mandalay Bay
www.mandalaybay.com
3950 Las Vegas Boulevard
South.
Tel: 632-7777 or
877-632-7000.
Fax: 632-7108. **$$$**

MGM Grand
www.mgmgrand.com
3799 Las Vegas Boulevard
South.
Tel: 891-7777 or
800-929-1111.
Fax: 891-1030. **$$$**

The Mirage
www.mirage.com
3400 Las Vegas Boulevard
South.
Tel: 791-7111 or
800-627-6667.
Fax: 791-7414. **$$$**

Monte Carlo
www.monte-carlo.com
3770 Las Vegas Boulevard
South.
Tel: 730-7777 or
800-311-8999.
Fax: 730-7250. **$$$**

The New Frontier
www.frontierlv.com
3120 Las Vegas Boulevard
South.
Tel: 794-8200 or
800-421-7806.
Fax: 794-8445.
Longest-established
hotel on the Strip, with a
venerable history Elvis
first played here.**$$**

New York-New York
www.nynyhotelcasino.com
3790 Las Vegas Boulevard
South.
Tel: 740-6969 or
800-693-6763.
Fax: 740-6920. **$$$**

Paris Las Vegas
www.paris-lv.com
3655 Las Vegas Boulevard
South.

Tel: 946-7000 or
888-266-5687.
Fax: 946-4405. **$$$**

**Riviera Hotel and
Casino**
www.theriviera.com
2901 Las Vegas Boulevard
South.
Tel: 734-5110 or
800-634-6753.
Fax: 794-9451 **$$**

**Stardust Hotel and
Casino**
www.stardustlv.com
3000 Las Vegas Boulevard
South.
Tel: 732-6111 or
800-634-6757.
Fax: 732-6296. **$$**

**Stratosphere Tower
Hotel and Casino**
www.stratlv.com
2000 Las Vegas Boulevard
South.
Tel: 380-7777 or
800-998-6937.
Fax: 383-5334. **$$**

(T.I.) Treasure Island
www.treasureisland.com
3300 Las Vegas Boulevard
South.
Tel: 894-7111 or
800-944-7444.
Fax: 894-7414. **$$$**

**Tropicana Resort and
Casino**
www.tropicanalv.com
3801 Las Vegas Boulevard
South.
Tel: 739-2222 or
800-634-4000.
Fax: 739-2469. **$$$**

The Venetian
www.venetian.com
3355 Las Vegas Boulevard
South.
Tel: 414-1000 or
888-283-6423. **$$$$**

MOTEL CHOICES

Howard Johnson
1401 Las Vegas Boulevard.
Tel: 388-0301 or
800-325-2344.
Near the Convention
Center; with a pool. **$–$$**

King Albert Motel
185 Albert Avenue.
Tel: 732-1555 or
800-553-7753.
Pool, kitchenettes, and
a laundromat. **$**

Motel 6
195 East Tropicana Avenue.
Tel: 798-0728.
Three blocks from the
Strip, near the airport.
Pool, plenty of parking,
and a food shop. **$**

Viva Las Vegas
www.vivalasvegasvillas.
1205 Las Vegas Boulevard
South
Tel: 384-0771 or
800-574-4450.
Funky, light-hearted
motel near the Strat
Tower with themed
rooms, a wedding
chapel, parking. Great
vibes and great rates.**$**

DOWNTOWN

CASINO HOTELS

Binion's Horseshoe Hotel and Casino
129 Fremont Street.
Tel: 392-1600 or
800-237-6537.
Fax: 382 5750.
Home of the famous World Series of Poker. Shopping, pool, seven restaurants, buffet, room service, and cable TV. **$**

California Hotel and Casino
www.thecal.com
12 Ogden Avenue.
Tel: 385-1222 or
800-634-6505.
Fax: 388-2610.
Hawaiian decor. Shopping, swimming pool, concierge desk, three restaurants, room service, and cable TV. **$**

Castaways Hotel, Casino and Bowling Center
www.castaways.com
2800 Fremont Street.
Tel: 385-9123.
Fax: 385-9154.
Bingo parlor, 105 bowling lanes, business services, swimming pool, airport shuttle, concierge desk, three restaurants, buffet, room service, cable TV, and data port. **$**

El Cortez Hotel and Casino
www.jackiegaughan.com
600 East Fremont Street.
Tel: 385-5200 or
800-634-6703.
Fax: 385-1554.
Salon, huge casino, concierge desk, restaurant, and room service. One of the last places in Vegas with penny slot machines. **$**

Fitzgeralds Casino and Hotel
www.fitzgeralds.com
301 Fremont Street.
Tel: 388-2400 or
800-724-5824.
Fax: 388-2478.
Rooms with computer ports, safe, and 25 inch TVs with cable and movies, airport shuttle, four eating places, buffet, room service. **$**

4 Queens Casino and Hotel
www.fourqueens.com
Tel: 385-4011 or
800-634-6045.
Fax: 387-5185.
Two restaurants, room service, and cable TV. Good slot machines. **$**

Fremont Hotel and Casino
www.fremontcasino.com
200 East Fremont Street
Tel: 385-3232 or
800-634-6460.
Fax: 385-6229.
Shopping, five restaurants, room service, and cable TV. **$**

Golden Gate Hotel and Casino
1 Fremont Street.
Tel: 385-906 or
800-426-1906.
Fax: 393-9681
Built in 1905, this is the oldest hotel and casino in Las Vegas. Noted for its 99¢ shrimp cocktails. Two restaurants, cable TV, and a coffeemaker in each room. Sun–Thurs **$**, Fri–Sat **$$**

Golden Nugget
www.goldennugget.com
129 East Fremont Street.
Tel: 385-8362 or
800-634-1454.
Fax: 386-8362.
The most upscale of the Downtown properties. Shopping, salon, exercise facilities, swim-

ming pool, airport shuttle, five restaurants, buffet, room service, cable TV. **$$**

Lady Luck Casino and Hotel
www.ladyluck.com
206 North Third Street.
Tel: 477-3000 or
800-523-9582.
Fax: 366-9602.
Suites with Jacuzzis, an attractive garden with poolside rooms, four restaurants, room service, and cable TV. **$**

Las Vegas Club Casino Hotel
www.vegasclubcasino.net
18 East Fremont Street.
Tel: 385-1664 or
800-634-6532
Fax: 387-6071.
Sports-themed hotel at the corner of Main Street. Concierge desk, three restaurants, room service, cable TV. **$**

Main Street Station Brewery and Hotel
www.mainstreetcasino.com
200 North Main Street.
Tel: 387-1896 or
800-713-8933.
Fax: 386-4466.
Casino with antique woodwork and stained-glass windows. Concierge desk, three restaurants, cable TV. **$**

Jackie Gaughan's Plaza Hotel and Casino
www.jackiegaughan.com
1 Main Street.
Tel: 386-2110 or
800-634-6575.
Fax: 382-8281.
The Plaza is a few steps from the Greyhound station. Exercise facilities, swimming pool, wedding chapel, airport shuttle, concierge desk, three restaurants, and cable television in every room. **$**

Downtown

MOTEL CHOICES

City Center Motel
700 East Fremont.
Tel: 382-4766.
Pool, sundeck, 58 rooms, and a restaurant located opposite. **$**

Crest Budget Motel
207 North Sixth Street
Tel: 382-5642.
Complementary coffee and breakfast, cable TV, free and pay-for movies, microwave oven. **$**

Days Inn Downtown
707 East Fremont.
Tel: 388-1400
Slot parlor, elevated pool, sundeck, and a restaurant. **$**

Downtowner Motel
129 North Eighth Street.
Tel: 384-1441
Kitchenettes; free donuts and coffee. **$**

PRICE CATEGORIES

Rates are for a hotel room, using the lowest standard rate. Suites start at a higher rate.
$$$$ $150+
$$$ $100–$149
$$ $50–$99
$ under $49

BEYOND THE STRIP

There are many properties offering rooms and suites, gaming and other entertainment at lower rates than the huge hotels and mega-resorts. Perimeter hotels in the greater Las Vegas area have become popular with locals and visitors who want to enjoy what the resorts have to offer without having to deal with the traffic and the crowds on the Strip. Some are very upscale and most have similar amenities offered by the Strip resorts.

HOTELS

Amerisuites Hotel
www.amerisuites.com
4520 Paradise Road.
Tel: 369-3366 or
800-833-1516.
Fax: 369-0009.
Located half a mile from the airport, amenities include exercise facilities, business services, a pool, airport shuttle, concierge desk, cable television and VCR, data port, and a coffee maker in each room. **$$**

Arizona Charlie's Hotel and Casino
www.azcharlies.com
740 South Decatur Boulevard.
Tel: 258-5200 or
800-342-2695.
Fax: 258-5192.
The original Arizona Charlie's (there's another on the way to Boulder City), located about a mile west of the Strip and about 11 miles (18 km) from the

airport. Wedding chapel, swimming pool, airport shuttle, five restaurants, buffet, and cable TV. **$**

Cancun Resort
8335 Las Vegas Boulevard South.
Tel: 614-6200.
Fax: 614-6206.
A non-gaming property located 5 miles (8 km) from the airport south of the Strip, Cancun Resort has a penthouse suite and villas with private balconies. Services include exercise facilities, swimming pool, concierge desk, cable TV, VCR, Jacuzzi, and data port. Call for rates.

Best Western Mardi Gras Inn
www.mardigrasinn.com
3500 Paradise Road.
Tel: 731-2020 or
800-634-6501.
Fax: 733-6994.
About 3 miles (4 km) from the airport, the hotel has a casino, salon, business services, swimming pool,

airport shuttle, concierge desk, cable TV, and data port. **$$**

Boardwalk Hotel and Casino
www.boardwalklv.com
3750 Las Vegas Boulevard South.
Tel: 735 2400 or
800-635-4581.
Fax: 739-8152.
Located on the Strip Boardwalk between Bellagio and the Monte Carlo. Wedding chapel, shopping, exercise facilities, swimming pool, concierge desk, three restaurants, buffet, and room service. Great value considering its location. **$$**

The Carriage House
www.carriagehouselasvegas.com
105 East Harmon Avenue.
Tel: 798-1020 or
800-221-2301.
Fax: 798-1020.
Condominium suite hotel, one block from the Strip near the MGM Grand. This non-gaming hotel has in-room movies, kitchenettes, pool, whirlpool, sports

Beyond the Strip

court, airport shuttle, concierge desk, restaurant, room service, and cable TV. **$$$**

Club de Soleil
www.clubdesoleil.com
5499 West Tropicana Avenue.
Tel: 221-0200 or
877-476-5345.
A non-gaming hotel with a French-Mediterranean theme. Pool, tennis courts, exercise facilities, a masseuse, concierge desk, cable TV and VCR, Jacuzzi. About 5 miles (8 km) west of the airport. **$$**

Convention Center Courtyard by Marriott
www.marriott.com
3275 Paradise Road.
Tel: 791-3600 or
800-321-2220.
Fax: 796-7981.
Opposite the Convention Center, this Marriott offers meeting rooms, exercise facilities, business services, pool and spa, concierge desk, cable TV, and a restaurant. It has no gaming. **$$$**

Convention Center Marriott Suites
www.marriott.com
325 Convention Center Drive.
Tel: 650-2000 or
800-228-9290.
Fax: 650-9466.
A comfortable hotel for business travelers and tourists who prefer suites. Three miles (5 km) from the airport, it has exercise facilities, business services, swimming pool, concierge desk, cable TV, restaurant, and data port. **$$$**

Crowne Plaza Las Vegas
4255 South Paradise Road.
Tel: 369-4400 or
800-227-6963.
Fax: 369-3770.
Just east of the Strip, this non-gaming, all-suites hotel is 3 miles (5 km) from the airport. Exercise facilities, business services and meeting rooms, pool, airport shuttle, concierge desk, restaurant, room service, cable TV, and data port. **$$$**

Desert Paradise Resort
www.desertparadiseresort.com
5165 South Decatur Boulevard.
Tel: 579-3600 or
877-257-0900.
Fax: 579-3673.

About a mile west of the Strip, Desert Paradise is an all-suites non-gaming hotel. Located 5 miles (8 km) from the airport, it has exercise facilities, business services, swimming pool, spa, fitness center, concierge desk, and cable TV. **$$**

Doubletree Club
www.doubletree.com
7250 Pollock Drive.
Tel: 948-4000 or
800-222-TREE.
Fax: 948-4100.
Non-gaming hotel with free shuttle to the Strip and airport. Fitness center, pool, on-site bakery, cafe. **$–$$**

Embassy Suites Convention Center
www.eslvcc.com
3600 Paradise Road.
Tel: 893-8000 or
800-362-2779.
Fax: 893-0378.
Located just three blocks from the Convention Center, this non-gaming, all-suites venue has a restaurant, room service, shopping, exercise facilities, swimming pool, cable TV and data port. **$$$**

Emerald Springs – Holiday Inn
www.holidayinnlasvegas.com
325 East Flamingo Road.
Tel: 732-9100 or
800-732-889.
Fax: 731-9784.
An attractive boutique non-gaming hotel, 2 miles (3 km) from the airport; with exercise facilities, business services, pool, airport shuttle, restaurant, room service, cable TV, and data port. **$$**

Gold Coast Hotel and Casino
www.coastcasinos.com
4000 West Flamingo Road
Tel: 367-7111 or

888-402-6278.
Fax: 385-7505.
At the Gold Coast, there's a bowling center, three lounges, a dance hall, and a theater. The guest rooms are comfortable and affordable. **$$**

Greek Isles Hotel and Casino
www.greekislesvegas.com
305 Convention Center Drive.
Tel: 952-8000 or
800-633-1777.
Fax: 952-8100.
Attractive Greek decor with taverna. There's a showroom and comedy lounge, wedding chapel, exercise facilities, business services, pool, airport shuttle, restaurant, cable TV, and data port. **$$**

Hampton Inn
www.hamptoninn.com
7100 Cascade Valley Court.
Tel: 360-5700 or
800-426-7866.
Fax: 360-5757.
Tucked away in the northwest portion of Las Vegas, about 15 miles (8 km) from the airport. A non-gaming venue, it has business services, pool, and cable TV. **$$**

Hard Rock
www.hardrockhotel.com
4455 Paradise Road.
Tel: 693-5000 or
800-693-7625.
Fax: 693-5010.
Three blocks from the Strip. Everyone knows the Hard Rock. This one has a beach club, spa, some luxury suites, and music memorabilia. **$$**

Hotel San Remo
www.sanremolasvegas.com
115 East Tropicana Avenue.
Tel: 739-9000 or
800-522-7366.
Fax: 736-1120.
Within walking distance of the Strip (but too hot

to walk in summer) with showroom, wedding chapel, business services, pool, concierge desk, restaurants, room service, buffet, Jacuzzi, and data port. **$$**

Key Largo Casino and Hotel
www.keylargocasino.com
377 East Flamingo Road.
Tel: 733-7777 or
800-634-6617.
Fax: 734-5071.
Casino, wedding gazebo, shopping, pool, airport shuttle, restaurant, cable TV, and data port. **$$**

Las Vegas Hilton Hotel and Casino
www.lv-hilton.com
3000 South Paradise Road
Tel: 732-5111 or
888-732-7117.
Fax: 732-5805.
Popular with visitors who are seduced by the luxury, the large bedroom closets, and marble-tiled bathrooms. **$$$**

The Orleans Hotel and Casino
www.orleanscasino.com
4500 West Tropicana Avenue.
Tel: 365-7111 or
800-675-3267.
Mardi Gras-themed hotel, offering New Orleans style with salon, exercise facilities, business services, pool, Jacuzzi, concierge desk, eight restaurants and buffet, room service, cable TV, and data port. **$$**

PRICE CATEGORIES
Rates are for a hotel room, using the lowest standard rate. Suites start at a higher rate.
$$$$ $150+
$$$ $100–$149
$$ $50–$99
$ under $49

The Rio All-Suites Hotel and Casino

www.keylargocasino.com
3700 West Flamingo Road.
Tel: 252-7777 or
800-752-9746.
Fax: 7252-8909.
Good value off the Strip, this huge, illuminated casino hotel has large, spacious rooms and the best buffet in town. Be sure to ask for a room in the Masquerade Tower. **$$$**

St Tropez – All Suite Hotel

455 East Harmon Avenue.
Tel: 369-5400 or
800-666-5400.
Fax: 369-8901.
A luxurious non-gaming all-suites hotel near the airport. Shopping, exercise facilities, business services, pool, airport shuttle, concierge desk, a restaurant, cable TV, VCR, data port, and coffee hour. **$$$$**

Silverton Hotel and Casino

www.silvertoncasino.com
3333 Blue Diamond Road.
Tel: 263-7777 or
800-588-7711.
Fax: 896-5635.
Near the airport, a Western-themed hotel with cocktail lounge and entertainment. Pool, restaurants and buffet, room service, and cable TV. Pool, kitchenettes, laundromat. **$**

Westward Ho Hotel and Casino

www.westwardho.com
2900 Las Vegas Boulevard South.
Tel: 731-2900 or
800-634-6803.
Fax: 731-6154.
Five miles (8 km) from the airport, with suites for up to six guests, seven pools and Jacuzzis, concierge desk, restaurants, a buffet, cable TV. **$–$$**

BEYOND LAS VEGAS

HOTELS

Towards Boulder

Arizona Charlie's East Hotel and Casino

www.azcharlies.com
4575 Boulder Highway.
Tel: 951-5900 or
800-362-4040.
East of Las Vegas, part way to Boulder City and Hoover Dam. About 6 miles (10 km) from the airport, amenities include a casino, airport shuttle, buffet , five restaurants, and cable TV in each room. **$**

Boulder Station Hotel Casino

www.boulderstation.com
4111 Boulder Highway.
Tel: 432-7777 or
800-638-7777.
Fax: 432-7744.
Boulder Station is about 15 miles (25 km) from the airport. It has movie theaters, childcare, business services, swimming pool, airport shuttle, concierge desk, 12 restaurants, buffet, room service, and cable TV. **$$**

Sam's Town Hotel and Gambling Hall

www.samstown.com
5111 Boulder Highway.
Tel: 456-7777,
800-634-6371.
Fax: 454-8107.
On Boulder Highway 7 miles (11 km) east of the airport. A beautiful, huge atrium offers patio dining, waterfalls, and a nightly laser show. Pool, eight restaurants and buffet, cable TV, and childcare. **$$**

Boulder City

Boulder Dam Hotel

www.boulderdamhotel.com
1305 Arizona Street.
Tel: 293-3510.
Fax: 293-3093.
This quaint, historic and centrally located hotel offering bed and breakfast has a restaurant, room service, shop, a charming museum, exercise facilities, cable TV, and data ports.
$$–$$$

Hacienda Hotel and Casino

www.haciendaonline.com
US Highway 93.
Tel: 293-5000 or
800-245-6380.
Fax: 293-5608.

Three restaurants, 24-hour shop, buffet, swimming pool, theater, Jacuzzi, and helicopter rides. **$$**

Henderson

Fiesta Henderson Casino Hotel

777 West Lake Mead Drive,
Tel: 558-7000 or
800-899-7770.
South-of-the-border theme hotel about 10 miles (16 km) from the airport. The Fiesta has a swimming pool, Jacuzzi, three bar-lounges, restaurants and buffet, cable television, and data port in each room. **$**

Residence Inn – Henderson Green Valley

www.marriot.com
2190 Olympic Avenue,
Tel: 434-2700 or
800-331-3131.
This is an all-suite hotel with no gaming facilities located 5 miles (8 km) from the airport. There's an excellent sports court suitable for basketball, tennis, or volleyball; exercise facilities; a swimming pool; airport shuttle; cable television and

Beyond Las Vegas

VCR; as well as a data port in each room. **$$$**

Sunset Station Hotel

www.sunsetstation.com
1301 West Sunset Road,
Tel: 547-7777 or
888-786-7389.
Mediterranean style with a bar based on the style of Spanish architect Gaudí. Eight miles (13 km) from the airport, this hotel has a casino, a microbrewery, multi-screen movie theater and an outdoor amphitheater. **$$–$$$**

PRICE CATEGORIES

Rates are for a hotel room, using the lowest standard rate. Suites start at a higher rate.

$$$$	$150+
$$$	$100–$149
$$	$50–$99
$	under $49

ACTIVITIES

NIGHTLIFE, SHOPPING, AND SPORTS

NIGHTLIFE

Vegas's nightlife is the heartbeat of the city. Aside from gaming and the shows at the hotels and resorts, there are many lounge acts, nightclubs, and dance halls. In Las Vegas, you must be 21 or older to frequent nightclubs, casinos, and bars. For a select list of gay clubs, *see page 238*.

Comedy

Catch a Rising Star Comedy, Excalibur, 3850 Las Vegas Boulevard South. Tel: 597-7777 or 800-937-7777. Fax: 597-7009. www.excaliburcasino.com
Presenting a new show every week.

Comedy Stop at the Trop Tropicana Resort and Casino, 3801 Las Vegas Boulevard South. Tel: 739-2222 or 800-634-4000. Fax: 739-2469. www.tropicanalv.com
Nightly. Some of the best comedians in the country.

Crazy Benny's X-treme Comedy Howard Johnson's, 3111 West Tropicana Avenue. Tel: 360-5576.
Nightly, reservations required. Crazy Benny puts on an outrageous, unpredictable adult comedy show.

Dr Naughty: X-rated Comedy Hypnotist, Bourbon Street, 120 East Flamingo Road. Tel: 228-7591.
Monday–Saturday nights. Not for the faint hearted. An adult show.

Hip Nosis: Playin' with your Head, O'Shea's, 3555 Las Vegas Boulevard South. Tel: 737-1343.
Every night hypnotist Justin Tranz has fun presenting an adult act.

I Love Lafong Bourbon Street, 120 East Flamingo Road. Tel: 228-7591. Nightly.
Impersonations of stars, ventriloquist comedy, and more.

Improv Comedy Club Harrah's, 3475 Las Vegas Boulevard South. Tel: 369-5111 or 800-392-9002.
www.harrahs.com
Tuesday–Sunday nights. Presenting some of the new faces in comedy.

Riviera Comedy Club Riviera Hotel and Casino, 2901 Las Vegas Boulevard South. Tel: 794-9433. www.theriviera.com
This is the original comedy showcase in Las Vegas.

The Second City Flamingo Las Vegas, 3555 Las Vegas Boulevard South. Tel: 733-3111.
www.flamingolasvegas.com
Tuesday–Sunday, plus additional shows some evenings. Second

City has been a starting point for many US comedy actors, writers, and directors including Joan Rivers, Dan Akyroyd, John Candy, and John Belushi. Enjoy some of the finest improvisational comedians.

Live Entertainment

The Bar at Times Square New York-New York, 3790 Las Vegas Boulevard South. Tel: 740-6969. Features dueling pianos.

Carnival Court Harrah's, 3475 Las Vegas Boulevard South. Tel: 369-5111.
Admission free. Enjoy live bands throughout the day and into the wee small hours.

Club Rio 3700 West Flamingo Road, Tel: 252-7777. Wednesday–Saturday. Live entertainment and celebrity DJs at one of Las Vegas's hottest music, dance, and video clubs.

Drink 200 East Harmon. Tel: 796-5519.

TICKETS

Tickets for big shows can be purchased online at:
www.vegas.com
www.lasvegas.com
www.lasvegasshows.com

With numerous dance floors and rooms for music, and concerts. There is a small cover charge.

House of Blues
Mandalay Bay, 3950 Las Vegas Boulevard South. Tel: 632-7600. Nightly, live entertainment including high-class performers like the Blues Brothers, Sheryl Crow, and Bob Dylan. Book early for big stars.

The Joint
Hard Rock Hotel, 4475 Paradise Road. Tel: 693-5000. Big-name entertainment and the Hard Rock Center Bar.

Kickin' Back Lounge
Key Largo Casino and Hotel, 377 East Flamingo Road. Tel: 733-7777. Live entertainment nightly.

La Piazza, Cleopatra's Barge, Caesars Palace, 3570 Las Vegas Boulevard South. Tel: 731-7110. Listen or dance nightly to live acts.

La Playa Lounge
Harrah's, 3475 Las Vegas Boulevard South. Tel: 369-5111. Admission is free for live bands every day and night.

Lagoon Saloon
The Mirage, 3400 Las Vegas Boulevard South. Tel: 791-7111. Nightly. Piano bar and saloon.

Le Cabaret
Paris Las Vegas, 3655 Las Vegas Boulevard South. Tel: 946-7000. Live entertainment show lounge.

Loading Dock Lounge
Palace Station Hotel, 2411 West Sahara. Tel: 367-2411. Varied and often interesting music to listen and dance to.

Minstrels Lounge
Excalibur, 3850 Las Vegas Boulevard South. Tel: 597-7777. Two live bands for listening or dancing, and a video poker bar.

Napoleon's
Paris, 3655 Las Vegas Boulevard South. Tel: 946-7000. Enjoy live music as well as the cigar and pipe lounge, with collections of fine cognac and cigars.

Nefertiti's Lounge
Luxor, 3900 Las Vegas Boulevard South. Tel: 262-4000. Live entertainment and dance.

Nightclub at Las Vegas Hilton
3000 Paradise Road. Tel: 732-5755. Wednesday–Sunday 11pm–2am. No cover charge for dancing to some of the city's best bands.

The Railhead
Boulder Station, 4111 Boulder Highway. Tel: 432-7777. Live headline entertainment with free blues on Monday.

Rain
The Palms, 4321 West Flamingo Road. Tel: 942-7777. This impressive, enormous venue is a concert hall, a nightclub and a special-events facility.

Roundtable Showroom
The New Frontier, 3475 Las Vegas Boulevard South. Tel: 794-8200. Two different shows performing at any time.

Nightclubs

Baby's Nightclub
Hard Rock Hotel, 4475 Paradise Road. Tel: 693-5000. Thursday–Saturday. Men pay; women are allowed in free.

The Beach
365 Convention Center Drive. From 10pm. A popular singles party place that occasionally presents live concerts.

C2K Mega Club
The Venetian, 3355 Las Vegas

Boulevard South. Tel: 933-4225. Wednesday–Sunday 11pm–dawn. One of Las Vegas's hottest dance clubs. Men pay more in admission than women.

Coyote Ugly Bar and Dance Saloon
New York-New York, 3790 Las Vegas Boulevard South. Tel: 212-8804. Nightly from 4pm. Hot nightspot with bar-top dancing and fire-breathing coyotes.

Gilley's Dance Hall
New Frontier, 3120 Las Vegas Boulevard South. Tel: 794-8200. Nightly from 4pm. Dance to Country & Western music, try to ride a mechanical bull, and participate in crazy contests.

Light
Bellagio, 3600 Las Vegas Boulevard South. Tel: 693-7111. Thur through Sun until around 4am. State-of-the-art sound and lighting, with Top-40 hits and dance music. A sophisticated atmosphere, two bars and two VIP areas.

Ra
Luxor, 3900 Las Vegas Boulevard South. Tel: 262-4000. Outstanding sound and lighting system, two full bars, a dance floor, stage, and a live DJ. One of Las Vegas's liveliest nightspots.

Rumjungle
Mandalay Bay, 3950 Las Vegas Boulevard South. Tel: 632-7408. From 11pm. Interactive entertainment and dining, with volcanic mountains of rum rising in the illuminated bar. Various music from salsa to romantic, techno to hip hop. "Tasteful" attire only.

Shadow
Caesars Palace, 3570 Las Vegas Boulevard South. Tel: 731-7110. Afternoons during the week and weekend evenings. Enjoy cocktails, appetizers, and top-shelf liquor while viewing silhouetted dancers performing behind a screen.

Studio 54
MGM Grand, 3799 Las Vegas Boulevard South. Tel: 891-1111. Tuesday–Saturday until the early mornings, enjoy a two-story dance club blending cutting-edge

house music with the latest pop and rock. Beautiful women swing over the dance floor releasing a shower of glitter on dancers below. Distinctive acts nightly.

Cocktail Lounges

All the Las Vegas hotel and casino venues have a lounge, as do most of the restaurants. These are a few with different atmospheres.

Bix's
4455 South Buffalo. Tel: 889-0800.
Upscale in both atmosphere and crowd, Bix's has a classy bar and well-decorated tables. It also has wine and cigar rooms.

Ghostbar
The Palms, 4321 West Flamingo. Tel: 942-7777.
An indoor and outdoor lounge on the 55th floor with tremendous views attracting a stylish crowd.

J.C. Wooloughan
J.W. Marriott, 221 North Rampart. Tel: 869-7725. Irish pub open all day Saturday and Sunday as well as each evening.

Hideaway Lounge
(T.I.)Treasure Island, 3300 Las Vegas Boulevard South. Tel: 894-7111. Daily. Call for times.

Velvet Lounge
Warner Bros. Stage 16, The Venetian, 3355 Las Vegas Boulevard South. Tel: 414-1699.
Daily Wednesday–Saturday from 3pm, live music 6–10pm. Fantastic view of the Strip in a candlelit atmosphere. Food available.

SHOPPING

Las Vegas's array of shopping prospects spans the spectrum from the merely affordable to the lavishly expensive. Major casinos try to outdo each other with their glitzy shopping arcades, but there are loads of great shopping possibilities everywhere. The sales tax on goods in Clark County is 8.25 percent.

Shopping Malls

Some of the best shopping in Las Vegas can be found in the huge malls, many of which include entertainment and dining facilities. At the time of going to press, all the stores here have premises in the mall or shopping arcade listed, but if you're interested in a specific shop, be sure to call ahead first or check the web to make sure the place has not moved.

Boulevard Mall
3528 South Maryland Parkway (between Flamingo and Desert Inn roads). Tel: 732-8949.
www.malibu.com. 10am–9pm.
Charlotte Russe, Dillards, The Children's Store, Footlocker, Gap, JC Penny, Victoria's Secret, Macy's, Marshalls, and Sears.

Desert Passage at the Aladdin
3667 Las Vegas Boulevard South. Tel: 876-0710.
www.desertpassage.com
Ann Taylor Loft, bebe, Build-A-Bear Workshop, Cutter & Buck, Illuminations, North Beach Leather, Sephoria, Sur la Table, Tommy's Bahama, Z Gallerie.

Fashion Outlets of Las Vegas
Primm, Nevada (around 35 miles/56 km south of Las Vegas on Interstate 15). Tel: 874-1400.
www.fashionoutletlasvegas.com
Versace, Banana Republic Factory Store, DKNY, Gap, Burberry, Last Call from Neiman Marcus, Polo Ralph Lauren, Williams Sonoma Marketplace, Tommy Bahama, Coach, Escado.

Fashion Show Mall
3200 Las Vegas Boulevard South (at Spring Mountain Road). Tel. 369-0704.
www.thefashionshow.com
Premiere mall on the Strip.
Ann Taylor, Dillards, Louis Vuitton, Macy's, Neiman Marcus, Nordstrom, Robinsons-May, Saks Fifth Avenue, The Sharper Image, Victoria's Secret, and Williams-Sonoma.

Forum Shops at Caesars
3500 Las Vegas Boulevard South

(adjacent to Caesars Palace). Tel: 893-4800.
www.shopsimon.com
Armani, Bertolini's, Christian Dior, The Cheesecake Factory, The Disney Store, Estée Lauder, FAO Schwartz, Ferragamo, Bucci, Hugo Bass, Virgin Records Megastore, Fendi, Polo, and Guess.

Galleria at Sunset
1300 West Sunset Road (intersection of Sunset/Stephanie roads, Henderson). Tel. 434-0202. www.galleriaatsunset.com
Ann Taylor, bebe, Chevy's, Dillards, Eddie Bauer, JC Penny, Juxtapose, Limited Too, Mervyn's California, Gap and Victoria's Secret.

Grand Canal Shoppes
3355 Las Vegas Boulevard South (in The Venetian Hotel/Casino).
Tel: 414-4500. www.venetian.com
Canyon Ranch Spa Club, Burberry, Davidoff, Sephora, Ann Tylor, Banana Republic, bebe, Lladro, Movada, and the eatery Postrio.

Las Vegas Outlet Center
7400 Las Vegas Boulevard South at Warm Springs Road. Tel: 896-5599. www.belz.com
Burlington Brands, Calvin Klein, Casual Corner, Famous Footwear, Jones New York, Levis, Nike, Osh Kosh B'Gosh Pfaltzgraff, Reebok.

Las Vegas Premium Outlets
875 S. Grand Central Parkway. Tel: 474-7500. www.premiumoutlets.com/lasvegas
On the way to downtown Las Vegas, with good discounts on upscale fashions: A/X Armani Exchange, Dolce & Gabbana, Polo Ralph Lauren.

Resort Shopping

Most the larger resort casinos have shopping areas that provide guests with almost everything they'll need, but a boutique in a hotel other than your own may have the perfect souvenir to remind you of your Las Vegas visit. Most of the shops open at 10am, and close 5pm–10pm.

CLOTHES CHART

The chart listed below gives a comparison of United States, European, and United Kingdom clothes sizes. It is always a good idea, however, to try on any article before buying it, as sizes between manufacturers can vary enormously.

● Women's Dresses/Suits

US	Continental	UK
6	38/34N	8/30
8	40/36N	10/32
10	42/38N	12/34
12	44/40N	14/36
14	46/42N	16/38
16	48/44N	18/40

● Women's Shoes

US	Continental	UK
4½	36	3
5½	37	4
6½	38	5
7½	39	6
8½	40	7
9½	41	8
10½	42	9

● Men's Suits

US	Continental	UK
34	44	34
—	46	36
38	48	38
—	50	40
42	52	42
—	54	44
46	56	46

● Men's Shirts

US	Continental	UK
14	36	14
14½	37	14½
15	38	15
15½	39	15½
16	40	16
16½	41	16½
17	42	17

● Men's Shoes

US	Continental	UK
6½	—	6
7½	40	7
8½	41	8
9½	42	9
10½	43	10
11½	44	11

Appian Way

Caesars Palace, 3570 Las Vegas Boulevard South. Tel: 731-7110. Some of the finest boutiques and shops, including Cartier Jewelry.

Avenue Shoppes

Bally's, 3645 Las Vegas Boulevard South. Tel: 739-4111
www.ballyslv.com
Specialty, clothing and jewelry stores.There's also a wedding chapel and three restaurants.

Carnaval Court

Harrah's, 3475 Las Vegas Boulevard South. Tel: 369-5000.
www.harrahs.com
The Art of Gaming, Carnaval Corner, Jackpot, and Ghirardelli Chocolates.

Circus Circus Shops

2880 Las Vegas Boulevard South. Tel: 734-0410.
www.circuscircus.com
An array of good shopping including Marshall Rousso, and other stores featuring gifts, clothing, ceramics, jewelry, and souvenirs. Good for kids' stuff.

Excalibur Stores

3850 Las Vegas Boulevard South.
Tel: 597-7777.
www.excaliburcasino.com
Excalibur Shoppe, Castle Souvenirs, Gifts of the Kingdom, Spirit Shoppe, Dragon's Lair, and Desert Shoppe. Good for children's souvenirs.

Las Vegas Hilton Stores

3000 Paradise Road.
Tel: 732-5111. www.lvhilton.com
Kidz Clubhouse, Candy Mania, Paradise Gift Shop, Landau Jewelers, Charisma Apparel and Footwear, Sports Zone Arcade, Ozone Business, and Regis Salon.

Palms Promenade

The Regent Las Vegas, 221 North Rampart Boulevard.
Tel: 869-7777.
www.regentlasvegas.com
Jewelry by Berger and Son, eyewear by Occhiali, the Markman Gallery, and Tolstoys.

Shopping le Boulevard

Paris Las Vegas, 3655 Las Vegas Boulevard South. Tel: 967-7000.
www.parislasvegas.com

Upscale French retail outlets fronting quaint cobblestoned streets.

The Shopping Promenade

(T.I.) Treasure Island, 3300 Las Vegas Boulevard South. Tel: 894-7111.
www.treasureisland.com
Toiletries to designer fashions.

Starlane Shops

MGM Grand, 3799 Las Vegas Boulevard South. Tel: 891-7777.
www.mgmgrand.com
Emerald City, Houdini Magic, Harley-Davidson, Pearl Factory.

Tower Shops

Stratosphere, 2000 Las Vegas Boulevard South. Tel: 380-7777.
Everything from gifts to clothing, souvenirs to novelties.

The Street of Dreams

Monte Carlo, 3400 Las Vegas Boulevard South. Tel: 791-7777.
www.montecarlo.com
Fine jewelry, designer clothing, eyewear, and souvenir boutiques.

The Street of Shops

Mirage, 3400 Las Vegas Boulevard South. Tel: 791-7111.
www.mirage.com
Childrenswear, swimwear, jewelry, casual wear, and designer attire.

Via Bellagio

Bellagio, 3600 Las Vegas Boulevard South. Tel: 693-7111.
www.bellagio.com
Chanel, Armani, Prada, Tiffany, Moschino, Hermes, Gucci.

Specialist Shops

The Attic

1018 South Main Street.
Tel: 388-4088.
Massive collection of vintage clothes and knick-knacks.

Gamblers General Store

800 South Main Street.
Tel: 382-9903.
Slot machines, videos, etc.

Gamblers Book Shop

630 South 11th Street.
Tel: 382-7555.

Tower/Good Guys WOW! Store

4580 West Sahara
Tel: 364-2500.
Out-of-the-way but huge electronics and CD emporium.

SPORT

Las Vegas is a sports enthusiast's playground. Lake Mead's deep blue waters and 550 miles (885 km) of shoreline provide a recreation center for all types of outdoor activities including scuba diving, swimming, boating, water skiing, and fishing.

Golf

Golf is almost as much a part of Las Vegas history as is gaming. There are enough challenging courses to make the sport, for some outdoors and active people, the main reason to visit. Here is a selection of those open to the public:

Angel Park
100 South Rampart Boulevard. Tel: 254-4653 or 888-851-4114 www.angelpark.com
Two 18-hole Arnold Palmer courses and one par-3 course featuring holes with similar shot values as at the world's most famous par 3s.

Badlands
9119 Alta Drive. Tel: 382-4653, 800-468-7918.
www.americangolf.com
Two-time PGA winner Johnny

Miller designed Badlands in consultation with Chi Chi Rodriguez, with three nine-hole courses.

Bali Hai
3220 East Flamingo Road. Tel: 450-8000 or 888-397-2499 www.waltersgolf.com
Located near the south end of the Las Vegas Strip, the course has numerous water features, towering palms, and tropical plants.

Bear's Best
1635 Village Circle. Tel: 385-8500
Jack Nicklaus recreated 18 of his most famous holes worldwide.

Black Mountain
500 Greenway Road, Henderson. Tel: 565-7933.
www.golfblackmountain.com
In the shadow of Black Mountain, this par-72 course is one of the oldest in the city.

Callaway
6730 Las Vegas Boulevard South.
Tel: 896-4100.
www.callawaygolfcenter.com
This facility features a 113-stall driving range, Callaway performance center, St Andrews golf shop, and a lit par-3 golf course.

Craig Ranch
628 West Craig Road, North Las Vegas. Tel: 642-9700.
With thousands of trees, this 72-par course is a local favorite.

Desert Pines
3415 East Bonanza Road. Tel: 450-8000 or 888-397-2499.
www.waltersgolf.com
Just 15 minutes from the Strip, Desert Pines offers a country-club experience with more than 4,000 pines and white-sand bunkers.

Desert Rose
5483 Club House Drive. Tel: 431-4653. www.americangolf.com
A county facility with narrow fairways and smooth greens.

Eagle Crest
2203 Thomas Ryan Boulevard. Tel: 240-1320.
www.suncitygolf.com
Perfect for quick rounds in under three hours, the Summerlin course has an executive layout.

Las Vegas Golf Club
4300 W. Washington Avenue. Tel: 646-3000.
www.americangolf.com
There are several reachable par-5s on this par-72 layout. The oldest in Las Vegas, and one of the busiest.

Las Vegas National
1911 East Desert Inn Road. Tel: 796-0013.
www.americangolf.com
This par-71 course has hosted several LPGA and PGA Tour events. It is a traditional-style course with a lit range and lessons available.

Las Vegas Paiute Resort
10325 Nu-Wav Kaiv Boulevard. Tel: 658 1400 or 888-921-2833 www.lvpaiutegolf.com
Owned and operated by southern Paiute Native Americans at the base of Mount Charleston, three challenging nationally acclaimed courses.

Legacy
130 Par Excellence Drive, Henderson. Tel: 897-2187 or 888-851-4114.
www.thelegacygolf.com
The Devil's Triangle, a three-hole series on the back nine, can make or break the round on this par-72.

Painted Desert
5555 Painted Mirage Road. Tel: 546-2570.
www.americangolf.com
A rugged and arid 18-hole desert-style course.

Reflection Bay
75 Montelago Boulevard, Henderson. Tel: 740-4653.
www.lakelasvegas.com
A Jack Nicklaus-designed par-72 course on the shore of the man-made Lake Las Vegas.

Revere at Anthem
2600 Hampton Road, Henderson Tel: 259-4653.
Designed by Billy Casper and Greg Nash, the Revere flows down a natural desert canyon.

Rio Secco
2851 Grand Hills Drive. Tel: 889-2400. www.playrio.com
Said to be one of the world's top golf resorts, the 7,000-yard (6,700-meter) course is fre-

CAMPING & HIKING

Hiking and camping are a wonderful way to experience southern Nevada outside the dark gaming dens of Sin City.

Some of the larger casinos in Las Vegas maintain RV parking lots in town where visitors driving RVs are encouraged to stay, but there are also some spectacular camping areas around Las Vegas that highlight the desert side of the city. Most of the marinas at Lake Mead also operate camping areas for a nominal fee.

The United States Forest Service on Mount Charleston maintains some outstanding camping areas and trails that can take adventurous guests up to heights of 11,819 ft (36,000 meters).

The temperature on Mount Charleston is generally much, much cooler than in Las Vegas and so can be a welcome retreat from the heat. The mountain is home to unique vegetation and animal life. During a stay on the mountain, it's not uncommon for campers to spot deer, elk, coyote, squirrels, or a number of different types of birds.

quented by Tiger Woods and is home to the Butch Harmon School of Golf.

TPC at The Canyons
9851 Canyon Run Drive.
Tel: 256-2000. www.pgatour.com
This beautiful desert course is host to the Invensys Classic at Las Vegas, the first professional PGA tournament won by ace golfer Tiger Woods.

Tennis

There are hundreds of tennis courts in Las Vegas. Andre Agassi, who was born and raised here, learned how to play in the desert heat of southern Nevada. Many casinos have courts and offer lessons, while numerous courts throughout the metropolitan area are free.

Casino Courts

Bally's/Paris
3645 Las Vegas Boulevard South.
Tel: 739-4111. Ten outdoor courts, seven of which are lit. Non guests pay slightly more than guests.

Flamingo Las Vegas
3555 Las Vegas Boulevard South.
Tel: 733-3444. Four lit outdoor courts to the northeast of the hotel. Reasonable fees consider-

ing it's the Strip.
Las Vegas Hilton
3000 Paradise Road. Tel: 732-5648. Six courts with four lit on the pool deck area. For guests only.

Monte Carlo
3770 Las Vegas Boulevard South. Tel: 730-7777. Four lit courts, all open to the public. The fee is fairly reasonable.

Jackie Gaughan's Plaza
No. 1 Main Street. Tel: 386-2110. Four lit courts Downtown. Call for reservations and fees.

Riviera Hotel
2901 Las Vegas Boulevard South. Tel: 734-5110. Lit courts. Guests of the hotel play for free; non guests allowed for a fee.

Public Courts

There are numerous public parks around the metropolitan area that have tennis courts available to the public. Many are free of charge when the park is open (generally 7am–11pm daily). They are usually on a first-come first-served basis, and players simply drive around and look for an open court.

Lorenzi Park Courts
3075 West Washington Avenue.
Tel: 229-4867. Reservations are recommended for these eight lit courts. There is a fee charged.

Paradise Park
4770 South Harrison. Tel: 455-7777. Two free lit courts on Tropicana Avenue just east of Eastern Avenue.

Paul Meyer Park and Community Center 4525 New Forest Drive. Tel: 455-7723.

Sunrise Park/Community Center 2240 Linn Lane. Tel: 455-7600.

Sunset Park
2601 East Sunset Road. Tel: 260-9803. Located east of Las Vegas Boulevard South, there are eight lit courts. Call for opening hours, reservations, and cheap prices.

Whitney Park, Community and Senior Center 5700 Missouri Street. Tel: 455-7573.

Winchester Park and Community Center 3130 South McLeod Street. Tel: 455-7340.

YMCA
4141 Meadows Lane. Tel: 877-9622. Lessons are available at this public facility which has five lit courts; small fee.

Car Racing

600 Racing Inc
6825 Speedway Boulevard Suite B 102. Tel: 642-4386.

Richard Petty Driving Experience
6975 Speedway Boulevard.
Tel: 643-4343.

Derek Daly Academy
7055 Speedway Boulevard.
Tel: 643-2126.

Freddie Spencer's High Performance Driving School
7055 Speedway Boulevard.
Tel: 643-1099.

Cycling

Downhill Bicycling Tours
7943 Cadenza Lane. Tel: 897-8287. A bus drives riders up to the 8,000-ft (2,438-meter) mark on Mount Charleston, and you ride 18 miles (30 km) back down the mountain through several different layers of desert and mountain environments.

Escape Adventures Mountain Bike and Hiking Tours

8221 West Charleston Suite 101. Tel: 596-2953. www.escapeadventures.com Providing rental bikes and guides, the company conducts tours to Mt Charleston and Red Rock Canyon.

Red Rock Downhill Bicycle Tours
1250 American Pacific Drive Suite 1711, Henderson. Tel: 278-7617. Fax: 947-215. Experienced guides lead safaris down Red Rock Canyon on 21-speed mountain bikes.

Horseback Riding

Bonnie Springs Old Nevada
1 Gunfighter Lane, Blue Diamond. Tel: 875-4191. Red Rock riding stables with desert tours available.

Silver State Old West Tours
Tel: 798-7788. Scenic trail including daily guided rides, sunset and sunrise tours, and Western BBQs.

Cowboy Trail Rides
800 North Rainbow Suite 204. Tel: 387-8778. Fax: 248-9336. www.cowboytrailrides.com Singles to large groups guided on horseback to breathtaking views.

Hot-Air Ballooning

Adventure Balloon Tours
P.O. Box 97. Tel: 800-346-6444. www.smilerides.com

D and R Balloons
3275 Rosanna St. Tel: 248-7609. www.lasvegasballoonrides.com

The Ultimate Balloon Adventure
2013 Clover Path Street. Tel: 800-793-9278. www.lvhd.com

Rafting

Black Canyon River Raft Tours
1297 Nevada Highway, Boulder City. Tel: 800-696-7238. www.rafts.com

Western River Expeditions
7258 Racquet Club Drive, Salt Lake City, Utah, 84121. Tel: 800-453-7450. www.westernriver.com

Skiing

Las Vegas Ski & Snowboard Resort
Office: 3620 North Rancho Drive Suite 103. Resort: Highway 156 Lee Canyon, Mount Charleston. Tel: 645-2754; Fax: 645-3391. Snow report: 593-9500. www.skilasvegas.com Around 35 miles (56 km) northeast of Vegas off Highway 95, this resort is open from around Thanksgiving to Easter. Fees and hours vary.

Cedar Breaks Lodge
P.O. Box 190248, Brian Head, Utah 84719. Tel: 888-282-3327. www.cedarbreakslodge.com

A major ski resort in southern Utah around four hours' drive north of Vegas on Interstate 15. Lifts, resort area, and rooms.

Elk Meadows
P.O. Box 511, Beaver, Utah 84713. Tel: 435-438-5433. www.elkmeadows.com Around five hours north of Las Vegas on Interstate 15, a small resort famous for its powder.

Skydiving

Skydive Las Vegas
1401 Airport Road, Suite 4, Boulder City. Tel: 759-3483 or 800-875-934. Fax: 293-5684. www.skydivelasvegas.com Specializes in first-time jumpers and tandem jumps with a 46-second freefall.

Las Vegas Gravity Zone
Tel: 456-3802. A family-owned school for first-time jumpers. Member of the U. Parachute Association.

Flyaway Indoor Skydiving
200 Convention Center Drive. Tel: 731-4768. www.flyawayindoorskydiving.com

Water Skiing/Sailing

In winter it is possible to ski in the morning, then water ski in the afternoon. Most, however, prefer to leave water skiing until the water warms up to 85°F (30°C), generally around the first of June.

Forever Resorts
Callville Bay, Lake Mead Cottonwood Cove, Lake Mohave. Tel: 800-255-5561. Renting everything from luxurious houseboats to powerboats. Prices very greatly.

Las Vegas Bay Marina
Las Vegas Bay, Lake Mead Drive. Tel: 565-9111. Houseboats, tracker patio boats, Bayliner ski boats and personal watercraft can be rented. There is a restaurant and lounge.

Lake Mead Resort and Marina
322 Lakeshore Rd, Boulder City. Tel: 293-3484.

A–Z

DIRECTORY

Admission Charges

Museums and attractions have hefty admission prices, often around $15. The best shows in town are expensive, too, usually over $100. To see a major star, expect to pay much more.

Budgeting for your Trip

Almost everything except for admission and show prices can be done cheaply, from dining at a $6.99 all-you-can-eat buffet, to staying in a decent motel for as little as $25. Sin City is also a place that likes to do deals, and car rental firms and even major casinos offer extremely low prices, usually in the hot summer months. Always bargain.

Business Hours

Las Vegas is a 24-hour city. Casinos, hotels, many liquor stores, bars, numerous restaurants, grocery stores, and other shopping outlets never close. Banks keep regular hours, generally 9am to 5pm, but some branches are open on Saturday and a few even on Sunday. Most major shopping malls are open from 10am to 10pm every day including Christmas Day and New Year's Day.

Climate

Located in the Mojave Desert, Las Vegas has relatively hot and dry weather most of the year. Most of the city's annual rainfall of about 4.13 inches (10.64 centimeters),

comes in winter. The monsoon period in the Mojave Desert falls from July through September with frequent thunderstorms bringing lightning and heavy downpours. The drenching rains, though fleeting, can create dangerous flash floods, and motorists and pedestrians are cautioned never to cross running water, flooded washes, or roads after a storm.

The average monthly temperature is 56°F (13°C)–80°F (27°C). Summer temperatures are often over 100°F (38°C) in the day and 75–85°F (26–30°C) at night, but heatwaves of 117°F (47°C) can occur in Las Vegas. The heat is dry as the city has low humidity.

Although it rarely drops much below freezing, the Las Vegas Valley occasionally has winter snow. An average year sees 212 clear days, 82 partly cloudy days and 71 cloudy days. The mildest Las Vegas weather is generally from October through April or May.

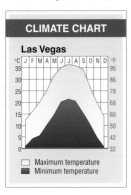

CLIMATE CHART

Las Vegas

- ☐ Maximum temperature
- ■ Minimum temperature

What to Bring

Dress is almost universally casual, although some upscale restaurants require smart attire. While light clothes are essential for summer, warm coats and sweaters are needed in winter and a jacket may be advisable for cooler summer nights. Rain can be expected in winter and spring. During the hot season, wear a hat and sunglasses.

Crime & Safety

Las Vegas is a relatively safe city despite the fact that it is awash in cash. In addition to the Metropolitan Police Department, which patrols nearly all areas, there are separate police departments in North Las Vegas, Henderson, and Boulder City. Other police agencies include Nevada Gaming Control officers, who keep gaming on the up and up, and the Federal Bureau of Investigation (FBI), which investigates federal crimes.

Every casino has its own armed security force to protect customers and the casino's interests. If you have any problem inside the hotel, your first stop should be with security, although the chances of retrieving lost property are not good.

At no time should you leave any cash or belongings unattended. There are those who prey on the unsuspecting. For the most part, visitors to Las Vegas are safe in all casino areas including the street in front of the resorts, but, as in most cities, it is unwise to travel at night in areas that are not well lit.

Customs

Meat or meat products, illegal drugs, firearms, seeds, plants, and fruits are among prohibited goods. Also, do not bring in any duty-free goods worth more than $400 (US citizens) or $100 (foreign travelers). Visitors over 21 may import 200 cigarettes, 3 lb (1.3 kg) of tobacco or 50 cigars, and 34 fl oz (1 liter) of alcohol.

Non-residents may import, free of duty and internal revenue tax, articles worth up to $100 for use as gifts for other persons, as long as they remain in the US for at least 72 hours and keep the gifts with them. This $100 gift exemption or any part of it can be claimed only once every six months. It can include 100 cigars, but no alcohol. Do not have the articles gift wrapped, as they must be available for customs inspection.

If you are not entitled to the $100 gift exemption, you may bring in articles worth up to $25 free of duty for your personal or household use. You may include any of the following: 50 cigarettes, 10 cigars, 150 ml of alcohol, or 5 fl oz (150ml) of alcoholic perfume or proportionate amounts. Articles bought in duty-free shops in foreign countries are subject to US customs duty and restrictions but may be included in your exemption. However, if you stop off in Vegas for a couple of days "in-transit," these may be confiscated.

For a breakdown of customs allowances contact the United States Customs Service, PO Box 7407, Washington, DC 20044. Tel: 202-514-4316.

D isabled Travelers

If you have a physical disability and need special accommodation requirements, your reservation agent or hotel ADA coordinator can help you find a room. Most showrooms have assistive listening devices and wheelchair accommodations, as do quite a few restaurants and hotel lounges.

For more information you should contact the properties concerned directly. Many casinos have slot machines and table games with wheelchair access.

If you rent a car, you should bring your hometown parking permit, or request a free 90-day permit through the city of Las Vegas at the Parking Permit Office, tel: 229-6431.

Lift-equipped shuttles are available to and from McCarran International Airport, which also has TTYs for the hearing impaired.

E ntry Requirements

A passport, a passport-sized photograph, a visitor's visa, proof of intent to leave the US and, depending on your country of origin, an international vaccination certificate are required of most foreign nationals. Visitors from a few European countries staying less than 90 days no longer need a visa. Vaccination certificate requirements vary, but proof of immunization against smallpox or cholera may be necessary. Canadian and Mexican citizens, and British residents of Canada and Bermuda, are normally exempt but it is wise to check.

Since September 11, 2001, security measures are in place,

ELECTRICITY

The US uses a 110-120 volt 50 cycle alternating current (AC). Transformers or plug adaptors can be bought in many Las Vegas shops.

EMERGENCY NUMBERS

- **All emergencies**: 911
- **Police:**
Metropolitan Police Department, 400 Stewart Avenue.
Tel: non-emergency 795-3111
or 229-3111.
North Las Vegas Police Department, 1301 East Lake Mead Boulevard, North Las Vegas. Tel: 633-9111.
Henderson Police Department, 240 South Water Street, Henderson. Tel: 565-8933.
Boulder City Police Department, 1005 Arizona Street, Boulder City. Tel: 293-9224.
Nevada Highway Patrol
Tel: 486-4100.
Nevada Gaming Control, 555 East Washington. Tel: 486-2000.
- **Ambulance Dispatch Center**
Tel: 384-3400.
- **Alcoholics Abuse Hotline**
Tel: 800/222-0199.
- **Alcoholics Anonymous**,
1431 East Charleston Avenue.
Tel: 598-888.
- **Domestic Violence Hotline**
Tel: 646-4981.
- **Drug Abuse Prevention**
Tel: 799-8402.
- **Gamblers Anonymous**
Tel: 385-7732.
- **Poison Control**
Tel: 732-4989.
- **Rape Crisis Hotline**
Tel: 366-1640.
- **Suicide Prevention Hotline**
Tel: 877/885-4673.

and are subject to change without notice. Foreign nationals should always carry photo ID.

G ay & Lesbian Travelers

The **Gay and Lesbian Center**, 953 East Sahara Avenue, Suite B 25, tel: 733-9800, is generally staffed seven days a week. The office provides a guide to local bars which includes:
Badlands Saloon, 953 East Sahara Avenue. Tel: 792-9262.

An easy-going neighborhood bar with very friendly staff.
Cobalt, 900 Karen Avenue.
Tel: 693-6567. Attracts all types with a variety of special shows and programs.
FreeZone, 610 East Naples Drive. Tel: 733-6701. The most popular bar for women, but also a hit with men on boys' nights and weekends. Check out the *What a Drag* show.
Hamburger Mary's, 4503 Paradise Road. Tel: 735-4400. A great place to grab some food and hang out for both the gay and straight crowd. Holds tons of special events.
Las Vegas Eagle, 3430 East Tropicana Avenue. Tel: 458-8662. Home of the "infamous" Underwear Nights on Wednesday and Friday.
Las Vegas Lounge, 900 Karen Avenue. Tel: 737-9350. Las Vegas's only transgender bar. Has fantastic, splashy shows and a great crowd.
Sasha's, 4640 Paradise Road. Tel: 735-3888. The most diverse live entertainment in town. Featuring the longest-running drag-show cast.
Spotlight Lounge, 957 East Sahara Avenue. Tel: 696-0202. A favorite with locals. Lots of community events, and friendly laid-back staff.

H ealth & Medical Care

Health care is extremely expensive, so visitors should always have comprehensive travel insurance to cover any emergencies.

Hospitals

Desert Springs Hospital Medical Center, 2075 East Flamingo Road. Tel: 733-8800.
Lake Mead Hospital and Medical Center, 1409 East Lake Mead Boulevard, North Las Vegas. Tel: 649-7711.
St Rose Dominican Hospital, 102 East Lake Mead Drive, Henderson. Tel: 616-5000.
Summerlin Hospital Medical Center, 657 Town Center Drive. Tel: 233-7000.
Sunrise Hospital and Medical Center, 3186 South Maryland Parkway. Tel: 731-8080.
University Medical Center, 1800 West Charleston Boulevard. Tel: 383-2000.
Valley Hospital, 620 Shadow Lane. Tel: 388-4000.

I nternet

Many resorts have in-room internet facilities; a few of the best have business centers. Local libraries and a few 24-hour supermarkets also have computers for basic surfing.

Maps

Flexi-maps, available from Insight guides, provide key sites and a handy, laminated finish.

Media

Print

There are two major daily newspapers in Las Vegas, the *Las Vegas Review-Journal* and the smaller *Las Vegas Sun*. Although the papers are editorially separate, they share advertising and printing facilities. Several other alternative publications are available, including weekly newspapers and magazines, most of which are free.

Television

There are numerous TV stations in Vegas as well as the national CBS, NBC, and ABC. There is also the FOX network, and the UPN network, an entertainment channel; a local government channel; and a few Spanish channels.

Money Matters

Credit cards are accepted almost everywhere, although not all cards at all places. Along with out-of-state or overseas bank cards, they can also be used to withdraw money at ATMs (automatic teller machines), which are commonplace in casinos. These are marked with the corresponding stickers (i.e. Cirrus, Visa, MasterCard, American Express, Plus, etc.)

If you plan to cash travelers' checks, be sure to bring along your passport.

Currency

US dollars (US$). Automated teller machines (ATMs) are located throughout the city and in most major casinos, many of which also accept travelers' checks and cash foreign currency. There are many check-cashing services, which accept foreign checks.

Tax

Shoppers in Clark County pay about 8.25 percent in taxes for all non-food items, or for food items purchased already prepared such as in a restaurant. There is often a slight difference between the tax in Clark County, the city of Las Vegas, Henderson, North Las Vegas, Boulder City, Mesquite, Laughlin, and other areas of the state.

Photography

Taking photographs is an imperative for most visitors who otherwise find it hard to explain Las Vegas to friends and family back home. There are numerous camera shops that handle all types of film and equipment, and there are places to have film developed in an hour on almost every street corner and in most supermarkets Downtown or on the Strip.

Photography inside casinos or showrooms is strictly prohibited. In the early days there was such a stigma attached to gaming that customers would get upset if anyone took photographs, in case a picture of them sitting at a blackjack table appeared in their newspaper. Particularly obliging pit bosses or security guards might give you a wink and turn their backs *if you ask first*.

In showrooms, the performers and casino big shots believe that while customers have paid for the right to watch a live performance, it doesn't give them the

right to take pictures, or, a big fear, perhaps sell the photo to others. Many showbusiness people have spent large sums of money registering the right to make money off their faces, and they don't want just anyone taking their picture.

In some shows, like the daredevil Cirque du Soleil performances, a photographic flash going off at a critical moment could be hazardous for the acrobats themselves, so cameras are banned. However, some performers, such as Wayne Newton at the Stardust, will walk through and greet the audience, and photography is positively encouraged.

Postal Services

Postal authorities are available to respond to questions or concerns 24 hours a day, seven days a week by calling 800/275-8777. There are branches of the post office throughout the Las Vegas Valley, but the main post office is located at 101 East Sunset Road, a stone's throw from McCarran Airport.

Religious Services

There are more than 500 churches and synagogues in Las Vegas representing more than 40 faiths. Casino gaming chips are found in donation baskets nearly every day at two Roman Catholic churches a few hundred yards from the Strip.

PUBLIC HOLIDAYS

Although Las Vegas recognizes all major public holidays in the US, it makes little difference to the casual visitor. Most government offices, including federal, county, and city, close on holidays, but the majority of businesses that cater to tourists never close. Most major holidays occur on the Monday closest to the celebration date. On most 3-day weekends, Vegas becomes very crowded.

● **New Year's Day** January 1
● **Martin Luther King Day** Third Monday in January
● **President's Day** Third Monday in February
● **Labor Day** First Monday in September
● **Independence Day** July 4
● **Veterans' Day** November 1
● **Christmas Day** December 25

TELEPHONE NUMBERS

Unless otherwise stated, all telephone numbers in this book begin with the code **702**. When dialing within Las Vegas, the code is not used. When calling outside the area, even if the code is still 702, you must dial it in full. The area code throughout the rest of Nevada is **775**.

■ime Zones

Pacific Standard Time (Pacific Daylight Time in summer). Vegas is in the same time zone as California; 8 hours behind London and 3 hours behind New York.

Tipping

Far more than in other US cities, tipping is the grease that keeps the machine of Las Vegas operating. Most tipping (bellman per bag; cocktail waitress; daily maid service) is in the $1–$3 range, but sometimes a larger tip will move things along. No table at a big hotel restaurant? Try a $10 or $20 bill. Valet parking full? Start with $5 and work upwards, but always discreetly.

Restaurant tipping is between 15 and 20 percent of the total bill before taxes. Be aware that some restaurants add this to the bill automatically, so check first.

Tourist Information

Tourist Offices

There are public tourist offices throughout Clark County. These provide excellent information for Las Vegas travelers and often have discount coupons for any number of activities in the area. They can all be accessed through the Internet at **www.lasvegas24hours.com**, the website of the Las Vegas Convention and Visitors Authority (LVCVA). Everything you need to know about Las Vegas can be found here including an events calendar, detailed maps of the area, and visitor and convention information.

The tourist offices are:
Las Vegas Visitor Information Center, 3150 Paradise Road. Tel: 892-7573.
Las Vegas Chamber of Commerce, 3720 Howard Hughes Parkway. Tel: 735-1616. Fax: 735-2011.
Boulder City Visitor Information Center, 100 Nevada Highway, Boulder City. Tel: 294-1252.

■eights & Measures

The US uses the Imperial system of weights and measures. Metric weights and measures are rarely used in Las Vegas.

What to Read

American Billionaire by Richard Hack. Millennium Press, 2001.
The Anza Borrego Desert Region by Lowell and Diana Lindsay. Wilderness Press, 1978.
Behind the Tables by Barney Vinson. Gollehon, Grand Rapids, 1986.
Chip-Wrecked in Las Vegas by Barney Vinson. Mead Publishing, 1994.
The Dirt Beneath the Glitter: Tales from Real Life Las Vegas edited by Hal K. Rothman and Mike Davis. University of California Press, 2002.

The First 100, edited by A.D. Hopkins & K.J. Evans. Huntington Press, 1999.
Hiking Southern Nevada by Bruce Whitney. Huntington Press, 2000.
How to Win at Gambling by Avery Cardoza. Cardoza Publishing, 1993.
The Las Vegas Pauites: A Short History by John Alley. Las Vegas Tribe of Pauite Indians, 1977.
Loaded Dice by John Soares. Taylor Publishing, 1985.
The Man Who Invented Las Vegas by W.R. Wilkerson III. Ciro's Books, 2000.
The Money and the Power: the Making of Las Vegas and its Hold on America by Sally Dention and Roger Morris. Vintage Books, 2002.
The New Gambler's Bible by Arthur S. Reber. Three Rivers Press, 1996.
The Players: The Men Who Made Las Vegas edited by Jack Sheehan. University of Nevada Press, 1997.
Saints in Babylon: Mormons in Las Vegas by Kenric F. Ward, 2002.
Searchlight: The Camp That Didn't Fail by Harry Reid. University of Nevada Press, 1998.
Wilderness Emergency by Gene Fear. Survival Education Association, 1972.

Other Insight Guides

Insight Guide: Los Angeles Captures the energy and glamour of America's movie capital.

Compact Guides are mini encyclopedias for visitors in a hurry.

Berlitz Guides are pocket-size and perfect for easy reference.

LAS VEGAS STREET ATLAS

The key map shows the area of Las Vegas covered by the atlas section. An index of street names and places of interest shown on the maps can be found on the following pages. For each entry there is a page number and grid reference

Map Legend

	Freeway with Exit
	Freeway (under construction)
	Divided Highway
	Main Road
	Secondary Road
	Minor road
	Track
	International Boundary
	State Boundary
	National Park/Reserve
✈	Airport
✝	Church (ruins)
✝	Monastery
🏰	Castle (ruins)
∴	Archaeological Site
∩	Cave
★	Place of Interest
🏠	Mansion/Stately Home
※	Viewpoint
	Beach
	Freeway
	Divided Highway
	Main Roads
	Minor Roads
	Footpath
	Railroad
	Pedestrian Area
	Important Building
	Park
●—●	Monorail
🚌	Bus Station
ⓘ	Tourist Information
✉	Post Office
✝	Cathedral/Church
☪	Mosque
✡	Synagogue
🛆	Statue/Monument
▯	Tower

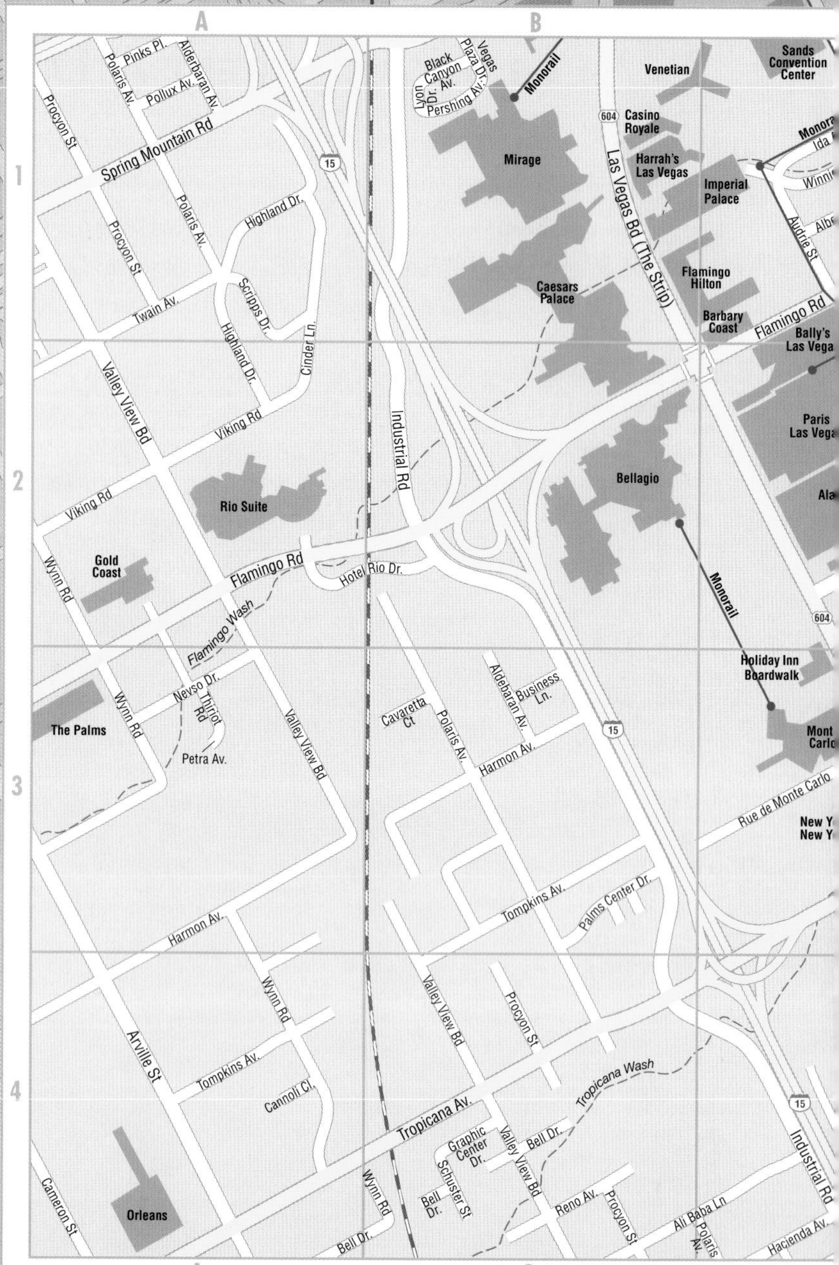

A

B

Sands Convention Center

Pinks Pl.

Polaris Av.

Aldebaran Av.

Pollux Av.

Black Canyon Av.

Vegas Plaza Dr.

Pershing Av.

Lyon Dr.

Monorail

Venetian

Procyon St.

Spring Mountain Rd

[15]

604

Casino Royale

Monorail

Ida

Polaris Av.

Highland Dr.

Scripps Dr.

Mirage

Las Vegas Blvd (The Strip)

Harrah's Las Vegas

Winni

Procyon St.

Imperial Palace

Audrie St.

Albe

Twain Av.

Highland Dr.

Cinder Ln.

Flamingo Hilton

Viking Rd.

Valley View Bd

Caesars Palace

Barbary Coast

Flamingo Rd

Bally's Las Vega

Viking Rd.

Industrial Rd

Paris Las Vega

Wynn Rd.

Rio Suite

Bellagio

Ala

Gold Coast

Flamingo Rd

Hotel Rio Dr.

Flamingo Wash

Monorail

604

Nevso Dr.

Holiday Inn Boardwalk

The Palms

Wynn Rd.

Thjot Rd.

Petra Av.

Valley View Bd

Cavaretta Ct.

Polaris Av.

Aldebaran Av.

Business Ln.

[15]

Mont Carlo

Harmon Av.

Rue de Monte Carlo

New Y New Y

Tompkins Av.

Palms Center Dr.

Harmon Av.

Wynn Rd.

Valley View Bd

Procyon St.

Arville St.

Tompkins Av.

Cannoli Cl.

Tropicana Av.

Bell Dr.

Tropicana Wash

[15]

Industrial Rd

Graphic Center Dr.

Valley View Bd

Bell Dr.

Cameron St.

Bell Dr.

Wynn Rd.

Bell Dr.

Schuster St.

Reno Av.

Procyon St.

Ali Baba Ln.

Polaris Av.

Hacienda Av.

Orleans

A

B

University of Nevada, Las Vegas

Marjorie Barrick Museum

Gym Dr.

Flamingo Wash

Hughes Pw.

Hughes Center Cr.

Flamingo Rd

Koval Ln.

Howard

Hospitality Ct.

Charlotte Dr.

Fredda St.

Debbie Way

Paradise Rd

Tropicana Wash

Harmon Av.

Thomas and Mack Center

Hard Rock Hotel

Swenson St.

Naples Dr.

Rochelle Av.

La Cienega St.

Deckow Ln.

Salton St.

Sadie St.

Lana St.

Harmon Av.

La Mar Cr.

Monterey

Grand Dr.

Monterey Cr.

Tropicana Av.

Audrie St.

Monorail

Harmon Av.

MGM Grand Adventures Theme Park

Koval Ln.

Deckow Ln.

Paradise Rd

Liberace Museum

Showcase Mall

MGM Grand

Tropicana Av.

Island Way

Duke Ellington Way

San Remo

Tropicana

Reno Av.

Haven St.

McCarran International Airport

xcalibur

Monorail

Ali Baba Ln.

Giles St.

Hacienda Av.

Bethel Ln.

Danville Ln.

Haven St.

Las Vegas Blvd (The Strip)

Luxor

604

Mesa Vista Av.

Hacienda Av.

Mandalay Bay

Diablo Dr.

Four Seasons

0   500 yds

0   500 m

N

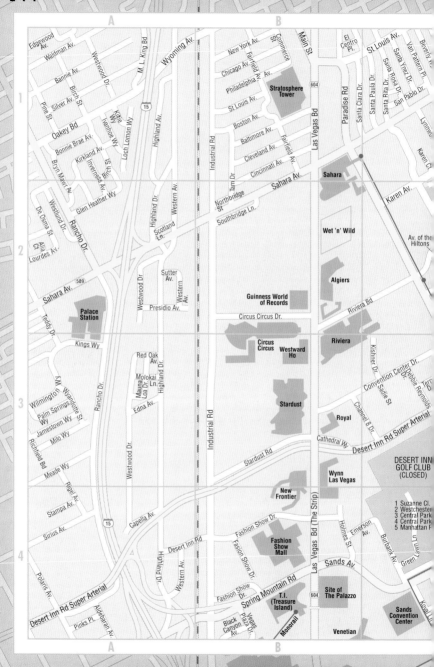

A B

1

2

3

4

Edgewood Av.
Waldman Av.
Westwood Dr.
Bannie Av.
Birch St.
Silver Av.
Pine St.
Oakey Bd
Bonnie Brae Av.
Kirkland Av.
Inverness Av.
Bryn Mawr Av.
De Osma St.
Alta Lourdes Av.
Sahara Av.
Westlund Dr.
Glen Heather Wy.
Rancho Dr.
Teddy Dr.
Palace Station
Kings Wy.
Wilmington Av.
Palm Springs Wy.
Jamestown Wy.
Milo Wy.
Richfield Bd
Meade Wy.
Stampa Av.
Sirius Av.
Polaris Av.
Pinks Pl.
Aldebaran Av.
Desert Inn Rd Super Arterial

M. L. King Bd
Wyoming Av.
Kittie Wy
Ivanhoe Wy.
Loch Lomon Av.
Highland Av.
Highland Dr.
Scotland Ln.
Western Av.
Sutter Av.
Western Av.
Presidio Av.
Westwood Dr.
Red Oak Av.
Molokai Dr.
Mauna Loa Dr.
Highland Dr.
Edna Av.
Rancho Dr.
Westwood Dr.
Capella Av.
Highland Dr.
Desert Inn Rd
Western Av.
Fashion Show Dr.

Industrial Rd
Tam Dr.
Northbridge St.
Southbridge Ln.
New York Av.
Chicago Av.
Philadelphia Av.
St Louis Av.
Boston Av.
Baltimore Av.
Cleveland Av.
Cincinnati Av.
Sahara Av.
Guinness World of Records
Circus Circus Dr.
Circus Circus
Westward Ho
Stardust
Stardust Rd
New Frontier
Fashion Show Mall
Fashion Show Dr.
Black Canyon Av.
Vegas Plaza Dr.
Spring Mountain Rd
Monorail

Commerce
Main St.
Fairfield Av.
Fairfield Av.
Stratosphere Tower
Las Vegas Bd
Las Vegas Bd (The Strip)
Sahara
Wet 'n' Wild
Algiers
Riviera Bd
Riviera
Royal
Wynn Las Vegas
Holmes St.
Sands Av.
Site of The Palazzo
T.I. (Treasure Island)
Venetian

El Centro Pl.
Paradise Rd
St Louis Av.
Beverly
Van Pattin Av.
Santa Clara Dr.
Santa Paula Dr.
Santa Rita Dr.
Santa Ynez Dr.
San Pablo St.
Karen Av.
Karen Av.
Av. of the Hiltons
Kishner Dr.
Convention Center Dr.
Debbie Reynolds Dr.
Sadie St.
Channel 8 Dr.
Cathedral Wy.
Desert Inn Rd Super Arterial
DESERT INN GOLF CLUB (CLOSED)
1 Suzanne Cl.
2 Westchester
3 Central Park
4 Central Park
5 Manhattan
Emerson Av.
Burbank Av.
Green
Sands Convention Center

15
604
589
604

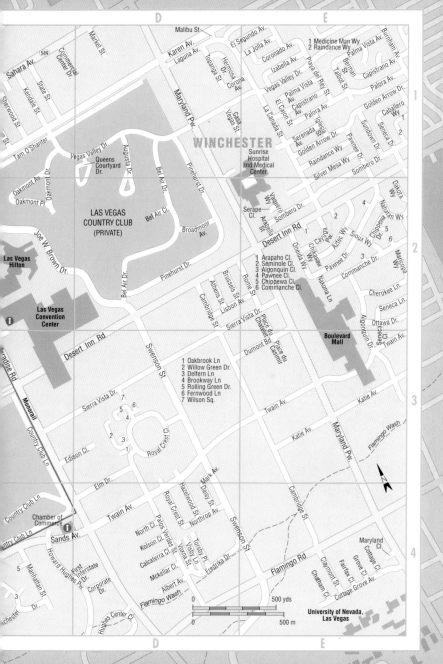

D

589
Sahara Av.

Malibu St

WINCHESTER

Sunrise Hospital and Medical Center

LAS VEGAS COUNTRY CLUB (PRIVATE)

Las Vegas Hilton

Las Vegas Convention Center

Desert Inn Rd.

1 Medicine Man Wy
2 Raindance Wy

1 Arapaho Cl.
2 Seminole Cl.
3 Algonquin Cl.
4 Pawnee Cl.
5 Chippewa Cl.
6 Commanche Cl.

1 Oakbrook Ln
2 Willow Green Dr.
3 Delfern Ln
4 Brookway Ln
5 Rolling Green Dr.
6 Fernwood Ln
7 Wilson Sq.

Boulevard Mall

Chamber of Commerce

Flamingo Rd.

500 yds

500 m

University of Nevada, Las Vegas

E

STREET INDEX

ART & PHOTO CREDITS

GENERAL INDEX

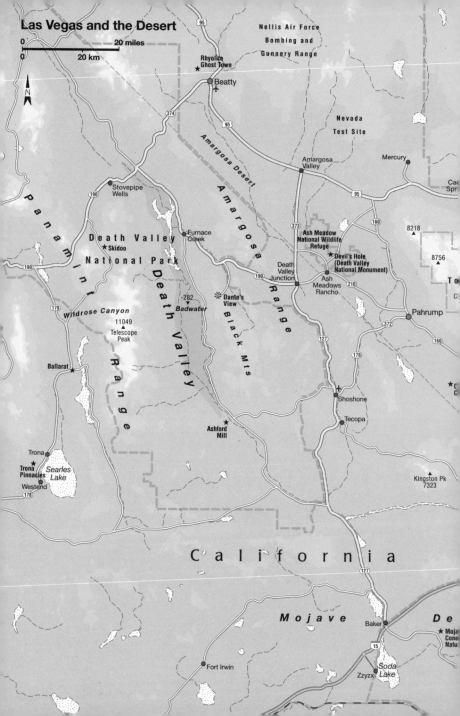